Meeting the Standards in Primary Mathematics

Tony Brown

RoutledgeFalmer
Taylor & Francis Group

LONDON AND NEW YORK

First published 2003
by RoutledgeFalmer
11 New Fetter Lane, London EC4P 4EE

Simultaneously published in the USA and Canada
by RoutledgeFalmer
29 West 35th Street, New York, NY 10001

RoutledgeFalmer is an imprint of the Taylor & Francis Group

© 2003 Tony Brown

Typeset in Bembo by
Newgen Imaging Systems (P) Ltd, Chennai, India
Printed and bound in Great Britain by
St Edmundsbury Press, Bury St Edmunds, Suffolk

British Library Cataloguing in Publication Data
A catalogue record for this book is available
from the British Library

Library of Congress Cataloging in Publication Data
A catalog record for this book has been requested

ISBN 0–415–24986–4

Contents

Figures

Tables

Series editor's preface

This book has been prepared for students training to be teachers who face the challenge of meeting the many requirements specified in the governments Circular 02/02, *Qualifying to Teach: Professional Standards for Qualified Teacher Status* (DfES/TTA). The book forms part of a series of publications that sets out to guide trainees on initial teacher training programmes, both primary and secondary, through the complex package of subject requirements they will be expected to meet before they can be awarded Qualified Teacher Status.

Why is there a need for such a series? Teaching has always been a demanding profession, requiring of its members enthusiasm, dedication and commitment. In addition, it is common sense that teachers need to know not only what they teach but how to teach it most effectively. Current trends in education highlight the raising of standards (particularly in the areas of literacy and numeracy), the use of new technologies across the curriculum and the development of key skills for lifelong learning. These run alongside Early Learning Goals, Baseline Assessment, the requirements of the National Curriculum, the National Literacy and Numeracy Strategies, PSHE and citizenship work, Standard Assessment Tasks (SATs), interim tasks, GCSE examinations, post-16 assessment.... The list seems endless. Such demands increase the pressure on teachers generally and trainee teachers in particular.

At the primary school level, since the introduction of the National Curriculum there is an even greater emphasis now than ever before on teachers' own subject knowledge and their ability to apply that knowledge in the classroom. Trainees have to become Jacks and Jills of all trades – developing the competence and confidence to plan, manage, monitor and assess all areas of the National Curriculum plus religious education. The increasing complexity of the primary curriculum and ever more demanding societal expectations makes it very difficult for trainees and their mentors (be they tutors in the training institutions or teachers in schools) to cover everything that is necessary in what feels like a very short space of time. Four of the books in this series are aimed specifically at the trainee primary teacher and those who are helping to train them:

- *Meeting the Standards in ... Primary English*
- *Meeting the Standards in ... Primary Mathematics*
- *Meeting the Standards in ... Primary Science*
- *Meeting the Standards in ... Primary Information and Communications Technology*

For those training to be secondary school teachers, the pressures are just as great. They will probably bring with them knowledge and expertise in their specialist subject, taken to degree level at least. However, content studied to degree level in universities is unlikely to match closely the needs of the National Curriculum. A degree in medieval English, applied mathematics or biochemistry will not be sufficient in itself to enable a secondary trainee to walk into a classroom of 13- or 16-year-olds and teach English, mathematics or science. Each subject at school level is likely to be broader. For example, science must include physics, chemistry, biology, astronomy, and aspects of geology. In addition there is the subject application – the 'how to teach it' dimension. Furthermore, secondary school teachers are often expected to be able to offer more than one subject. Thus, four of the books are aimed specifically at the secondary level:

- *Meeting the Standards in … Secondary English*
- *Meeting the Standards in … Secondary Mathematics*
- *Meeting the Standards in … Secondary Science*
- *Meeting the Standards in … Secondary Information and Communications Technology*

All of the books deal with the specific issues that underpin the relevant Teacher Training Agency requirements identified in Circular 02/02. The very nature of the subject areas covered and the teaching phases focused upon means that each book will, of necessity, be presented in different ways. However, each will cover the relevant areas of:

- subject knowledge – an overview of what to teach, the key ideas underpinning the relevant subject knowledge that the trainees need to know and understand in order to interpret the National Curriculum requirements for that subject;
- subject application – an overview of how to interpret the subject knowledge so as to design appropriate learning experiences for pupils, organize and manage those experiences and monitor pupils' progress within them.

The former is not presented in the form of a textbook. There are plenty of good quality GCSE and A-level textbooks on the market for those who feel the need to acquire that level of knowledge. Rather, the subject knowledge is related to identifying what is needed for the trainee to take the National Curriculum for the subject and translate it into a meaningful package for teaching and learning. The latter is structured in such a way as to identify the generic skills of planning, organizing, managing, monitoring and assessing the teaching and learning. The content is related to the specific requirements of Circular 02/02. The trainee's continuing professional development needs are also considered.

The purpose of the series is to give practical guidance and support to trainee teachers, in particular focusing on what to do and how to do it. Throughout each book there are suggested tasks and activities that can be completed in the training institution, in school or independently at home. They serve to elicit and support the trainee's development of skills, knowledge and understanding needed to become an effective teacher.

Dr Lynn Newton
University of Durham
May 2003

Acknowledgements

There are so many people to thank for their advice and encouragement. Colleagues from the College of St Mark & St John have always supported my work and given freely of their time to advise and guide my thinking.

Apologies to anyone I might have overlooked, and grateful thanks to the members of the primary education team, Alan Meechan, Annie Fisher, Dee Tod, Laura Osborne, Pat Stinton, Paul Foster, Robert Guyver, Steve Pratchett and Tim Rose.

Two colleagues in particular, Joanna Haynes and Henry Liebling have contributed so much to my thinking and my understanding of children and learning that they must be singled out for special thanks for their unwavering friendship and advice: thank you Henry, for your thorough reading of the earlier drafts and for your valuable comments.

My daughters, Hannah and Alice know just when and how to encourage me. Their enthusiasm for my work has done much to keep me going through the tough bits. Also, I want to acknowledge the creative spirit of Julie Jo Elle Gregory: a truly inspiring person and committed writer whose personal story and lived experience has done much to encourage me in my own life and work.

Using this book

The demands on trainees are complex and this necessarily results in a book with many different elements to it. Hopefully I have managed to keep it as simple as possible whilst making it only as complex as necessary. There are probably only a minority of people who would want to read it in the order that it appears: and it certainly was not written in this order.

Starting with the Standards

Some readers will want to look closely at the Standards to assess the challenges facing them and the achievements that are expected. You could use the various landscape pages in the final part of the book to identify those Standards that you can already meet. If this is your preferred starting point then Part IV will be a good place to begin. The pages in this part of the book are designed to be photocopied for your personal use.

Starting with the maths

For many primary trainees, the study of mathematics produces some nervousness, if not anxiety. For some people, this is related to their own learning experiences in school, whilst for others, anxiety is related to uncertainty about the level of knowledge currently demanded in training as a result of the introduction of the National Numeracy Strategy (NNS).

My experience is that trainees who identify strongly with *learners who are anxious about maths*, often make very good mathematics teachers when they have developed their own subject knowledge and pedagogy. The most effective teachers are often those who have combined their sensitivity to the needs of the learner, with a thorough revision of the mathematics needed for effective teaching and learning. You could start by looking at the mathematics curriculum presented in Part II.

Starting with the pedagogy

I am using *pedagogy* here to mean the study and practice of teaching – *professional know-how*. In this book, most of the discussion on pedagogy is built around examples of mathematics and examples of mathematical activities that have proved to be effective for learning. Reading some of the pedagogical discussions might be a good place to start for readers who like to flick through a book and browse different sections before reading in depth.

It is impossible to provide an example of every area of mathematics being taught using every conceivable pedagogical strategy. What I have done in the book is to take a wide range of pedagogical strategies, like visualising numbers and shapes in your mind's-eye, and to illustrate the use of the strategy with an example.

The challenge for the trainee is to develop their pedagogical understanding in one area of maths, or with one age group, and then learn how to adapt it to new teaching and learning contexts. Applying what we already know to new circumstances is one of the most difficult learning processes for all of us and it will be one of the toughest (but most interesting) aspects of your professional development in mathematics.

Getting a sense of location

I have put the whole process of training into a context that explores the current situation critically, that is, I have expressed my views on the recent developments in training and the curriculum changes that have taken place, in order to present as clear a picture as possible, but from the perspective of someone who has been involved in Initial Teacher Training. If this is a useful starting point for you, then read on, or start with some of the essential reading listed below.

Essential reading

http://www.canteach.gov.uk/ (Teacher Training Agency).
http://www.dfes.gov.uk/index.htm (Department for Education and Skills).
http://www.ofsted.gov.uk/ (Office for Standards in Education).
http://www.qca.org.uk (Qualifications and Curriculum Authority).
Claxton, G. (1999) *Wise Up: The Challenge of Lifelong Learning*. London: Bloomsbury.
DfEE (1999) *The National Numeracy Strategy: Framework for Teaching Mathematics*. London: DfEE.
DfEE (1999) *National Numeracy Strategy: Mathematical Vocabulary*. London: DfEE
DfES/TTA (2002) *Qualifying to Teach: Professional Standards for Qualified Teacher Status*. London: Teacher Training Agency.
Headington, R. (2000) *Monitoring, Assessment, Recording and Accountability: Meeting the Standards*. London: David Fulton.
NNS/QCA (1999) *Teaching Mental Calculation Strategies*. London: Qualifications and Curriculum Authority.
NNS/QCA (1999) *Teaching Written Calculation Strategies*. London: Qualifications and Curriculum Authority.
Parsons, E. (ed.) (1999) *GCSE Mathematics Revision Guide* (Higher Level). Coordination Group Publications.
QCA/DfEE (1999) *Mathematics: The National Curriculum for England*. London: HMSO.
QCA (1999) *Early Learning Goals*. London: Qualifications and Curriculum Authority.
QCA (2000) *Curriculum Guidance for the Foundation Stage*. London: HMSO.
TTA (2000) *Using ICT to meet Teaching Objectives in Mathematics*.

Welcome to your teaching career

The route to your teaching career is through successful work in schools and completion of your training course. Your training should lead to the successful coverage of the Standards. The Professional Standards for Qualified Teacher Status (QTS) were published by the Teacher Training Agency in *Qualifying to Teach* (TTA, 2002). They replace the earlier ones published in 1998. Trainees in all training routes now have to prove themselves in three broad areas:

- *Professional values and practice*;
- *Knowledge and understanding*;
- *Teaching*.

These are shown in detail in Part IV of this book. You must meet all the Standards to gain QTS. Most of the Standards will be met in school settings during periods when you are observed carrying out a range of professional activities, not only teaching classes of children, but also carrying out other professional duties throughout the school.

Helping you to meet the Standards

This book has been written to support you whichever route you choose into teaching. It makes practical suggestions about how to meet the Standards in your mathematics teaching. It focuses on ways to strengthen your subject knowledge of mathematics and it discusses strategies for effective teachers of primary mathematics.

Mathematics has an interesting – if not infamous – history as a school subject. For many students it is the subject that they love to hate. And, it is perfectly acceptable even in the new millennium, to claim publicly that, 'Maths is my worst subject!'. Culturally, this attitude to maths needs to be turned around, and I suspect, most of this is going to be down to teachers in classrooms, on a daily basis, working in exciting ways with children until they say, 'Wow! More maths please!'.

It is unacceptable that after six or so years of formal state education, the best we can manage are the bemused, scornful and negative attitudes to maths that currently pervade all too many classrooms in the early years of secondary education. Things *are* changing however, and there are strong claims being made that the Daily Maths Lesson (dubbed the Numeracy Hour by journalists) is helping to change children's attitudes to maths in very positive ways.

This book will:

- promote maths as an enjoyable, curious and puzzling – though difficult – subject to teach and learn;
- guide you through the mathematics curriculum;
- help you understand the pedagogy of mathematics teaching;
- develop your subject knowledge;
- guide you through the Standards and show you how to meet them.

Routes into teaching

This book will be of interest to any trainee who hopes to become a primary school teacher, regardless of the route taken into training. Traditional routes to primary school teaching have been the undergraduate four-year degree (Bachelor of Education) and the one-year post-graduate certificate of education (PGCE). A glance through university prospectuses will illustrate the recent moves towards diversification, which include BA (Ed.) degrees, and part time PGCE programmes.

All undergraduate courses are two-in-one arrangements with an academic element – the degree, awarded by the university and additionally a training component which will lead to the university recommending successful trainees for QTS. This status is formally awarded by the TTA. Formal recognition by the TTA then permits the trainee to gain membership of the General Teaching Council (GTCE in England http://www.gtce.org.uk/ and GTCW in Wales http://www.gtcw.org.uk/) as a Newly Qualified Teacher (NQT). Membership of the GTC is a requirement for teaching in state schools. In Scotland the General Teaching Council of Scotland administers the registration of teachers and a two-year probationary period. (In England the General Teaching Council is in its infancy but will regulate the quality of teachers already in school.)

In addition to training courses, there are new routes that are not courses in the traditional sense. There are school-based training options which attract a salary during the training period. In England and Wales there is a Graduate Training Programme (GTP) and a less well-known Registered Teacher Programme (RTP). These are both employment-based routes and operate through the TTA. http://www.canteach.gov.uk/ in England, and the National Assembly in Wales. Many traditional providers like universities and colleges of HE are now managing GTP programmes.

As a trained teacher, you will be required to register with the GTC if you wish to teach in state run schools. You will have to agree to uphold the rules and values of the GTC, which are summarised in the section called *Professional Values and Practice* in the 2002 Standards, and which are available in full on the Council's website. *Qualifying to Teach* (DfES/TTA: 2002) is the official document that contains all the Standards you need to meet by the end of your training.

Why have we got the Standards?

The government's stated purpose is to ensure the continued improvement of standards in education, through regulation and control of the curriculum and assessment, and standards of entry to the profession. An important milestone is the Education Reform Act (ERA) of

1988. This legislated for changes in the way schools were run and it freed schools to some extent from the direct control of Local Education Authorities (LEA) – allowing them to manage their own budgets, for example. This legislation also introduced the National Curriculum (NC) and it was this aspect of the Act that probably had the biggest impact on teachers' professional lives.

The ERA legislation changed the curriculum from something that was largely the responsibility of individual schools into something that was produced by, monitored by, and assessed by national government, through a number of different quasi-governmental bodies like the National Curriculum Council. Many of these bodies have since disappeared or been replaced in the intervening years.

Probably the best known of the current players is the Office for Standards in Education (OFSTED). Others include the TTA and the government's own Department for Education and Skills (DfES). To these, we can add the Quality and Curriculum Authority (QCA) which has produced curriculum guides mainly for science and the non-core subjects and where responsibility for formal assessment is located. More recently, we have seen the emergence of the Task Forces for the National Numeracy and Literacy Strategies.

Recent changes in arrangements for training

I think it is important to acknowledge that the expectations and the demands placed on students in teacher training have never been higher. Trainees are now expected to know and be able to do things that were once only expected of qualified and experienced teachers. These heightened expectations have raised teaching standards, and both trainees and trainers have responded well.

By the end of their training, most trainees are now very effective in classrooms. Many were surpassing the Standards required by Circular 4/98 which governed teacher training until September 2002 when they were replaced by the Professional Standards (TTA, 2002).

So, why have the demands on students increased so much in recent years? One reason for the changes in the training process stems from the fact that children are increasingly seen as belonging to society, rather than people who have not yet joined the 'real world'. The curriculum has expanded in response to personal, moral, social and health agendas. Every teacher now has responsibility for ensuring that educational provision is inclusive and for teaching part of the citizenship curriculum.

Current political thinking and research evidence (Hay McBer, 2000) argues that teachers and schools *can* shape the future of society by influencing the thinking and behaviour of pupils in significant ways. Some of the biggest changes brought about by the 2002 regulations, were intended to enable trainees and newly qualified teachers to make a big contribution to the government's commitment to pupils' social and educational inclusion. The new Standards and requirements introduce for the first time, expectations about professional responsibilities and the values that underpin professional behaviour.

Resources and further reading

http://www.canteach.gov.uk/teaching/ (Teacher Training Agency for routes into teaching).
http://www.gttr.ac.uk/ (Graduate Teacher Training Registry GTTR – applications online for graduates).
http://www.dfes.gov.uk/index.htm (Department for Education and Skills).

www.gtce.org.uk (General Teaching Council).

Ashdan, C. and Overall, L. (1998) (eds) *Teaching in Primary Schools*. London: Cassell.

Croll, P. and Hastings, N. (1996) (eds) *Effective Primary Teaching: Research based Classroom Strategies*. London: David Fulton.

Day, C. (2000) (ed.) *The Life and Work of Teachers: International Perspectives in Changing Times*. London: Falmer Press.

Ghaye, A. and Ghaye, K. (1998) *Teaching and Learning Through Critical Reflective Practice*. London: David Fulton.

MacGrath, M. (2000) *The Art of Peaceful Teaching*. London: David Fulton.

Moseley, J. (1995) *Circle Time*. Lame Duck Publishing.

Pollard, A. (ed.) (1996) *Readings for Reflective Teaching*. London: Cassell.

Pollard, A, (ed.) (1997) *Reflective Teaching in the Primary School*. London: Cassell.

Richards, C., Simco, N., Twiselton, S. (1998) (eds) *Primary Teacher Education: High Status? High Standards?* London: Falmer Press.

Selley, N. (1999) *The Art of Constructivist Teaching*. London: David Fulton.

Sharron, H. (1994) *Changing Children's Minds*. Sharron Publishing.

Smith, A. (1996) *Accelerated Learning in the Classroom*. Network Educational Press.

Turner-Bisset, R. (2001) *Expert Teaching: Knowledge and Pedagogy to Lead the Profession*. London: David Fulton.

PART I

Putting your training in context

1   Teachers as critical professional thinkers

There are critics of the new Standards, many of whom cite the language of compliance as limiting opportunities for teachers to exercise independent professional judgements. There is always a potential cost to trainee teachers and their pupils, of following prescriptive government agendas. It is important to realise that neither the previous Standards nor the new Professional Standards contained in *Qualifying to Teach* explicitly require or encourage teachers to have any understanding of, or be critical of government policies, despite the fact that these increasingly dictate teachers' professional roles and responsibilities.

There is no requirement for critical awareness of how government policies may impact on the education service or on teachers' effectiveness; no requirement that teachers will innovate in a creative, sensitive and caring way; no requirement that teachers will develop a personal vision of teaching and learning. The requirements contained in the regulations relate to compliance with government requirements rather than mediation of the government's agendas for schools and education through professional decision making, and some commentators see this as a continuing limitation.

Many argue that a teacher's informed judgement does not develop out of compliance, but only from creative mediation between complex and sometimes contrary demands. A fully trained teacher will exercise a personal, professional and critical perspective on government expectations and will try to mediate government demands by creatively modifying their own professional behaviour in a world which they recognise as containing conflicting demands, limited resources, and where they acknowledge the limits to their own current levels of expertise.

> The DfES and TTA aim to produce caring, concerned, respectful teachers anxious to promote inclusion and educational achievement but only in ways fully congruent with current government thinking.
>
> The other missing dimension … is any understanding of how or why these statutory requirements, frameworks, etc. have been developed (and changed over time) and any indication that they are contestable, that they could be different, and that they could be (and are being) challenged in some quarters.
>
> (Simco and Wilson, 2002: 4–5)

During the 1960s one Secretary of State for Education is reported to have said, 'It cannot be for the Secretary of State to tell teachers how to teach.' Times have certainly changed and politicians 'discovered' education several years ago. Today all political parties claim an interest in education to further their political ends and have staked their success partly on improvements to education. Schools, teaching, learning, and teacher training, are no longer seen as beyond the reach of political influence, or as unalterable aspects of community life. Today the most powerful education managers are the central government and the non-elected groups it creates, such as the Teacher Training Agency (TTA). It is the Secretary of State for Education who now has the responsibility for determining the Standards for training and to a large extent is able to define what and how teachers should teach.

> The Standards and Requirements ... replace Df EE Circular 4/98 and have the same legal standing. They set out:
>
> - the Secretary of State's Standards, which must be met by trainee teachers before they can be awarded Qualified Teacher Status;
> - the Requirements for training providers and those who make recommendations for the award of Qualified Teacher Status.
>
> Only those trainee teachers who have met all of the Standards will be awarded QTS. The Standards and Requirements contained in this document come into effect from 1 September 2002.
>
> (Df ES/TTA, 2002: Contents)

For those who wish to engage in this debate, teaching offers an exciting future: there is much to play for. One thing is for certain: those who wish to work in schools cannot exempt themselves from being a part of the current social and political processes that are shaping schools in particular and society in general.

Politicians of all persuasions now believe that directly influencing education by setting the agenda for change in schools is an important way of achieving social, cultural and financial objectives at a national level. They see the work that teachers do with pupils as having a direct impact on future economic performance and increased material prosperity and as influencing social cohesion, law and order, health, and citizenship.

As a teacher in training and as a fully qualified teacher, you will be accepting a part in this process. Many people from very different walks of life will have expectations of you in your role as a teacher, and see it as their right to comment on and judge the effectiveness of your work in school.

One inevitable question is, 'Where are the children in all this?' Your interest in teaching is almost certainly based on your enjoyment of working with people and a desire to nurture individual children's learning.

In this book, I try very hard not to lose sight of the fact that your personal goals will include wanting to be an influential teacher who makes a positive contribution to the lives of children: someone who wants to build strong relationships with them. Good teachers do make a positive contribution to the lives of children, and the aim of this book is to help you to make a difference as you train to teach children in school.

The education debate

From 1976, successive governments have claimed the Standards debate as a main part of their agenda and positioned themselves as more authoritative than educators (teachers, academics, researchers and members of professional educational associations) in the determination of what constitutes appropriate standards in education. The purpose of education has never been the subject of widespread agreement in Britain and very different views continue to be adopted by different groups.

Likewise, the purpose of teaching mathematics in schools has been regularly explored by different groups over the last 150 years but no common consensus has been achieved, as Professor Margaret Brown's commentary shows:

> Ernest (1991), Ball (1990) and Brown (1996) describe the clash in philosophies of education and of numeracy/mathematics which troubled policy decisions in this period [1976–1995]; these were in fact only recent manifestations of differences which had pertained over the previous 150 years.
>
> (Brown, 2001: 7)

Brown continues with the observation that 'other countries such as Japan are much more measured in their implementation of reforms, valuing more greatly the expertise and views of teachers, educators and researchers…' (ibid.).

Some initiatives like the long-awaited General Teaching Council for England (GTCE) are instructive. They appear to shift some of the responsibility for education from central government but in fact bring little diminution of the very substantial powers of the Secretary of State built up over the last few years.

Having claimed Standards to be a national issue, successive governments have been able to dictate what is to be included in debates on standards in education. What is excluded from government agendas is as informative as what they choose to put up for discussion.

English children are now among the most tested in the world. The tests are also used to pass judgement on the standards of teachers and schools. The disadvantages of inflating the assessment process in this way are only just beginning to be discussed, with the debacle over Advanced Subsidiary (AS) level examinations in 2001 and the apparent manipulation of A-level results in 2002.

The wider issues of the benefits and drawbacks to children's learning, to parents, the education establishment and employers, have yet to be seriously explored. Many primary and secondary teachers now cram children for Statutory Assessment Tasks (SAT) tests. Those who do not teach to the tests, risk their school dropping in the published league tables. (Wales by contrast has stopped Key Stage 1 SAT tests and abolished the publication of league tables as 'unhelpful' in raising standards.)

Music, drama, physical education (PE), art, history, geography and Information Communications Technology (ICT) have all suffered as the time spent in school is increasingly dominated by English and mathematics, and as the government's view of what is appropriate for children to do at school has dominated the debate. The concern of educators is that the requirement of schools to provide children with a broad, balanced, relevant and differentiated curriculum (*Better Schools*, DES, 1985) cannot currently be met.

Social and educational inclusion

The exclusion debate has been replaced by a debate about how to secure inclusion for all pupils. Few schools can hope to completely achieve the aims of inclusion, equal opportunity and widening participation in life-long learning for all pupils. Most schools, however, do have ambitions to create fairer and more inclusive environments for learning and person growth. They have had to ensure that they provide sensible frameworks for meeting legal requirements such as child protection, which give effective support and guidance to teachers and other professionals involved in school. Pupil underachievement and disengagement remain big issues in many schools and mathematics is a subject that can make a big contribution to pupils' engagement with the learning agenda. The Professional Standards contained in *Qualifying to Teach* are intended to create a climate of opportunity for trainees to develop the skills needed to be effective in the areas of social and educational inclusion.

At the end of their training, trainees are asked to provide the TTA with data about the effectiveness of their training. This is gathered through the TTA annual surveys. In recent years, many Newly Qualified Teachers (NQTs) have indicated that at the end of their training, they felt inadequately prepared to make a full contribution to schools' aims and practices relating to inclusion. In particular, the data indicated that a large proportion of trainees wanted more guidance and experience in order to:

- support children with special educational needs;
- engage effectively with children from minority ethnic groups;
- teach pupils for whom English is an additional language.

The new Standards and requirements attempt to address these concerns. From September 2002, courses of training should address these concerns both generically, and within subject areas like mathematics, where teachers face very particular and difficult challenges. How you teach mathematics can lead directly and quickly, either to pupils' disaffection and underachievement, or to inclusion and excellence. Mathematics is perhaps the school subject which engenders the strongest positive and negative feelings in us and many of us can speak more passionately about the way we experienced mathematics teaching than we can about any other school subject.

The Standards contained in *Professional Values* (Section 1 of *Qualifying to Teach*) are not particularly explicit about how professional values can influence inclusion. In Section 2, *Knowledge and Understanding*, there are two Standards that relate to inclusion:

- understand how pupils' learning can be affected by their physical, intellectual, linguistic, social, cultural and emotional development (2.4);
- understand their responsibilities under the SEN Code of Practice, and know how to seek advice from specialists on less common types of special educational needs (2.6).

In Section 3, *Teaching*, there are nine Standards related to inclusion:

- use teaching and learning objectives to plan lessons, and sequences of lessons, showing how they will assess pupils' learning. They take account of and support pupils' varying needs so that girls and boys, from all ethnic groups, can make good progress (3.1.2);
- select and prepare resources, and plan for their safe and effective organisation, taking account of pupils' interests and their language and cultural backgrounds, with the help of support staff where appropriate (3.1.3);
- identify and support more able pupils, those who are working below age-related expectations, those who are failing to achieve their potential in learning, and those who experience behavioural, social and emotional difficulties (3.2.4);
- with the help of an experienced teacher, they can identify the levels of attainment of pupils learning English as an additional language. They begin to analyse the language

demands and learning activities in order to provide cognitive challenge as well as language support (3.2.5);

- have high expectations of pupils and build successful relationships, centred on teaching and learning. They establish a purposeful learning environment, where diversity is valued and where pupils feel secure and confident (3.3.1);
- differentiate teaching to meet the needs of pupils, including the more able and those with special educational needs, with guidance from an experienced teacher where appropriate (3.3.4);
- able to support those who are learning English as an additional language, with the help of an experienced teacher where appropriate (3.3.5);
- take account of the varying interests, experiences and achievements of boys and girls, and pupils from different cultural and ethnic groups, to help pupils make good progress (3.3.6);
- recognise and respond effectively to equal opportunities issues as they arise in the classroom, including challenging stereotyped views, bullying or harassment, following relevant policies and procedures (3.3.14).

It is clear that the TTA has taken advice and acted to bring together the government's commitment to inclusion and widening participation, and the expressed concerns of trainees and trainers, that professional values must be an identifiable part of the training process, even though the assessment of trainees' professional values will be difficult. The General Teaching Council (GTC) has suggested that difficulties over assessing professional values can be overcome by looking at professional behaviour and assessing how it contributes to professionalism. The TTA Standards explicitly require that:

> Those awarded Qualified Teacher Status must understand and uphold the professional code of the General Teaching Council.
>
> (*Qualifying to Teach*, DfES/TTA, 2002: 6)

Resources and further reading

www.triangle.co.uk/ciec (Contemporary Issues in Early Childhood Education).

www.bernardvanleer.org (Van Leer Organisation – Early Childhood Matters).

www.becta.org.uk/news/reports/primaryfuture/index.html (Becta (2001), *Primary Schools of the Future – Achieving Today*).

Briggs, M. and Pritchard, A. (2002) *Using ICT in Primary Mathematics Teaching*. Exeter: Learning Matters.

Brown, M. (2001) Numeracy Policy (in) M. Askew and M. Brown (eds) Teaching and learning primary numeracy: policy, practice and effectiveness. *BERA Review*. British Educational Research Association. Southwell: Nottinghamshire.

Department for Education and Science (1985) *Better Schools* (presented to Parliament by the Secretary of State for Education and Science. London: HMSO.

DfES/TTA (2002) *Qualifying to Teach: Professional Standards for Qualified Teacher Status and Requirements for Initial Teacher Training*. London: DfES/TTA.

MacGilchrist, B. *et al.* (1997) *The Intelligent School*. London: Paul Chapman Publishing.

Pollard, A. (1997) *Reflective Teaching in the Primary School*. London: Cassell.

Simco, N. and Wilson, T. (eds) (2002) *Primary Initial Teacher Training and Education: Revised Standards, Bright Future?* Exeter: Learning Matters.

2 Mathematics and the curriculum

There is a lot of technical information about Key Stages, levels and so on that inevitably becomes introduced as part of any discussion about schooling and the curriculum. It might be helpful to represent this in a diagram for ease of reference. There are plenty of overlapping labels and definitions, and the beginnings and ends of some periods of schooling are quite fuzzy.

By contrast, some labels, like the Key Stages, are fairly well defined. Levels of attainment were not so detailed in the early versions of the National Curriculum (NC), but have become much more sharply defined since the publication of the National Numeracy Strategy (NNS), partly as a result of political pressure to raise standards. When he was Secretary of State for Education, David Blunkett chose to define a national objective for attainment in mathematics. This was set at 75% of children achieving Level 4 in the Statutory Assessment Tasks (SAT) tests by the end of Key Stage 2 (KS2) in Year 6 (Y6). Until May 2003 when it dropped plans for national targets, the Government had insisted that targets for 2004 would be for 85% to achieve level 4 or better and for 35% to achieve level 5 or better.

Such decisions inevitably have a knock-back effect. In order to achieve the desired target, the 'pitch' of the teaching in the preceding years needs to be set to accommodate it. For example, the pitch outlined in the NNS (Section 1: 42) suggests that work for most children will be mainly set at Level 1 in Y1 but starting on some work at Level 2.

I have incorporated this data in the Figure 2.1. Where there is an emphasis in any one year, this is shown in bold. For example, the pitch of work for most of the children in Y1 is shown as L **1**/2.

The origin of this decision to set targets is twofold. One is the political desire to demonstrate success in raising educational attainment. The other is comparative research data for pupil performance over a range of different countries. It does appear from research into teaching and learning in other countries, that we have a much larger proportion of under-achieving children in our classes in Britain than can be found in classrooms in such dissimilar countries as Germany, Taiwan and Hungary. There might be good reasons for this (other than assuming that the teaching is 'better' in these other countries), which could include different types of special needs, support outside normal lesson time, for example, or different ways of organising classrooms and teaching.

The publication of data, particularly the very large 'TIMSS'[1] (The Third International Mathematics and Science Study) created an educational and political consensus in the late 1990s about the need to address the reasons why there is a relatively large proportion of under-achieving children in British classrooms, and whether attainment could be improved by changing some very established teaching methods. The NNS was intended to become one way in which the situation could be improved. The Framework together with the

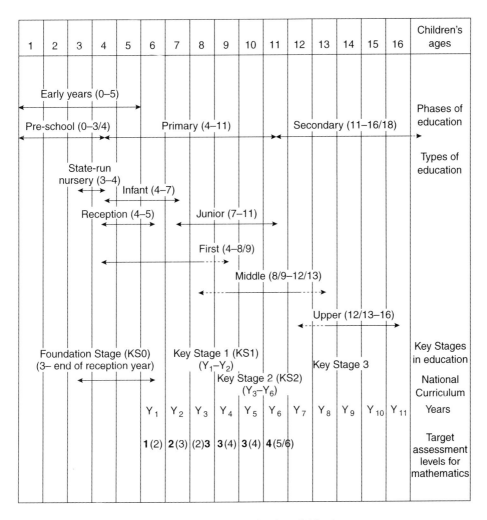

Figure 2.1 The terminology of primary education related to children's ages.

accompanying videos and other methods of curriculum intervention such as the deployment of consultants and Leading Maths Teachers (LMT) were aimed at creating support for change.

Section 1 of the NNS Framework is an important read for trainees, because it presents the general philosophy of the Strategy in a pragmatic way and sets the scene for the intended change in the way mathematics is to be taught and learnt.

How has the debate developed?

In some respects there has been a less than satisfactory debate about what a balanced primary curriculum for the second millennium should look like. For those trainees interested in teaching primary mathematics – the main intended readership for this book – it is the discussion about curriculum balance which is long overdue.

Is there a need for mathematics to take approximately half of the curriculum time every morning? What should be covered in mathematics lessons? Should the primary mathematics curriculum be a basic preparation for broader more interesting work in secondary schools? Do all children need to be taught mathematics to the current level expected by the end of KS2? How can we best explore these arguments?

Quality and quantity do not often go hand in hand; more often the relationship is an inverse one. It may be that less time spent on maths and less maths curriculum coverage, may allow teachers and children to become more competent and confident albeit with a smaller range of mathematical ideas. The key issues are whether we can establish a consensus in terms of coverage, depth of understanding and application.

As well as being taught as a separate subject, mathematics can play an extensive and important role in the non-core subjects if opportunities are created. There is by no means full agreement about the amount of time that should be spent teaching mathematics in primary schools and what the mathematics curriculum should look like, particularly for very young children. This was well illustrated by the arguments for and against the use of calculators in school.

The developments that have come to pass, were not planned against an overall philosophy of what children need in their first years of education, but were introduced piecemeal, sometimes by competing factions. As a society we may well have an unrealistic wish that schools will solve our problems for us, and it has been left to teachers and schools to implement the individual changes and to mediate the different expectations and requirements in what has become a curriculum that is not only intended to teach children but to respond to national social anxieties.

There is a strong government view but less of a general consensus about what the overall primary curriculum should look like. We can see that this is a difficult discussion when we look back to earlier curriculum development initiatives and consider their success. It becomes even more difficult if we argue that the purpose of primary education is to prepare children for their future: especially if we try to describe that future and if we remind ourselves that the youngest primary children of 2003 will be entering the labour market in about 2015. Anyone prepared to describe what such a labour market might look like is brave indeed.

The NC structure was conceived in the mid-1980s. It formalises what has to be learned in state (not private) schools, mainly in terms of traditional subject knowledge areas, with additional elements like citizenship and Special Educational Needs (SEN) added separately at a later date. The current curriculum model is based on a reductionist approach: each of the NC subject orders presents a selected subset of information based on a 'traditional' subject curriculum. Most children in English primary schools are not taught much about Welsh, or Scottish history and even fewer learn about Irish history or British history and involvement in Ireland, for example. An alternative position is to argue for the development of an informed world view, starting from personal experience and including a move beyond self-interest and the immediate environment at the same time as a knowledge of self and location is being explored.

Successive governments have expressed concern that those leaving full-time education should be highly employable. Education is seen by government as an important factor in making the country commercially competitive. Increasingly, employability includes the ability to use many different types of electronic data processing devices. We all need to be able to select the relevant information from huge amounts of data, much of it superfluous and presented in many different formats. The use of Information Communications and

Technology (ICT) in mathematics is challenging but exciting developments like interactive whiteboards present really powerful opportunities for teaching mathematics.

The introduction of a standardised curriculum in 1989 widened the curriculum in the country's weakest schools to include a regular programme of art, music, history, geography, and more notably, science, design technology and ICT. Children's *entitlement* to a broad, balanced and relevant curriculum was more comprehensively acknowledged and achieved, though this balance has been subsequently disturbed with the introduction of the Literacy and Numeracy Strategies. Their arrival in schools has led to a decrease in the proportion of time available for non-core subjects.

In mathematics, long-term and medium-term planning became a whole school process with much greater emphasis on teacher collaboration and the inclusion of Teaching Assistants (TA) and other adult helpers in the planning process. It became easier to ensure continuity of the curriculum across the primary years and Key Stages. Progression within the curriculum became easier to manage with the publication of a NC which spelled out coverage and depth. This has continued with the detailed curriculum of the NNS contained in the Framework. As with many externally driven initiatives, one consequence was a loss of creativity and spontaneity in what was taught. Gradually, as teachers have internalised both the philosophy and the expectations, they have learnt to mediate creatively between the official expectations and the needs of children.

The NNS includes an expectation that teachers should observe good practice and have opportunities to watch each other teaching mathematics lessons. Many teachers have also had the opportunity to watch a LMT at work and most have seen videos illustrating a wide range of teaching styles. Many teachers now routinely observe colleagues in their own school.

As a result of this opening up of the 'how-to' debate, teachers have been able to raise the quality of discussion about pedagogy (the way they use their professional skills to create opportunities for effective teaching and learning). Many teachers now have a stronger belief in themselves as effective teachers of maths. From the late 1990s there developed a more critical, analytical climate, where teaching decisions are more openly discussed informally between colleagues in staff rooms, with subject leaders within schools, and as part of professional training and development. Teaching of mathematics is now more widely seen for what it is: a difficult but rewarding challenge. Teachers now have greater access to strategies and strategic thinking about how to maximise their classroom effectiveness.

Teachers are expected to be familiar with, and use, a large number of official documents produced by a wide range of different bodies. The NC is the legal framework that sets out the primary school mathematics curriculum. The curriculum applies to almost all primary children from Y1 to Y6, except a very few who have been 'disapplied'. Most children with SEN including many in Special Schools, follow the NC Programmes of Study. This often means breaking down the content into very small steps to ensure every chance of success, even if this is in terms of achieving Levels 1 or 2 by age 16.

The *Foundation Stage Guidance* (QCA, 2000) is written for teachers of children aged 3–5. This has a section specifically on mathematics, and is presented in a developmental format, with suggestions for different activities, many of which are based around social games and activities like cooking, climbing, playing with large toys.

A government appointed Numeracy Task Force, with its own Director developed the NNS. It is aligned to the NC so that schools which use the NNS know they are meeting the requirements of the NC. Where the NC prescribes the 'what' of the mathematics curriculum, the NNS Framework suggests the 'how', the 'when' and the 'why' through its guidance pages, examples of activities, its increasingly rich web-based resources, and its more recently published Unit Plans.

Neither the Foundation Guidance nor the NNS have legal status; that is, they provide non-statutory guidance and schools are not required by law to follow them. However, OFSTED's (Office for Standards in Education) response to these guidelines has been to look for their use in schools and to assess their impact on school standards. Where they are not used, OFSTED requires schools to demonstrate that the alternative methods used are just as effective.

National Curriculum

Mathematics, with its multicultural heritage, its relevance to business and the world of work, and its application in other subjects like science, has a significant contribution to make to the wider school curriculum. Trainee teachers need to be aware of the wider aspirations written into the NC (DfEE, 1999a,b) as well as being aware of the general structure and content of the NC document. Trainees need to understand the detail of the Orders for Mathematics, because these set out the values associated with teaching mathematics in primary schools.

> Aim 1: The school curriculum should aim to provide opportunities for all pupils to learn and to achieve.
>
> Aim 2: The school curriculum should aim to promote pupils' spiritual, moral, social and cultural development and prepare all pupils for the opportunities, responsibilities and experiences of life.
>
> (DfEE, QCA, 1999: 11)

The four main aims of the NC (DfEE, QCA, 1999: 12–13) are:

- to establish an entitlement;
- to establish standards;
- to promote continuity and coherence;
- to promote public understanding.

While the government sees these four main purposes as constant and unchanging over time, it also sees an effective school curriculum as developing over time, responsive both to national and local needs.

National Curriculum content

The NC is the legal basis for the curriculum. Mathematics is presented like the other NC subjects, under a series of Programmes of Study which detail what is to be taught at each Key Stage. The revised (1999) mathematics Programmes of Study now begin at 2 rather than 1. Originally, there was a separate programme of study (Ma1) for teaching children how to use and apply their knowledge and skills in Ma2 (number and algebra), Ma3 (shape, space and measures) and Ma4 (handling data). Using and applying is now embedded within the content programmes of study.

In the revised version, the skills of *using and applying* are presented as the first part of each of the remaining programmes of study. For each programme of study, teachers should ensure that children are taught the using and applying skills of problem solving, communicating and reasoning.

Problem solving is at the heart of learning mathematics. As part of using and applying it should feature in virtually every lesson that is taught. When children are taught and encouraged to solve problems; they face challenges, extend their individual thinking skills and make sense of the mathematics in a particular context. A problem solving climate encourages them to identify the mathematics and resources they need for their work, the operations they need to use to tackle problems. Children need to be taught to select and use the appropriate skills and this takes time, but we need to provide opportunities for children to make decisions about how to tackle mathematical problems. They should be expected to explain their reasoning, demonstrate their methods and explore the reasons for wrong answers.

Communicating is vital for developing mathematical ideas, for challenging misconceptions and for improving the skills of reasoning. There should be opportunities in every lesson for children to communicate their ideas, their reasoning and their methods both orally and in other ways. Children need opportunities to communicate with their teacher, with other adults and with each other. We help children communicate when we encourage them to think about the audience. They will need to organise their work if they are to communicate effectively to their audience and they will need to refine the ways in which they record what they have done. This means carefully considering the use of diagrams and symbols in order to best communicate their ideas. By discussing in whole class and group settings, children are helped to interpret different strategies, solutions and ways of working.

Children's *reasoning* is supported when teachers help them to express their ideas in increasingly general ways and to make general mathematical statements. Reasoning is strengthened when children explore patterns particularly in their own results as part of problem-solving activities, and learn to apply logical thought to the work they do.

The revised (1999) NC met the demands of the day, in that the whole of the NC documentation was dramatically slimmed down following a review by Lord Dearing. The drawback was that the later versions became a brief reminder of the legal requirements. They were not documents that teachers could use to plan lessons. Concerns about children's attainment and inadequate teaching styles, led to a National Numeracy Project and eventually to the NNS, written to support the teaching of mathematics. The impact of the Strategy has been evaluated by OFSTED in their publication (*The National Numeracy Strategy: The First Three Years*, 1999–2002).

The Strategy emphasises number and calculation but includes all other content areas. It includes video and supplementary written material: much of which has been warmly welcomed. A significant part of the Strategy was the national process of dissemination. This has made it much more successful than earlier curriculum development projects. The appointment of Regional Directors and NNS consultants working within Local Educational Authorities (LEAs) ensured dissemination of the material and the success of training courses for heads and governors of schools, then mathematics coordinators and staff. The recent publication of Planning Units will transform teachers planning in school and should free up some of the time currently used for planning, allowing it to be devoted to developing more effective teaching programmes.

Many NNS numeracy consultants were appointed from within LEAs because of their expertise in teaching mathematics and their strong local knowledge. A further powerful feature of the Strategy was the identification of LMT, who give considerable time to supporting the initiative by allowing local teachers to visit them and observe them giving demonstration lessons. The pedagogical dialogue between LMT and visiting teachers has done much to communicate good practice in mathematics teaching.

National Curriculum and assessment

The NC is also the legal basis for the assessment of children's performance. The government's interest in raising standards in mathematics begins with the National Curriculum Attainment Targets and the levels of attainment set out in the back section of the printed version of the NC on pages 8–15. The criteria are divided into levels of increasing attainment.

> An attainment target sets out the 'knowledge, skills and understanding that pupils of different abilities and maturities are expected to have by the end of each Key Stage. … Each level description describes the types and range of performance that pupils working at that level should characteristically demonstrate. …The level descriptions provide the basis for making judgements about pupils' performance at the end of the Key Stages…
>
> In deciding on a pupil's level of attainment at the end of a Key Stage, teachers should judge which descriptions best fits the pupil's performance.
>
> (DfEE/QCA, 1999: Curriculum and Standards, p. 1)

The Attainment Targets (AT) cover the following areas:

1   Using and Applying mathematics;
2   Number and Algebra;
3   Shape, Space and Measures;
4   Handling data (which does not apply to KS1).

As an example of Level 1 work in number and algebra, we might look for evidence that a child can; count, order, add and subtract numbers when solving problems involving up to 10 objects. The child should be able to; read and write the numbers involved. It is important to emphasise that this information is for assessment purposes. It should not be used to define the total curriculum experience of the child. Although it might be possible to teach simply by following the ATs the consequence is likely to be that children will not learn the mathematics they are taught. The ATs define what must be addressed but to ensure that children engage in deep learning rather than superficial remembering, the experiences that teachers provide must go beyond the ATs.

Many schools see a five-day numeracy programme each week as inappropriate and some use at least one per month for work that has quite a different flavour. Others have a week of different activities each term: an Art Week or an Eisteddfod that incorporates mathematical activity as well as celebrating musical and poetic accomplishment.

Statutory reporting arrangements

At least once each year (the legal minimum) and usually each term, teachers assess their children's performance against the NC *levels of attainment* in a process called levelling. Following the guidance given in the Dearing review of 1995, teachers assess the level of performance of each child annually throughout each Key Stage, using a 'best fit' model. This is recorded as the *Teacher Assessment* and must be communicated to parents as part of the school's requirement to provide parents with (at least) one report annually.

At the end of each Key Stage, children also take SAT tests. The two types of assessments give different pictures of the end of KS attainment for a child. The teacher assessment is broader and is drawn from more detailed evidence. The SAT test is administered with the intention of comparing and ranking all children in that age group, nationally. A second purpose is to compare schools by publishing 'league tables' which show the proportion of children at KS2 who have achieved Level 4.

Each year, local education authorities and the governors of individual schools, are required to set targets for the coming year. These local targets feed into a national target set originally by David Blunkett in his role as Secretary of State for Education during the first Labour administration. Estelle Morris, during her period as Secretary of State, retained most of Blunkett's intentions, except that unlike her predecessor, she did not promise to resign if the government's targets were not met by Blunkett's deadline of 2004. Her resignation and subsequent replacement by Charles Clark was nevertheless prompted by issues relating to assessment and the way they are used to define Standards at a national level.

Note

1 'The Third International Mathematics and Science Study (TIMSS) is the largest and most ambitious international study of student achievement ever conducted. In 1994–95, it was conducted at five grade levels in more than 40 countries (the third, fourth, seventh, and eighth grades, and the final year of secondary school).

Students were tested in mathematics and science and extensive information about the teaching and learning of mathematics and science was collected from students, teachers, and school principals. Altogether, TIMSS tested and gathered contextual data for more than half a million students and administered questionnaires to thousands of teachers and school principals.

Also, TIMSS investigated the mathematics and science curricula of the participating countries through an analysis of curriculum guides, textbooks, and other curricular materials. The TIMSS results were released in 1996 and 1997 in a series of reports, providing valuable information to policy makers and practitioners in the participating countries about mathematics and science instruction and the achievement of their students.' http://timss.bc.edu/timss1995.html

Resources and further reading

There are number of useful websites that support trainees: http://www.standards.dfes.gov.uk/numeracy/

http://www.cleo.ucsm.ac.uk/content/maths/nationalnumeracy/cumbria/

www.ofsted.gov.uk/public/docs00/nnsinterim.pdf (Interim Report by OFSTED on the effectiveness of the NNS can be found here.)

Ainley, J. (1996) *Enriching Primary Mathematics with IT*. London: Hodder and Stoughton.

Briggs, M. and Pritchard, A. (2002) *Using ICT in Primary Mathematics Teaching*. Exeter: Learning Matters.

Coles, D. and Copeland, T. (2000) *Numeracy and Mathematics across the Primary Curriculum*. London: David Fulton.

O'Brien, T. C. (2002) *Problem Solving (1–6)*. (Ginn Numeracy Extras) Oxford: Ginn&Co.

Office for Standards in Education (OFSTED) (2002) *The National Numeracy Strategy: The First Three Years*. London: OFSTED.

QCA/DfEE (1999) *National Curriculum: Key Stages 1 and 2*. London: HMSO.

QCA (2000) *Curriculum Guidance for the Foundation Stage*. London: HMSO.

TTA (2000) *Using ICT to Meet Teaching Objectives in Mathematics*.

3 Curriculum development in mathematics

To be an effective primary teacher your knowledge of individual subjects such as mathematics needs to be integrated within your overall understanding of professional practice. This is a challenging task for anyone and is sometimes made more difficult by the contradictory demands made on teachers. If you understand the context in which you will be working, you are more likely to be able to put your knowledge of mathematics to better use in your teaching and more likely to see how meeting the Standards for mathematics contributes to becoming a professional primary teacher.

The current state of affairs in school is highly complex and not easy to understand. It is important to realise that any institution and state schools are no exception, has an associated history and ideology. This chapter provides a historical context which maps out, but doesn't necessarily justify, how we got to where we are today.

The curriculum has both a form and a substance, is historically determined – at least in part – and could be something other than it is today. It is as it is, partly because of historical tradition and partly because teacher-educators and other policy makers have shaped its form.

As far as I know only Caleb Gattegno has developed a theory of the learning of mathematics based on concepts of economy and only Dave Hewitt (1994) has attempted to develop this into a theory of 'economy of learning and teaching'.

What we have as far as a contemporary mathematics curriculum is concerned is something that saw its genesis in the nineteenth century when mathematics was introduced into many schools as an extra-curricular subject. (At Eton maths teachers were not full members of staff and according to the school rules were not to be 'capped' by the boys.)

We have a European history of philosophical and mystical scientific exploration going back at least as far as Pythagoras (e.g. with Pythagorean societies holding secret meetings to this day, in Plymouth). We have a twentieth-century curriculum with four distinct origins, the first based in practical work and shopkeeping, and which for me, led to lessons in mensuration – a separate subject at my secondary school. The second – classical Euclidean geometry, replete with propositions, axioms and proofs – a topic on which David Fielker wrote extensively in the 1980s in a series of articles for *Mathematics Teaching* called *Removing the Shackles of Euclid*. The third – a 'new maths' curriculum which appeared in England in the 1970s – was developed out of the work of Whitehead and Russell, *Principia Mathematica* (1910) which developed the use of set theory as a starting point for definitions of mathematics of number. Finally, the work of Piaget, first in biology and subsequently in child development, where he established an empirical basis for a theory of human interaction on the external physical world.

There are extensive sources of material. The Centre for Mathematics Education at the Open University for example, has produced an enormous number of resources and courses for the study of teaching and learning mathematics. Rudy Rucker (1988) in *Mind Tools* explored the idea of an essential toolkit for working mathematically. Jerome Bruner led the development of Piaget's ideas on constructivism and also promoted the work of Vygotsky, who wrote from a social constructivist perspective in his native Russia in the 1930s and was translated into English only some thirty years later.

The current National Numeracy Strategy (NNS) has a distinct flavour of Vygotskian social constructivism, arguing as it does that language and discourse form the crucial base on which we construct meaning. The contemporary mathematics curriculum of the NNS Framework is conceived as a series of experiences where maths topics are mediated through interaction with an expert curriculum guide. Learning is the result of children's interactions with the external world, mediated by a sensitive and provocative teacher, whose promotion of discourse is the prime mover in the internalisation of experience into coherent mathematical knowledge and understanding.

This definition of curriculum is itself an accommodation of different views of knowledge: the first being that knowledge is an external body of content to be captured and internalised, the second, that the only way to create useful knowledge that can be acted upon is to construct it through one's own structuring of the mind in response to external events. In this case, although the content of our knowledge base (what we know about multiplication tables or solving an equation) is comparable with what others know, what we have come to know, as a result of experience, has been produced by us individually and uniquely as a result of our singular interaction with the external world and our reflection on experience mediated through language and discourse.

No wonder then, that progression in the curriculum is such a slippery subject. If we accept the discussion made earlier (and some educators will of course resist it), which argues that the current curriculum is both a set of topics to be taught, and a way of working, the curriculum cannot sensibly be conceived as solely a progression through mathematical topics. As a culture we are still caught between these two ways of perceiving the curriculum and the purpose of education. In practice, we see the gap between teaching for understanding in the mathematics classroom and assessment through Statutory Assessment Tasks (SATs) which demands mainly recall and memorisation, and which is intended to measure children entirely in age-related groups, thus ignoring developmental issues. This type of testing also ignores the fundamental right of children to receive feedback and guidance on how to improve at all points in their education. Who should have the right to impose external demands like these on individual children is an interesting question that has not really been addressed as a democratic issue within education.

This confusion of what constitutes curriculum progression is partly due to our history. Since Victorian times, schools have been required to separate children by age, rather than by ability, partly for payment purposes for teachers when Victorian children met certain 'Standards'. Except in the smaller state schools, we continue to require a change of class teacher annually, for no particular reason other than tradition. In Steiner schools by contrast (after kindergarten), the teacher and class remain together during the primary phase.

We teach certain topics during each year, again largely for historical reasons, based on what typical children can manage to achieve in each year. So the curriculum is not geared to what each child needs, but rather to what children 'ought' to be taught if they are regarded as typical or average for their age group. Teachers are then required to explain the performance of children who are not well served by this system. We are forced to invent a language which describes children as very able, slow, above average, weak, etc. This discourse implicitly defines intelligence as fixed or relatively unchanging, despite research findings that provide considerable evidence to the contrary. The discourse also inhibits discussion about children's entitlement to a curriculum which is appropriate to their needs.

All the evidence coming from recent research into brain function is that the brain has immense potential for plasticity. Intelligence is plastic, it is shaped by a complex combination of circumstances but crucially by language, the degree to which neural connections can be easily formed and strengthened, motivation, confidence, self-esteem and social context. The NNS Framework tries to mediate these different views of learning by providing a spiral curriculum where children and teachers are able to take repeated opportunities to revisit ideas each term and half-term.

We have arrived at an exciting point in the development of the primary mathematics curriculum – but there is still a struggle to accommodate the dual conceptions of mathematics as: (i) a list of topics to be taught; (ii) an interactive process of engagement between teacher and learner.

At present, teachers can monitor and record children's progress with some degree of objectivity, but this part of their professional role receives less than appropriate status, because formal assessment of children's achievement has been hijacked for other purposes, including measuring teacher effectiveness and school success. The result of this multipurpose use of assessment is that we have something that does not work educationally for the individual child and the class teacher who is seeking to promote children's success in learning. What is important for children has been sidelined and what is focused on, in the formal assessment process, has become overly important and has led to a distortion of the purpose of education. Before 1988, schools and teachers could decide much of the curriculum for themselves. Religious Education (RE) was the only compulsory subject and the legislation dating from 1944 demanded that the RE curriculum be planned regionally following national guidelines. It should be taught from what was known as 'The Agreed Syllabus'. Parents had the right to remove their children from RE lessons and teachers could refuse to teach RE for personal religious reasons. Apart from some health and safety matters, teachers and schools were free to decide what to put in the school curriculum, and whether or not to teach a curriculum subject. Many chose not to teach science for example, and very few taught design or technology.

Many schools and Local Education Authorities (LEAs) emphasised certain curriculum areas: Oxfordshire was well-known for its creative arts initiatives. Schools varied considerably in the emphasis they placed on the other subjects of the curriculum. It is interesting that part of the present government's plans for helping gifted pupils through its Excellence in Cities initiative and its proposed city academies, implies that some schools (mainly secondary) will once again specialise in certain curriculum areas.

Local preferences versus curriculum entitlement

Prior to the introduction of the National Curriculum (NC) many primary schools developed a specialism, often in language, music, Physical Education (PE) or visual and tactile arts. Unfortunately, many schools did not, and their curriculum was dull, boring and mechanical. Some schools made outstanding provision for children's learning but too many children had a dreary diet of mainly arithmetic and English exercises, topped up with indifferent and unimaginative topic work.

The government of the day conceived of a basic curriculum for all children of school age in England, Wales and Northern Ireland (but not Scotland). The introduction of the NC proved enormously challenging and the huge number of published curriculum objectives went through three major revisions before a more manageable format was developed. The early versions of the NC were enormously difficult for teachers to implement and administratively disruptive for schools.

This curriculum was conceived as a subject-focused core curriculum of English (and Welsh, where it is a first language), mathematics and science, supported by the non-core curriculum subjects of: art, design and technology, history, geography, IT, music and PE (and Welsh in those parts of Wales where it is not the first language). RE continued as a compulsory (and therefore strictly speaking, a non-NC subject).

Current revisions have resulted in Curriculum 2000 with Information and Communications Technology (ICT) added (sometimes defined as a fourth core subject, sometimes ambiguously placed and seen as a non-core subject along with science).

If viewed from the perspective of entitlement, the story can be told very differently. Prior to the introduction of a NC, many children had had no access to a broad, balanced, relevant and differentiated curriculum. Only a few received a rich and interesting diet of: English, mathematics, science, music, history, geography, art or design technology. Some schools simply did not teach some subjects. Across the country, provision and quality were notoriously patchy. (Over many years, Her Majesty's Inspectors of Schools (HMI) had written extensively about the unacceptable variation in curriculum provision, particularly in respect of able pupils.)

In terms of children's entitlement, the NC offered a broader, more consistent and more challenging curriculum than teachers and schools had managed to provide prior to the 1988 Education Reform Act (ERA). The national picture improved considerably for a while. More recently children's entitlement has been threatened, first by the introduction of the Literacy Strategy, then by the Numeracy Strategy and by enhanced expectations in ICT.

Many schools report having had to replan their entire curriculum in order to accommodate the Literacy and Numeracy Strategies. Together, these two entirely dominate the morning timetables in a majority of schools, leaving only half the time in school for addressing the other subjects. History, geography, music, art, technology and PE have been hard hit and further curriculum reviews will be necessary if children's entitlement to a broad and balanced experience is to be restored.

From the 1960s to the 1980s

A curious influence on the school curriculum took place following the publication of *Children and their Primary Schools*, a report by the Central Advisory Council for England

(1967), generally known as *The Plowden Report* (named after Lady Plowden who chaired the proceedings). At the time of the report, lessons in many Junior Schools (7–11 age range) bore a striking resemblance to those in secondary schools: teaching was not very different from that of the 1930s. A class teacher delivered most lessons in a relatively formal way to the whole class, with children's responses mainly taking the form of a brief question and answer session, followed by lengthy written exercises in books.

In contrast, many infant schools (5–7 age range) looked and felt very different. A significant number had developed a curriculum that was heavily influenced by the very powerful kindergarten movement that had shaped schools in Europe (Britain included), during the 1920s and 1930s. British nursery schools had played an influential part in shaping European models of teaching between the two world wars. British infant schools were much more influenced by contemporary psychological theories of learning through play and child development, than were their junior school counterparts.

British education has constantly suffered from a simplistic polarisation of views. The 1970s was dominated by arguments about formal versus informal methods of teaching. One view of Plowden's influence was that it helped to establish children as participants in learning, legitimised play as a vehicle for learning, encouraged individualised learning and generally influenced the way schools were run. Those who disliked what they saw argued that it caused a decline in standards. They blamed Plowden for supposedly encouraging poorly supervised play and for discouraging formal teaching and learning.

In practice the situation was subtly different. It was the teacher's language about the curriculum that changed dramatically. Children's learning and child development tended to become a major element of infant teachers' discourse. Although the actual curriculum in primary schools and in particular in the 7–11 age range altered very little, a few schools hit the headlines.

In my work as a curriculum advisor, I visited hundreds of schools and classrooms in the 1980s. I found that only in about one in nine classrooms and schools was there any evidence that the changes recommended by Plowden had taken root. For the most part, it was teacher's knowledge, thinking and discourse that had changed, rather than the curriculum and children's experiences. The great changes that undoubtedly did take place in schools were brought about more by general changes in society, than by internally-led curriculum development.

There has been a steady move to a more formal curriculum for children, especially in the wake of the so-called Great Debate on Education inaugurated by the then Prime Minister Jim Callaghan in 1976. This certainly did lead to changes in the curriculum. In Britain, far from Plowden changing the junior school curriculum, which has become the popular view, the changes to classroom practice that have taken place have mostly arisen as the result of external influences and pressure. As politicians gradually learned to engage with educational issues, so there was a polarisation of the debate into a stereotype of progressive versus traditional education.

With some notable exceptions, most junior classrooms had in fact made very few changes to the way the curriculum was taught or the way in which teachers worked. There was one notable exception in the mathematics curriculum, where significant pedagogical changes took place rapidly in schools in the early 1970s where individualised workbooks and worksheet programmes were rapidly introduced. It was the introduction of individualised teaching programmes, couched in phrases that were distorted echoes of Piaget's language of individual development that brought to an end whole-class teaching in mathematics lessons. Interestingly, the inclusion of time for whole-class teaching is a central plank of the National Literacy Strategy (NLS) and the NNS.

Far from influencing the primary school curriculum in ways that some have argued, infant schools were themselves increasingly enmeshed in a remorseless formalising of the curriculum. In the 1970s and 1980s many infant classrooms offered a curriculum that was free from formal schemes. Many children were in schools that followed a play-based curriculum for the first two years, until children entered what was then known as the 'top infant' class (Year 2, Y2).

The introduction of the NC was originally conceived as starting in Y1. Schools had to introduce it much earlier when Office for Standards in Education (OFSTED) inspectors began to make it clear that they were looking for evidence of the NC being taught to children from the age of five. To meet these new external pressures, the traditional Early Years curriculum had to be largely abandoned. There were no opportunities to develop it through a process of curriculum review. In the last few years, until the introduction of the Foundation Stage Guidance, there was no evidence of a curriculum that reflected knowledge of child development or a curriculum based on children's immediate needs and interests.

Even in current documents and legislation, there is little direct reference to the dramatic developments in knowledge emanating from psychology, neuroscience or brain function. The official curriculum for the Early Years remains moribund and impoverished, restricted rather than helped by subject-focused curriculum constraints. The DfES website by contrast, acknowledges and publishes some exciting material including research findings that are far in advance of the thinking reflected in legislation and government curriculum materials.

Curriculum developments have created the conditions for a over-formal Early Years teaching regime in Britain that many now regard as inappropriate for young children and their development. No longer a leading European model, which others seek to follow, British Early Years provision has become a backwater, beset with controversy and very different in quality and intention from the provision in much of Europe where, in many countries, play-based kindergarten provision leads on to an informal school curriculum for children aged 4–5 and then to formal schooling only when children reach the age of six or in some countries seven. The Reggio Emilia curriculum provides a really dramatic contrast in cultural and social attitudes to pre-school education. These ideas are now much more easily accessible with the publication of *Experiencing Reggio-Emilia* (Abbott and Nutbrown, 2001). See also the pages on holistic education published by the informal education website infed.org. and the South Florida parenting magazine – http://www.sfparenting.com/top/1,1419, S-Sfparenting-Living-X!ArticleDetail-9697,00.html

It is very difficult to compare the results of educational experience of children in Britain and in Europe, especially in countries where formal education starts at seven. This later start could in fact be a factor in European children out-performing British children by age eleven. The evidence is not clear and not simple to interpret. A valuable source of information is a series of books by Robin Alexander and others on comparative education, which include *Culture and Pedagogy* (Alexander, 2000). The Highscope Project http://www.highscope.org/ which has been running in USA for many years has produced evidence of the benefit of early years education, with adults who were involved in Highscope programmes showing long-term gains as problem solvers and better adjustment to life challenges and society.

Although the introduction of a NC could be argued to have enhanced the quality and diversity of the curriculum for 7–11-year olds it did so at the expense of the Early Years curriculum, which became over-formal and inappropriate for 4–6-year old children. The introduction of the pre-school guidance called *Desirable Outcomes for Children* was a temporary measure, which was pedagogically flawed. It sat on the fence, espousing the need for the curriculum to be shaped by what is known about children's development, but written, like the NC, under subject headings. This situation was then only partially addressed through the introduction of a Foundation Stage and the publication of Early Learning Goals. The introduction of a Foundation Stage has not reunited Early Years practice in Britain and Europe nor allowed a cross-fertilisation of ideas that has been largely absent over the last few years except for projects like the Reggio Emilia Hundred Languages of Children exhibition, which has toured globally (http://ericeece.org/reggio/regtour.html) (Edwards *et al.*, 1998).

As children remain one of the largest groups who experience poverty in this country, Early Years provision needs to be child-centred and multidisciplinary, involving an integrated approach with teams which represent health, social and educational provision.

The 1990s

The NC of the early 1990s was unwieldy and difficult to manage. In 1995 Sir Ron Dearing was asked to carry out a review of the NC. This led to a reorganisation of the content. More importantly, Dearing forced the government to be explicit about teachers' legal responsibilities in regard to assessment of children and reporting to parents. The Dearing Review also guaranteed a five-year period of no curriculum change. Although this remained true as far as the NC content was concerned, SATs, and the style and focus of school inspections was continually under review and few teachers would say that the period from 1995 to 2000 was one of consistency and stability as promised by Dearing.

One of the features of the slimmed-down version of the NC was that it became much less useful for students in training. The early versions of the NC content were almost as detailed as the current NNS (although quite different in style since the NC focused on lists of content rather than emphasising mathematical strategies).

Trainees found the early versions of the NC very useful because they provided a detailed breakdown of the mathematics curriculum. The slimmed-down versions were much better for teachers who had gained several years' knowledge and experience of the maths curriculum but the value of the post-1995 revised programmes was much reduced for students entering training. The slimmed-down version of the NC didn't support teachers' planning in mathematics and it was clear that a pedagogical vacuum had been created. Teachers needed pedagogically appropriate materials if they were to have any hope of delivering the higher standards sought by politicians and curriculum developers. The NNS which emerged from the National Numeracy Project (NNP) was a natural vehicle for supporting and guiding curriculum enhancement in primary mathematics. A discussion of the scope and effect of the NNP can be found in Straker (1999).

Creating an effective climate for learning

What do we want to achieve in mathematics lessons? Initially, we may see the answer in terms of transmitting our own mathematical knowledge clearly and unambiguously to children. After all, don't we want children to grasp mathematical ideas with clarity? But when we review our own mathematical development, we realise that understanding and clarity were not always common features of the learning process: learning mathematics is often messy. Life and learning are more complex: and life in mathematics classrooms for many of us was tough, even when our teachers were careful to be precise, clear and supportive.

We need to sustain robustness and resilience in learners. Many start as resilient learners at four but become highly dependent and dysfunctional learners by fourteen. In contrast, we can help develop resilience in those who lack confidence in mathematics, but it is not easy. It is of course far better to nurture and maintain the resilience of younger learners as they grow, but it is clear that we simply do not achieve this with a large number of pupils. A very clear account of ways in which teachers can improve the ability and self-esteem of learners is given by Guy Claxton in *Teaching to Learn* where he discusses the research of Carol Dweck into the ways in which teachers create helpless-prone and mastery-oriented learners in their classrooms. See also *Wise Up* (Claxton, 1999).

Transmission and constructivist theories

It is obvious of course that there is a body of mathematical knowledge and skills, which primary children are expected to acquire. Initially, we are likely to see that we, as teachers, have greater knowledge and skills. A transmission model is not an unreasonable model to have when one begins teaching, but it fails to tell the whole story.

The last half-century has seen a steady development in two theoretical areas, constructivist theories of learning, and biological theories of brain function. In the simplest of terms, constructivist theories talk about concept development, while biological theories address knowledge acquisition in terms of electrical and chemical changes in the brain, which lead to the development of neural structures and pathways.

Learning is accompanied by changes in the structure of neural pathways, where responses to incoming information are processed initially through visual, aural, olfactory and kinaesthetic receptors, before being subtly subjected to change by internal emotional states. The resulting neural network patterns have to be used regularly if learners are to be confident in getting reliable access (recall) to the data stored by these changed neural pathways and clusters. The repetition needed for strengthened neural pathways can come from rote learning but the pathways are much more likely to be strengthened if there is an emotional commitment to repetition: not least because children don't spend that much time doing mathematics in school in comparison to say watching television. In simple terms, it means getting children to want to do more mathematics because they love doing it, so that they do it even when they are not in school: a tough assignment for us, but achievable.

Constructivist theory includes social aspects of learning, and argues that knowledge of mathematics cannot simply be transmitted from one person to another. We cannot teach facts without also engaging with people's emotions.

Learners construct their own knowledge and therefore, confusion and error needs to be seen as a natural part of the learning process, rather than necessarily a lack of ability on the part of the teacher. There is such a thing as poor teaching however: and poor teaching does not help learning of course. It is just that it is sometimes harder to define what constitutes poor teaching when one is working within a constructivist paradigm framework than when one is working within a transmission paradigm.

Resources and further reading

http://www.sfparenting.com/top/1,1419,S-Sfparenting-Living-X!ArticleDetail-9697,00.html (South Florida parenting magazine).

http://www.highscope.org/ (Highscope Educational Research Foundation).

http://ericeece.org/reggio/regtour.html (Reggio Emilia Hundred Language of Children Exhibition).

Abbott, L. and Nutbrown, C. (eds) (2001) *Experiencing Reggio Emilia: Implications for Pre-school Provision.* Buckingham: Open University Press.

Alexander, R. (2000) *Culture and Pedagogy: International Comparisons in Primary Education.* Oxford: Blackwell.

Berger, A., Morris, D. and Portman, J. (2000) *Implementing the National Numeracy Strategy for Pupils with Learning Difficulties.* London: David Fulton.

Briggs, M. and Pritchard, A. (2002) *Using ICT in Primary Mathematics Teaching.* Exeter: Learning Matters.

Central Advisory Council for England (1967) *Children and Their Primary Schools* (Plowden Report). London: HMSO.

Dryden, G. and Vos, J. (2001) *The Learning Revolution.* Stafford: Network Educational Press.

Edwards, C. P., Gandini, L. and Forman, G. E. (eds) (1998) *The Hundred Languages of Children: The Reggio Emilia Approach – Advanced Reflections* (second edition). Greenwich, Conn.: Ablex Publishing Corporation.

Liebling, H. (1999) *Getting Started: An Induction Guide for Newly Qualified Teachers* (chapter 8: Learning Styles). School Effectiveness Series. Stafford: Network Educational Press.

Montague-Smith, A. (1997) *Mathematics in Nursery Education.* London: David Fulton.

Pollard, A, (ed.) (1997) *Reflective Teaching in the Primary School.* London: Cassell.

Pollard, A. (ed.) (1996) *Readings for Reflective Teaching.* London: Cassell.

Pound, L. (1999) *Supporting Mathematical Development in the Early Years.* Buckingham: Open University Press.

Rucker, R. (1988) *Mind Tools: the five levels of Mathematical Reality.* Harmondsworth: Penguin.

Selley, N. (1999) *The Art of Constructivist Teaching in the Primary School: A Guide for Students and Teachers.* London: David Fulton.

Smith, A. (1996) *Accelerated Learning in the Classroom.* Stafford: Network Educational Press.

Straker, A. (1999) The National Numeracy Project 1996–99. In: Ian Thompson (ed.) *Issues in Teaching Numeracy in Primary Schools.* Buckingham: Open University Press.

Thompson, I. (ed.) (1997) *Teaching and Learning Early Number.* Buckingham: Open University Press.

Vygotsky, L. (1962) *Thought and Language.* MIT Press.

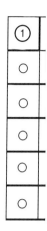

Figure 4.1

Figure 4.2

In the contex
duced by m
that many ch

The teach
here. This ca
square. Again
may find this
a table like t

Number
Square

4 Developing your personal knowledge base in mathematics

Mathematics is a hard subject to learn and to teach. We need to build up our own knowledge and understanding in several important ways.

1   Extending and reinforcing our content knowledge, for example, by learning about Arab architectural influence in Europe and the use of geometric patterns in buildings such as the Alhambra Palace. We need to develop our curriculum knowledge by tackling key mathematical ideas, such as the relationship between algebra and arithmetic. We may need to improve recall of known facts, and acquire, develop and hone our personal mathematical skills and strategies.
2   Developing general pedagogical knowledge, for example, by learning how to organise a three-part lesson along the lines suggested in the National Numeracy Strategy (NNS).
3   Developing pedagogical-content knowledge, by learning, for example, how to combine the use of elastic loops, Poleidoblocs, soap bubbles, Geostrips and shadows, to teach very different aspects of 2-D and 3-D shape.
4   Gaining knowledge of learners and their characteristics, by acquiring some knowledge of children's development, brain function and human motivational factors.
5   Employing a wide range of practical contexts for learning, by making good use of classrooms, playgrounds, school visits, table-top games and practical activities, in order to maximise learning.
6   Ensuring harmony between our beliefs and values about the purposes of education, and the very practical problems of ensuring that children have access to their educational entitlement through working with us, for example, by ensuring that children with special educational needs have access to a rich educational experience rather than a narrow training.

The Professional Standards state that trainees must be able to teach in at least two Key Stages (KS). Although some trainees may be on courses that combine KS2 and KS3, the majority are likely to be training for: (i) Foundation and KS1; (ii) KS1 and KS2.

The Professional Standards relate to mathematics and the other curriculum subjects through generic statements which set out what is expected of trainees in terms of knowledge and understanding.

For the Foundation Stage, ... [trainees] know and understand the aims, principles, six areas of learning and early learning goals described in the QCA/DfEE Curriculum

Children can go on to find the differences between successive square numbers (the difference between 1 and 4 is 3, between 4 and 9 is 5, …).

This can be created visually using small wooden or plastic shapes to show

$$1+3+5+7$$

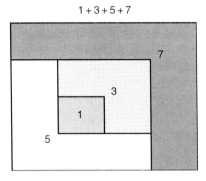

At some time in their school career, pupils will be taught that all this information about square numbers can be summarised in a very compact algebraic statement, written as:

$$y = x^2$$

This condensation of the above discussion into four written symbols, demonstrates the power of mathematics to encapsulate, symbolise and represent a huge quantity of subject knowledge. It is also a potential weakness of mathematics. For someone who is comfortable with mathematics, the expression $y = x^2$ is seen as a shorthand for what is already known, like an iceberg with the algebraic statement visible above the surface and all the connected knowledge and skills hidden beneath.

The algebraic statement is more than just a summary. Its use is governed by a powerful system of rules. It is an economic way of making a general statement about the relationship between two sets of numbers (a set of numbers represented by y and a second set by x: such that for every value that x might take, there is a value y which is derived by multiplying the value for x by itself to produce a square number). You can see how long winded a written English description of the meaning of the expression becomes, and how condensed the algebraic statement is in contrast.

Someone who is comfortable with algebraic expressions will know that it is possible to read $y = x^2$ as if it was a recipe or a set of instructions. 'Think of any number you like, and imagine the expression rewritten with your number in place of the x, for example, $y = 3.5^2$. Now carry out the calculation by squaring 3.5 and the result will be the value of y when $x = 3.5$ ($3.5 \times 3.5 = 12.25$).'

It is important to get a dynamic sense of what is happening as the numbers in the two sets change. If we can do this, we are more likely to get a feel for the mathematics involved. Kinaesthetic awareness can come from using a calculator which has a square function. The key pressings form a routine and each set of pressings can be associated with the visual readout.

Some people respond very well to diagrams that incorporate a sense of movement.

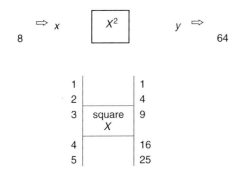

Someone who is comfortable with algebraic expressions will probably choose some key values of x that will help clarify the relationship more effectively than making $x = 3.5$ which doesn't provide much of a picture, except that values of y seem to be larger than the corresponding x (when x is about 3, y is about 12). Instead, we could choose 0, 1 and -1 as three values. We might intuitively do this based on our experience with arithmetic. We might recall that multiplying numbers by 0 and by 1 does something interesting. Just ask children if they want to learn the zero times table and the ones times table for homework and you will know from their response whether they know that 0 and 1 play special roles in multiplication. Here, we are trying to capitalise on this knowledge!

If also, we encourage children to get into the habit of making lists or tables of their findings, then we and they stand more chance of spotting patterns, and making sense of the mathematics that we are working on.

For $y = x^2$ a value of 0 for x produces a value of 0 for y. When x is given the value 1 then y becomes 1. Curiously, when we substitute -1 for x the corresponding value for y is still 1. If we make $x = 10$ then y becomes 100.

Possible values for x	-1	0	1	10
Resulting values for y	1	0	1	100

This work might not look at all like the starting point above, where we began by putting pegs in a pegboard. This is partly because the pegboard work was limited (without discussion) to the set of counting numbers (or positive integers). In contrast, $y = x^2$ can be applied to real numbers, that is, to positive and negative integers and numbers containing fractions or decimals.

The topic of square numbers can be studied in various ways using concrete and symbolic methods, and both arithmetic and algebraic representations. It is also possible to use a geometric representation. In the graph in Figure 4.3, positive and negative values of x give rise only to positive values of y and the graph has a certain pleasing symmetry which may be surprising on first exploration.

Access to the three representations, arithmetic, algebraic and geometric are crucial in building up an understanding of the topic, and an understanding of mathematics as a body of knowledge in which very different representations occur as a matter of course. Some representations are more difficult for children (and adults) than are others. Useful places to look

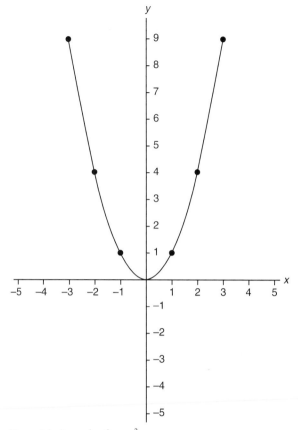

Figure 4.3 A graph of $y = x^2$.

for ideas are, Rudy Rucker's *Mind Tools* and *Primary Mathematics Today*, by Williams and Shuard.

Access to these different types of representation is something that we need to provide for children wherever possible. With topics like square numbers, there is an interesting pedagogical imperative facing us as teachers. We have to find a way to utilise arithmetic, algebraic and geometric representations of the mathematics in our work with young children. For many of us, it is this pedagogical imperative, this challenge of finding appropriate ways of helping children move between different mathematical representations of an idea, that motivates us to explore mathematics as teachers, when perhaps we did not enjoy mathematics as learners in school.

There is a pedagogical imperative to develop strategies rather than single approaches to tackling mathematical problems. A valuable book for adults those who wish to develop their strategies for tackling investigations and problem solving in mathematics is *Thinking Mathematically* (Mason *et al.*, 1982) with its detailed discussion of personal approaches, potential difficulties and how to manage them.

One strategy to adopt when faced with a mathematical problem or investigation is to ask ourselves the question, 'Can I represent this problem using numbers, algebra and geometry?' One important strategy is to learn to 'read' the mathematics, that is, to learn what to say out loud when one looks at a mathematical statement like:

$$\Box + 6.4 = 10$$

We need to teach children the sequence of eye scans and thought processes that are necessary to engage with this mathematical text. It is crucial to see that although there are many similarities with a piece of English text, mathematics is read differently, and reading mathematics requires as much teaching as scanning a sentence in English. In reading mathematics, left to right scanning is useful, but in the above case, it is important to read the meaning of the empty box as, 'I need to imagine a number in here later on, but not until I've glossed over it and read the rest of the sentence. But I will have to go back to it. … So, OK, something (in the box) and 6.4 together make 10. What do I need to imagine in the box?'

Of course this is not the only way to read the sentence. It is possible to read this as a mathematical equation. We can read it by looking at the $=$ sign and reading it as a balance point. Then we could read each side separately. 'This contains an equal sign and I'm going to balance the two parts of the sentence. Over on the right is a ten. Over on the left is 6.4 and a missing number. Together the 6.4 and the missing number must make 10 also.'

There are strategies that we can emphasise to learners.

1   Try anything sensible (a 'guesstimate') and then home in.
2   Learn how to 'transform' so that $\Box = 10 - 6.4$ is automatically seen as equivalent to $10 = \Box + 6.4$ and $6.4 = 10 - \Box$.
3   Draw a number line.

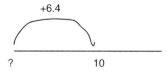

4   Think about using a different counting context (e.g. money). Something plus 64 pence makes a pound. Ah! It's 36 pence. Change from a pound for 64p? Have a look at our sunflower: it's grown 6.4 cm this week and it's now 10 cm tall. What was its height at the start of the week?

Number sentences can also be read as a set of instructions rather than an equation. 'Get an empty box and be ready to put a number in it. Add 6.4 to the number in the box in order to make 10.'

Modelling in classroom settings is the best way of teaching the reading process. As quickly as possible we step aside to allow competent children to model it to their peers, with our guidance, and less competent ones to try with more support from us. Modelling the reading of mathematics needs to be done, not just once or twice, but at least weekly, over the full primary age range. The encouragement of modelling by teachers and children is a strength of the teaching model promoted by the NNS.

Our learning is highly influenced by the associations and connections we make. We learn best when we tackle a topic in as many different ways as possible by:

- tackling different problems that relate to the same mathematical topic;
- working alone;
- working with others;
- verbally explaining our ideas;
- drawing diagrams;
- writing in prose;
- writing formulae;
- looking for general expressions.

When we work in different ways, we establish a wide range of mental images of the same mathematical topic. The more associations and connections we make between different facets of the topic, the more likely we are to be able to transfer our knowledge to new and different contexts.

When we come to teach the topic in a mathematics lesson, we will have a wider range of mental images to support us as we work. Mathematics learned in this way is more likely to appear familiar and accessible. We are more able to manage unusual or unanticipated questions posed by children. We are less likely to feel confused, and the mathematics is less likely to pose us difficulties.

The central role of language in mathematics learning

The principal roles of language are to help us make sense of the world and our lived experience, to structure our thinking and to communicate with others. We construct meaning through our internal use of language. This is not the same as sub-vocalising: the internal use of language is not synonymous with saying something to yourself inside your head.

It is easy for us to forget the complex role that language plays in the learning of mathematics. We can easily mistake language either for speaking or (especially in mathematics), for technical vocabulary. When we are teaching, we often focus on vocabulary (we need to introduce children to words and ideas like, square, rectangle, quadratic, square root, multiple, decimal, and so on). Teaching mathematical vocabulary should not take preference over helping children to think mathematically during lessons.

There is a strong interest in the role of discourse in children's learning (Bruner, 1996), which is reflected in the NNS. Discourse is seen as central to children's mathematical learning. The NNS view is that the learning of mathematics should be mainly through discussion and verbal exploration of ideas, with the children doing most of the talking and the teacher doing much of the listening. The mathematics National Curriculum (1999) also emphasises the role of language in learning:

> During Key Stage 2 pupils use the number system more confidently. They move from counting reliably to calculating fluently with all four number operations ... They

discuss and present their methods and reasoning using a wider range of mathematical language diagrams and charts.

(National Curriculum, 1999:67)

Auditing and your personal learning

Your training provider will expect you to carry out private study in mathematics. They want to help you get the most from your private study and they often do this by requiring you to carry out personal audits of your knowledge, skills and understanding. An effective audit is more than just a test of what you know, it should also map where you need to develop next. It should help you pinpoint pretty exactly:

- where you are secure in your maths knowledge;
- where there are gaps in your knowledge;
- which skills are rusty and need to be practiced;
- whether you have any misconceptions that are causing you difficulty.

Because of their personal experience and the nature of mathematics, many trainees initially underestimate their ability, particularly if it is a long time since they took public examinations like GCSE mathematics. At the beginning of your training, you may not remember all the mathematics that you will need. The seven-times table is likely to be the most difficult to recall, and it is interesting to think about why this might be. One area that most people need to work on is converting between fractions, decimals and percentages. Which conversions are easy and slick, which are laborious and slow? Which do you intuitively know? Which ones can you do but not explain? Notice the strategies that friends use. Try to get them to explain to you.

While you will quickly be able to pinpoint some areas that need addressing, you may need to have some misconceptions pointed out. An effective audit should be challenging but should also leave you feeling positive, because it will have helped you to identify specific areas of mathematics for personal work. It is not a good idea simply to try to 'brush up on everything': training courses are too short for indiscriminate study.

Your mentor or tutor should help you to set goals and targets for study, and you will probably receive some direct teaching intended to improve your mathematics, to help you revise important topics and prepare for the online mathematics QTS skills test.

Training providers often expect trainees to provide evidence of private study via a notebook, a learning log or a portfolio. Using your records as evidence, the training provider can monitor your mathematical development. A personal logbook can provide some of the evidence they will need to recommend you for QTS. More specifically, your learning logs or portfolios will need to provide evidence of:

1   Your knowledge and understanding of the National Curriculum and NNS for mathematics and the topics that children must be taught;
2   Your deeper understanding of these same mathematical topics, as you explore the mathematics beyond the level of difficulty that you will need to teach in the classroom.

Your portfolio or evidence base is your responsibility and you need to be clear about what your training provider expects of you, so that you are confident about the purpose of the evidence and efficient in collecting it.

Resources and further reading

Brown, T. and Liebling, H. (2003) *The Really Useful Maths Book*. London: Falmer Press.

Bruner, J. (1996) *Culture and Education*. Cambridge, MA: Harvard University Press.

Goulding, M., Rowland, T. and Barber, P. (2002) Does it matter? Primary teacher trainees' subject knowledge in mathematics. *British Educational Research Journal*. Vol. 28. No. 5 October 2002.

Mason, J., Burton, L. and Stacey, K. (1982) *Thinking Mathematically*. London: Addison-Wesley.

Mooney, C., Briggs, M., Fletcher, M. and McCulloch, J. (2002a) *Primary Mathematics: Teaching Theory and Practice*. Exeter: Learning Matters.

Nunes, T. and Bryant, P. (1997) *Learning and Teaching Mathematics*. Hove: Psychology Press.

Orton, A. and Frobisher, L. (1996) *Insights into Teaching Mathematics*. London: Cassell.

Thompson, I. (ed.) (1997) *Teaching and Learning Early Number*. Buckingham: Open University Press.

Thompson, I. (ed.) (1999) *Issues in Teaching Numeracy*. Buckingham: Open University.

Whitburn, J. (2000) *Strength in Numbers: Learning Mathematics in Japan and England*. London: National Institute of Economic and Social Research.

PART II
The mathematics curriculum

5   Number and the number system

The National Numeracy Strategy (NNS) has five strands, the first three of which are directly linked to the National Curriculum (NC) Programme of Study for number. (The fourth strand is linked to shape, space and measures. The fifth incorporates handling data.)

The three NNS number strands are detailed in the NNS Framework Section 1: 39–40. They are:

1   *Numbers and the number system*
    counting;
    properties of numbers and the number sequences, including negative numbers;
    place value and ordering, including reading and writing numbers;
    estimating and rounding;
    fractions, decimals and percentages, and their equivalence; ratio and proportion.
2   *Calculations*
    understanding number operations and relationships;
    rapid mental recall of number facts;
    mental calculation, including strategies for deriving new facts from known facts;
    pencil and paper methods;
    using a calculator;
    checking that results of calculations are reasonable.
3   *Solving problems*
    making decisions: deciding which operation and method of calculation to use (mental, mental with jottings, pencil and paper, calculator…);
    reasoning about numbers or shapes and making general statements about them;
    solving problems involving numbers in context: 'real life', money, measures.

This chapter introduces content knowledge about the differences between cardinal and ordinal counting and the use of sets for exploring classification of numbers. There is a discussion of the curriculum knowledge contained in the number section of the NC Programmes of Study, which has to be taught in school. There is considerable discussion of pedagogical knowledge and effective ways of teaching different aspects of the number curriculum.

The curriculum taught to young children in schools is changing in an interesting way. Historically, the introduction to mathematics in pre-school and primary schools was to help children develop their skills of recognising and making sets of objects using a wide range of large toys, table-top games such as dominoes and other activities which led to the counting of sets of objects with increasing accuracy.

Although this is still a recognisable feature of Foundation and Key Stage 1 (KS1) classrooms, and is required as part of the Level 1 assessment of the NC, two things are changing:

1   Counting objects is no longer proposed as the main route into early number.
2   Knowledge of sets is no longer seen as the route to effective calculation.

There is an imperative within the NC and particularly within the NNS Framework, to move children from counting to calculation as swiftly as possible. The simplest way of illustrating what this means and why it is thought to be essential, is to pose a question: 'Why might a calculation like $3 + 9$ (even when asked orally) be more difficult for a child to tackle in an "unreconstructed", i.e. pre-NNS classroom than for a child of similar age and ability in a classroom where teaching focuses on calculation?'

The argument is that the calculation is relatively easier and may well be completed with greater speed and accuracy in a classroom committed to teaching calculation strategies because children are:

- not encouraged to collect 3 objects, count them, collect a further 9 objects, count these out, then put them together and count out the enlarged set to find the total 12;
- more likely to do the addition mentally, using fingers or a number line;
- more likely to choose to reverse the digits without being prompted (knowing the result to be unchanged), so as to start with the larger number and add the smaller number by counting on.

This requires that both the child and the child's teacher need to understand that the number system has an internal structure. Knowing the structure allows for economy of learning which in turn leads to greater accuracy and efficiency. Work with number lines and tracks go alongside work with sets (Figure 5.1). Children are taught to calculate using fingers and numbers lines. Set work is used for sorting and classifying objects, and developing children's cardinal knowledge of number but not for teaching calculation.

Working with sets should not be neglected. Set theory offers a powerful thinking tool for children, particularly in relation to logic, reasoning and proof. For example, using sets can help children move from collecting objects with similar qualities (something they find relatively easy) to being able to separate objects using difference criteria; this is 'red'… this is 'not-red' (which they find comparatively difficult). Working with sets can help children gain knowledge of the structure of the number system. They can sort square numbers, for example, into those which are even and those which are odd. Discussion about why some square

Figure 5.1 Number tracks now complement work that young children do with sets.

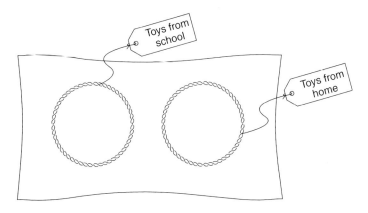

Figure 5.2 A large cotton sheet, two pieces of rope and some labels are ideal for sorting and classifying. They are a useful introduction to Venn diagrams.

numbers are odd is often more productive after children have experienced a practical activity where they have been asked to position physical numerals or number cards.

Young children enjoy collecting and sorting objects. Early activities need to be associated with children's immediate interests like sorting clothes, or teddies and themselves, by shoe colour or birthday month. Children enjoy sorting cut out numerals and this work can lead to a variety of number activities.

Figure 5.2 represents the situation where the whole universe (the totality of what we are interested in) must be placed within the rectangle. The universal set could be, 'All the teddy bears in this classroom'. Teddy bears belonging to Seema and her brother Assim, who have brought an assortment of teddies into class, could be put inside the two set rings. All other teddies that are in the classroom are therefore not Seema's and not Assim's. Seema puts her teddies in one set ring, Assim puts his in the other and they arrange the others outside the circles and within the rectangle – the universal set.

I might sort girls and boys, by using a large blanket as the universal set – big enough for us all to sit on, and two lengths of rope to make into circles. I might try shoes with laces and shoes without, people wearing socks and those who are not, those with trousers and those without, those who are tired and those who are not. Anything that provokes debate and for which initially at least, there is no ambiguity.

A really enjoyable way to explore matching and grouping in sets is through the CD-ROM *Zoombinis* by Brøderbund.

When they are secure at playing sorting games I may introduce greater ambiguity and look at the problem posed by trying to manage continuous rather than discrete data. This has to be done carefully. Eye colour and hair colour are ideas that children will offer. But if you have one child whose eye colour is very different from everyone else's and that child is newly arrived, then it is probably more important to emphasise similarities between the children for a while, rather than differences, especially if identifying differences lead to racial remarks and rejection.

I want to gently trip the children up; to pose problems and stop the learning being smooth. I want to provoke a minor and amusing problem, induce some puzzlement. I might say, 'I've got a problem that I can't work out. I wanted to put you into two sets, those wearing trousers and those wearing dresses but some people are wearing both today. I don't know what to do. Seema is wearing a beautiful dress so she needs to stand in one circle and she's also wearing trousers so she needs to stand in both.' Sometimes the children simply enjoy the joke of imagining Seema dashing between the two, or growing so tall that she can easily stand in both circles at the same time.

Alternatively, I might ask, 'Can we name these things?' And hold up a series of wooden cut out numerals, for example, 1, 7, 6, … 'I wanted to put the shapes that are curved in one set and those with straight sides in the other. I know what to do with 1 and with 6, but what can I do with 5?'

On occasions, the reaction is swift, even when working with very young children. Someone may simply walk out and rearrange the ropes to form an overlap. I pretend ignorance or disbelief and ask for further proof. If the explanation is sound: we all cheer and clap, if not, we celebrate the idea and then accept another suggestion.

I argue that it is more likely for learning to occur when children are invited to solve problems, than when a new idea is introduced explicitly by the teacher in an attempt to transmit knowledge, as in, 'Here is a new arrangement of the set rings. I want you to look carefully at what I've done, then I'll explain what it means….'

As the children meet new work in new classes, I want them to be referred back to sets and set theory with each new topic wherever possible. 'We are going to be working with positive integers from 1 to 100 today. Some of us are getting pretty good at recalling number facts for the 3- and 5-times table and today we're going to practice finding these numbers. If I ask you to use the set rings, can you find a way of sorting the multiples of 3 and the multiples of 5? Do we need some labels? Can anyone suggest a useful way of making a start? I've cards showing 1, 10, 12, and 15.'

We then take suggestions about making jottings, using calculators or not, moving the set rings around to produce intersections, trying to work out how many set rings to use and so on. When we have heard some advice on strategy from various children, individuals can opt for trying to solve the problem using some of the advice given. If the children find this too difficult, I may have to model the activity for them.

They could work in this way to test various arrangements of the sets and to see whether they have made the correct number of regions and intersections. Is there a region for 1, 3, 5, 15, 8, 9, 25 and so on? They need to understand that since the universal set is the set of positive integers such that $0 < x < 101$ (in other words x lies between 1 and 100) and every number should have one and only one region associated with it: in this case a region for all multiples of 3 and all multiples of 5. Is there a region for numbers which are not multiples of 3 *and not* multiples of 5? (Figures 5.3 and 5.4).

The use of sets is strongly visual, and can be strongly kinaesthetic too. If large cotton sheets or blankets are used with lengths of rope, then children can hold number cards and physically move around within the set: indeed if you pin the numbers onto them, they are the elements of the set.

For children to become effective users of sets we need to continually return to sorting and classifying as this is a fundamental skill for gaining access to the structure of the

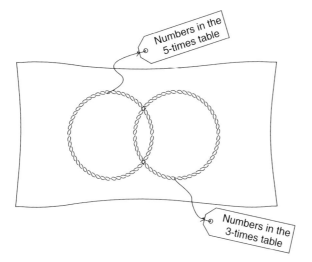

Figure 5.3 Two intersecting sets produce four regions.

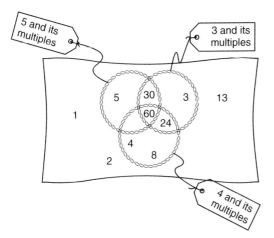

Figure 5.4 Three intersecting sets: how many regions?

number system. Children benefit from regular practice and we need to provide interesting problems to help them:

- think about numbers in terms of their various properties;
- use the results of classification to gain insights into the structure of the number system.

A Physical Education (PE) lesson with children, each of them wearing a numeral can lead to movement and mathematics. One set of activities could be about numeral recognition. Every number could be represented twice (one could be shown as spots, the other by the numeral. Put the numerals on the less confident children so the more confident can identify them).

- Find the person who is worth the same amount as you.
- Can you find someone who is two different from you?
- Join up with a partner so that you make an even total.

An enjoyable activity which helps introduce children to the structure of the number system is to look at truth tables for odd and even numbers under the four operations. When children are comfortably and consistently accurate with the arithmetic of addition and subtraction, they can be taught how to investigate from an algebraic perspective.

This could be started on a paper flipchart by the teacher in the manner suggested here or with an interactive whiteboard. I might start with a simple question. 'Can you help me add 3 and 8 please? I'm going to ask a funny question next and I want you to notice how strange it is. When I add 3 and 8 together, is the answer going to be odd or even? … Next, can you help me add 5 and 16 please? Don't bother telling me the answer; just say whether the result is odd or even? … My next numbers will be 7 and 6 but my question will be different this time! Here's my question. Please can you tell me, what is the same for all the pairs of numbers that we've added? What have they got in common? (We added 3 and 8, then 5 and 16, and now 7 and 6). What's the same each time? … Yes there are two numbers each time, what else? … What was my funny question? What did I want to know each time about the answers? What am I interested in? (odds and evens). And now please tell me about the results. So far, I added an even to an odd. I've done that three times and every time the answer has been odd. Will that always happen, do you think? What if I started with two odds, what might happen then? What if I started with two evens? Is there an investigation here that could keep us busy for a while? How would you like to work: alone, in pairs or in groups? What's a useful way of starting? What if you make mistakes in your addition?' (Figure 5.5).

Addition	Odd	Even
Odd	?	Odd + Even Result: Odd (3 + 8 = □)
Even	?	?

Figure 5.5 An incomplete truth table for addition of positive integers.

Multiplication	Odd	Even
Odd	?	Odd × Even Result: Even (3 × 8 = □)
Even	?	?

Figure 5.6 An incomplete truth table for multiplication of positive integers.

Some teachers may want to offer the children a way of summarising the information: others will prefer the children to develop their own ways of recording. The same approach can be used for multiplication. There are interesting problems that arise over subtraction and division because of course, neither is closed (i.e. although you start with positive integers you do not necessarily end up with them, e.g. $9 - 3 = 6$ but $3 - 9$ is negative 6, $3 \div 1 = 3$ but $1 \div 3$ is a non-terminating decimal).

The results for multiplication are counter-intuitive although the operation of multiplication is closed, that is, if you start with positive integers all the results will be positive integers.

Try tackling the truth table for multiplication (Figure 5.6). Decide quickly what your 'commonsense' answer would be, before working out the truth table. Look at a multiplication grid. Where are the odd numbers located? And the even numbers? If I multiply two integers (whole numbers) I can only get an odd integer product when I multiply odd by odd so if I pick two integers at random, what is the probability of their producing an odd product when I multiply them?

Learning economically

At various points, and whenever possible, I try to introduce children to the idea of economy in learning, through the learning of patterns rather than unrelated facts and relying on interpretation of patterns rather than trying to store facts in memory. Here I could say to them that when I am marking a piece of work and I look at a calculation, I know that if they have added 178 and 83 and got 262 I know it is *wrong* and I don't even have to calculate it, because an even and an odd must make an odd, and 262 is even.

A more important example of teaching economy perhaps, relates to memorising tables facts. I do not have to try to remember both 3×5 and 5×3, so long as I remember that reversing the order of the numbers does not change the result (using the commutative law for multiplication) (Figure 5.7).

Caleb Gattegno's theory of learning is a theory based on energy, and economy of energy use was a strong theme in his teaching and his theoretical work. One way of exploring the

×	1	2	3	4	5
1	1				
2		4	6	8	10
3			9	12	15
4				16	20
5					25

Figure 5.7 Part of a multiplication table for positive integers. ☐ Pay one Ogden for each of these facts; ■ Pay one Ogden for all of these facts; and ▨ Pay one Ogden for all these.

idea was in defining the Ogden (he simply borrowed one person's name from his current teaching group. When writing his ideas for publication, Gattegno referred to his most recent teaching group, of which Ogden had been a member). Gattegno argued that we can imagine expending one Ogden of energy for each item of knowledge that is effectively stored and which we can recall for later use.

I will expend one Ogden storing the fact that 15 is the result of the multiplication of 3 times 5. I expend another Ogden on remembering that 5 times 3 equals 15 and a further Ogden on remembering the fact that reversing any multiplicative pair will leave the result unchanged (5 times 3 and 3 times 5 give the same result). So paying one Ogden for commutativity saves me the cost of learning my tables facts as separate items. Further savings can be made. I use one Ogden for the identity element for multiplication (the identity for multiplication is 1, i.e. the number which when you multiply by it, leaves all other numbers unchanged. As an aside, what is the identity for addition? Which number, when added to any other number, leaves that number unchanged?)

To practise economy in learning requires us to emphasise connectivity to the full and to work with algebraic and general relationships wherever possible. So, algebraically,

$$a \times b = c \qquad c = a \times b$$
$$b \times a = c \qquad c = b \times a$$
$$n \times 1 = n \qquad n = n \times 1$$

It means taking learners beyond the lower level skill to look at the higher level strategy, and in this work on the number system, it means taking learners beyond the arithmetic and into the algebraic structure of the number system. It means emphasising structures and connections, and teaching in ways that help learners to minimise the number of separate pieces of knowledge to be learnt. Working economically in this way helps paint the wider picture at the same time as immersing learners in the detail.

Some learners find working without the big picture very disconcerting; 'Where are we going, what's the point?' Others prefer to approach things piecemeal, by collecting little bits of detailed evidence before they think big; 'Don't tell me too much all at once. I can't cope!' What is important is to help different types of learners towards a point where they can move more comfortably between the specific and the general, by gaining fluency and automaticity.

The real number system and the laws of arithmetic

The set of counting numbers 1, 2, 3, 4, ... which were extended to the set of integers with the inclusion of zero, $-4, -3, -2, -1, 0, 1, 2, 3, 4, 5, ...$ can now be further extended to become the real number system which includes fractions and decimals. I had two types of electronic calculator in my classroom which contained processors that used different types of logic, so they worked very differently. They produced different answers when you keyed in a mixed calculation like:

$1 + 2 \times 3$

Some children found their calculator gave an answer of 9 whilst others found they got 7. It made for an interesting lesson; a lot of healthy arguing, some scepticism about how reliable calculators are, and some increased attention to key presses. I then asked each group to explore other key presses in order to make their calculator produce the answer that the other sort of calculator had originally produced.

One group of children in my Y4 class decided that what was important was how you said the mathematical sentence. As one boy reasoned, if you say, 'One-add-two (long pause), times three', you mean something different from, 'One ... (long pause) add two-times-three. And it is important which bit you do first.'

When we put the calculators away and looked at writing and reading the sentences, I asked them to put brackets round the words that needed to be said first. The result was part of what adults call BODMAS – a mnemonic that reminds us of the rules of arithmetic, and in particular the order in which calculations should be done.

This lesson with my Y4 children showed them that:

1   The order in which calculations are done affects the result.
2   We can control the result by controlling the order in which calculations are done (by putting markers round the bit we want to do first).
3   You can not always trust a calculator to give you the answer you are expecting.

The convention that mathematicians have established is to put brackets round the bit that is to be done first. So reading BODMAS from left to right as B...O...D, etc., reminds us of the order in which to deal with a complex number sentence.

The difficulty that young children face is not just associated with the mathematics. They have been taught reading skills that emphasise left to right scanning. When reading a mathematical sentence, this is not necessarily the way to decode the meaning. You can be confident on working from left to right only when you have scanned the entire sentence and found that all the operations are the same. For example in:

$3 \times 4 \times 5 \times 2$

However, in the case of a sentence with mixed operators like:

$$3 + 4 - 2 \times 6$$

I need to put some reading markers in place, if I want the sentence to be read in a particular way. If I want the reader to obtain the answer 15 then I have to scatter some clues around and write the sentence in a way that shows my intention. If my clues follow the BODMAS rule then the reader who knows these rules can follow them and interpret my intention. B is for Brackets first, so I could rewrite my sentence as:

$$3 + (4 - 2) \times 6 \quad \text{or perhaps even} \quad 3 + ((4 - 2) \times 6)$$

to emphasise that I want the inside brackets to be tackled $(4 - 2)$ gives 2 and therefore (2×6) is the next stage in the calculation. This gives 12 and the last stage is therefore $3 + 12$.

Of course the same number sentence could provide an answer of -5 and in this case the intention could be shown by rewriting as:

$$(3 + 4) - (2 \times 6)$$

and now it does not matter which bracket is worked on first.

When reading mathematical sentences, the reader has to scan the whole sentence, spot the clues, and deduce the order in which to do the different parts of the calculation (by reference to the BODMAS rule: brackets first, and then the multiplication before the addition) (Figure 5.8). The *reading* task is quite a difficult one for children and is not easily learned by drawing on what is learnt about reading during English lessons – unless perhaps you enjoy reading poetry and are happy to contrast Coleridge's choice of word order with a more conventional one that we might use today, for sending a factual email report about Kubla Khan's new law:

> In Xanadu did Kubla Khan
> A stately pleasure-dome decree:
> Where Alph, the sacred river, ran
> Down to a sunless sea.

Children's analysis of text can be developed as part of English lessons by following guidance and suggestions in the *National Literacy Strategy*. Playing with word order and deconstructing text is valuable in developing the appropriate knowledge and skills for handling complex mathematical sentences but, without direct teaching in mathematics lessons, most

---

BODMAS rules

B = brackets   O = of   D = division   M = multiplication   A = addition   S = subtraction

Figure 5.8 Interpreting the BODMAS mnemonic.

children would not easily be able to apply the appropriate skills to mathematical contexts and learn to read mathematics accurately and with understanding. We can introduce stages between the teacher 'saying it all' and children being able to write the mathematics fluently and accurately in silence. We might for example try to have these stepping stones available.

- Say what is needed then ask children to repeat.
- Say what is needed and ask children to explain.
- Encourage children to say what is in their head and accept that it will be muddled and incomplete – you do the essential filling in.
- Encourage children to say what they are thinking and to write in English, rather than using mathematical symbols.
- Encourage them to use different representations of the same idea, for example, as shown here:

Say, 'Add three and five.'	Use a prefix operator and write $+ (3, 5)$ A common spoken language form in English. Also used in some computer languages.
Say, 'Take five pounds and seven pounds and add them.'	Use a postfix operator and write $(5, 7) +$ A common form of spoken language. Also used in some computer languages
Say, 'Three add four.'	Use an infix operator and write $3 + 4$ The standard written representation in school.

Commutative law

When we have a number sentence containing entirely addition operations or entirely multiplication operations we get the same result irrespective of the order in which we calculate. So,

$$6 + 8 + 4$$

can be tackled in any order. In fact, we draw children's attention to this commutative property by suggesting that they search for ways of combining numbers to make 10 (by adding the 6 and the 4) as part of their calculation strategy. The commutative property applies when multiplying. With:

$$2 \times 8 \times 3$$

the order does not matter as far as the result is concerned, although some people may find starting with (2×3) followed by the 8 will be the easiest.

So the general rule for any two numbers a and b is that:

$$a + b = b + a \quad \text{and} \quad a \times b = b \times a$$

And this is not the case for subtraction or division, and it might be best if you tried it out to make sure you are clear what is happening.

Associative law

In a number sentence the different parts can be regrouped without changing the answer. The emphasis in the NNS booklet (NNS/QCA, 1999) *Teaching Mental Calculation Strategies* is to teach children to exploit the associative and commutative laws to form the most efficient combinations of numbers to assist rapid and accurate mental calculation. As early as Year 1 (Y1) (children aged 5–6) the guidance suggests 'children should be able to use the following strategies, as appropriate, for mental calculations: … – reorder numbers in a calculation' (NNS/QCA, 1999: 6).

$$6 + 3 + 7$$

can be tackled by working directly from left to right. Many children may do just this, by applying their skills in scanning English sentences. We can add $(6 + 3)$ and then continue by adding the subtotal of 9 to the 7 to make 16. However, many teachers will emphasise the benefit of regrouping to make 10 wherever possible, and

$$(6 + 3) + 7 \text{ can be regrouped as } 6 + (3 + 7)$$

and the brackets signal that we will carry out $3 + 7$ as the first step. Children need to learn, and have a rapid recall of complements to 10 and then 10s' complements to 100.

It might be better perhaps, in the early stages of emphasising the value of using the associative law, to teach children to exercise their own preference for the order in which they like to tackle calculations, and so reveal their thinking to us.

When we invite them to add numbers in a different order, we are implying that they can change the order without affecting the total, but we may need to be more explicit than this, and show clearly that the end result is the same.

'Who would prefer to start by adding the 3 and the 6? OK! Tell me what you're saying to yourself in your head, … three and six make? … then what do we need to do? OK add the seven to the nine to make …? Who would prefer to start somewhere else? … OK. Let's check to see if we get the same final answer.'

The teacher can transform what the children say, by drawing a number line like the one shown. This allows the teacher to:

- demonstrate an effective way of supporting the children's thinking;
- make an explicit link between speaking and writing mathematical statements;
- provide a number sentence that can be read back to the children afterwards, so it acts as a useful recall mechanism;
- compare two number lines representing two different ways of carrying out the calculation to show that they provide two routes to the same answer.

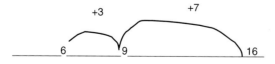

'Six and three more makes 9, hold it in your head, … nine add seven makes sixteen, well done. Now who would prefer to start by adding the 3 and the 7? OK. Start with the 7 because it's the larger number. Can you tell us what you say to yourself when you do this sort of sum?' …

And it is worth emphasising that with the number line, an addition will always take us further to the right of our starting numbers.

So it becomes very powerful for children to know that they can regroup the numbers in the sentence without changing the result, and to know it is their responsibility to decide the best order for themselves, and that this decision is part of what we mean when we talk about developing mental calculation strategies.

Many children and adults respond well to the use of metaphor. We can use Cuisenaire rods as metaphors. Let us look for three rods which together make 24. We could employ a PE metaphor and talk about the 'hop, step and jump' competition. In the competition the hops, steps and jumps will be of different distances, but the result is the total distance that the athlete covers. Using the metaphor with children might help us and them explore ways for making convenient hops, (small but really useful moves along the number line within or up to a decade), medium sized steps (perhaps across a single decade), and useful jumps (across several decades). So, calculating:

$$87 + 169 + 43$$

might result in one child saying: 'I'll start with 87 and add 43 because 7 and 3 make 10. That's like 80 add 40 and 10 more, so it is 130. Then I'll hop from 169 to 170 coz it's easier. Then I'll do 130 and 170 is 200 plus another 100 makes the answer 300, hop back 1. It's 299!'

Some children would not need their thinking to be supported by the hop, step and jump metaphor, so do not force it on them. Some may be able to go immediately to drawing:

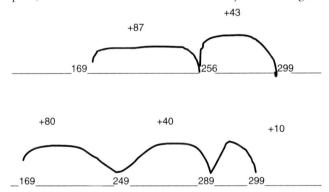

What we need to remind children is that when regrouping to carry out addition:

- regrouping does not change the answer;
- that some regroupings make mental calculation easier and less error prone, so hopping to the next decade is useful, stepping to a convenient multiple of ten can help, then jumping several decades or hundreds is often made easier;
- that people have idiosyncratic preferences about the way they group numbers for addition, what is easy for you might be a struggle for me and vice versa;
- the children should choose their own ways of grouping, but think simplicity;
- be open to finding new ways of combining numbers;
- aim at becoming fast and accurate over time;
- avoid counting and go for calculation wherever possible.

Multiplication

If we look at multiplication, we find it works in a similar way to addition:

$(4 \times 3) \times 2$ can be regrouped into $4 \times (3 \times 2)$ or $(4 \times 2) \times 3$ and

with the same result in each case. So multiplication obeys the commutative and associative laws. This is not true for subtraction or division. Try it, so that you see what actually happens.

Distributive law

When ordering food like fish and chips we are used to using the distributive law when we calculate the cost. If we buy fish and chips for a family of five (who all want the same!) with fish costing £2.20 and chips at 80p, then the easiest way to work out the cost might be to realise that the multiplication of 5 is *distributed* across the fish (£2.20) and the chips (£0.80). The cost is unchanged if we just calculate 5 times £3.

$$(5 \times £2.20) + (5 \times £0.80) \equiv 5 \times (£2.20 + £0.80) \equiv 5 \times £3$$

This is an example of multiplication distributed over addition. The law also applies to multiplication distributed over subtraction.

$$5(3.00 - 0.30) \equiv 5 \times £3 - 5 \times £0.30$$

Children can make good use of distributive laws when faced with as yet unknown multiplication facts. Even when $6 \times 7 = 42$ is not a currently known fact or perhaps is hard to recall, it can be derived, if one knows that 7 can be partitioned into 4 and 3 or into 5 and 2.

$$6 \times 7 = 6 \times (2 + 5) = 12 + 30$$

However, look what happens if we try to distribute division over addition or subtraction.

$$24 \div (8 + 4) \text{ is equivalent to } 24 \div 12$$

and gives us 2 as an answer. If we try to distribute the division over the addition we get $(24 \div 8) + (24 \div 4)$ and 9 as a result. So division cannot be distributed over addition when the division is to the left of the addition.

However, curiously if we started with:

$$(8 + 4) \div 24$$

and distribute the division to make

$$(8 \div 24) + (4 \div 24)$$

we do get the same result for both arrangements. Why not explore division distributed over subtraction – can you guess the outcome?

The NNS booklet (NNS/QCA, 1999) *Teaching Mental Calculation Strategies* argues that children need to practise number work regularly if they are to develop the following.

1   Efficient and accurate recall of known facts.
2   An awareness of possible connections between facts that need to be derived (what is the answer to 6×16?) and known facts (well, I know that $6 \times 8 = 48$ but how does that help me?).

3   The ability to connect known and derived facts through a strategy that can take them comfortably from one to the other (e.g. I need the answer to 6×16 I think I can get it because I know that 16 is double 8. So double 48 is 96).

Following a mental calculation agenda actually determines which strategies are important for teaching. The strategies needed are not the same ones as those needed to perform vertical pencil and paper methods. Doubling and halving strategies are useful though not crucial for pencil and paper work with vertical written calculations, but they are vital for lots of mental calculation work.

Counting numbers and integers

Counting systems are culturally influenced. The Babylonians used a sexagesimal (base 60) system for the counting of angle and time. According to Menninger (1969) the Babylonian priests were probably the ones responsible for introducing the key numbers 12, 60 and 360 through their astronomical texts. They used a system of fractions for astronomical calculations, which operated on base 60. Their language of fractions, translated into Latin, gave us the words minute and second:

> (pars) minuta prima (et) secunda,
> "first (and) second diminished part,"
>   (Menninger, 1969: 168)

We still use the numbers 60, 360, 12 and 7 as bases for counting. These bases are probably derived from the Babylonian's astronomical studies and are used today in addition to a decimal system.

> The number 60 … but also 360, came into our own culture … most probably occasioned by the sun's complete circuit through the heavens in roughly 360 days, from which we have the number of parts into which any circle is divided. … The solar day was divided into twelve two-hour periods in analogy with the twelve-fold division of the zodiac. Moreover, the seven known heavenly bodies were used not only for classifying and naming metals, colors, and parts of the body, but also for the cyclical ordering of days.
>   (Menninger, 1969: 168)

Cultural influences on number systems are brought about by:

- cultural activity (such as astronomical studies, navigation, use of ceremonial artefacts such as temples, …);
- commonly available materials (water, mud, clay, stone, wood, bone, silicon chip, etc.);
- dominant forms of communication (spoken, signed, cuneiform, hieroglyphic, written, electronic, …);
- representations and records of financial transactions (hieroglyphic, knotted string, wooden sticks, notched sticks, counting board, cowry shell, written numeral, on-screen symbol, …);
- preferences in groupings (binary, decimal, duodecimal, hexadecimal, vigesimal, sexagesimal).

In her book *Children Discover Arithmetic*, Catherine Stern (1949), recognised the cultural origins of counting systems and included them in an activity which she details (12–15), and which, in adapted form, I have used as an activity with trainees.

Stern provided ten apparently nonsensical sounds for the names of the first counting numbers from 1 to 10. My adapted practical activity sessions with students begin by providing these. (You may notice here that there is no zero – though I avoid drawing trainees' attention to this at the outset of the activity, since it is the dramatic effect of having a zero that I want students to consider.) Not everyone is aware that the inclusion of a zero creates a number system that can support calculation as well as the recording of numbers. The inclusion of place value and a zero (with its double function of standing for nothing and for nothing in this place) is the fundamental difference between the Arabic number system and others like the Roman numeral system which was not designed for calculation and was used to represent quantities.

As part of the activity, the multicultural origins of mathematics are made explicit when trainees are given information about the widely differing cultural origins of counting systems – care being taken to avoid creating inappropriate stereotypes. Menninger's authoritative book *Number Words and Number Symbols* is helpful here in providing hugely detailed accounts of counting and the recording of numbers, drawn from all over the world.

The students are invited to focus on a culture that interests them and consider how numbers might have been recorded in that culture (oral only, as in the early Armenian culture, clay tablets, sticks, knotted string, shells, …). They are reminded of the ten sounds and invited to think of appropriate ways in which the counting system might have been extended to larger numbers within that culture.

What the activity tends to do is force awareness of the need for simple structures that are easily remembered and the value of using pattern. It is an interesting activity to extend the count in this way, and it only becomes tedious when I ask for calculations using the four rules, because calculation without a place value system and a zero is very cumbersome and inefficient.

Other opportunities can come from traditional Chinese number symbols, or other systems that are unusual or relatively unfamiliar in Britain such as: Aztec, Japanese, Korean and Egyptian hieroglyphs. They can be provided in the form of paper jigsaws. The pieces can be cut up and used to construct a hundred square. Forced to read the unfamiliar symbols for clues, they have to work on the internal structure that the system possesses. It becomes noticeable how different the Arabic system is. Students gain a heightened awareness of the power of the place value system based on Arabic numerals and the opportunity it provides for recording quantities and for calculation at one and the same time.

The arithmetic of counting numbers

Young children tend to start to count from 1 rather than 0 and the first images of number lines offered to them tend to be number tracks beginning at 1. Carpet tiles with numerals painted on them provide a useful moveable number track, on which children can stand. Each numeral occupies a space and represents a number in a count. Plastic and wooden rules that are used in KS1 also tend to be marked as a track with square blocks of colour, one block for each number to be counted (Figure 5.9).

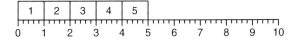

Figure 5.9 KS1 rulers tend to be number tracks marked off in centimetres.

In contrast, plastic or wooden rules for KS2 use length as a metaphor for number. The rulers begin at zero and each number is marked as a point along a line. The distance from zero represents the value of each number.

The set of natural numbers (1, 2, 3, 4, 5,...) are perhaps the most familiar to young children. They also see numerals used as labels. $0800,000,000$ is not the eight hundred millionth telephone line, it is a label for a particular subscriber or service, and (if you understand how telephones can be made to work) it is also an instruction, a connection code. Young children's ideas about numbers are likely to be the accumulation of their varied experience and the application of rational thinking. Young children's thoughts about numbers can include:

- numbers are things in themselves;
- number names can be attached as labels to objects;
- labels like half and quarter can be attached to objects (biscuits, cups of orange juice);
- counting starts at one;
- counting can go on for ever.

Young children will use numbers containing fractional parts but they may not associate them with the set of counting numbers. For example, four-and-a-half can exist in a child's language repertoire as an equivalent expression to, 'I'm nearly five years-old.' When children use numbers in this way they may not be using them in a numerical sense but as labels. Similarly, when playing with three cushions side by side on a sofa, with the child running and jumping on each in turn, the child (or adult) may call out one, two, three, as the child jumps on each one in turn. If the adult calls out bring me two, a young child is likely to bring the second cushion jumped on, rather than two cushions.

So several different notions of number occupy the young child's mind at the same time, and the mental connections and separations between these different views of number would appear to be governed as much by linguistic rules and social contexts as by numerical rules.

As teachers, we think about this set of natural numbers (1, 2, 3, 4, ...) as a system that is closed under addition. That is, adding can combine any two counting numbers and the result will always be a number that is a member of the same set. This is not so for subtraction of course. Seventy-five subtract twenty returns us to the same set of natural numbers, but the reverse does not. Twenty subtract seventy-five does not result in a natural number. With young children we may avoid this type of calculation, but with older children, we extend the number line with the introduction of zero and negative numbers, perhaps in relation to science lessons and the measurement of temperature.

Can you see that the set of natural numbers is closed for multiplication? Take any two numbers that exist in this system of counting numbers and multiply them. Is the resulting number going to be found on the existing number line? If you know that multiplication can be thought of as repeated addition, then you can deduce that multiplication has to follow the rule for addition.

What about division? Sixty divided by twenty gives an answer of three, which can be found on this number line. But what about twenty divided by sixty? The answer does not exist in this system. This system is not closed for division and our choice is either to avoid certain types of division, or modify the number line to allow for fractions.

Developing the number line

Developing the number line is something that happens during KS1 and KS2. The NNS *Framework* suggests that children in Y2 begin to place mixed numbers like $4\frac{1}{2}$ on a number line, recognising that the appropriate place is halfway between 4 and 5. The NC attainment target for Level 3 requires children to…

> begin to use decimal notation and to recognise negative numbers in contexts…
>
> (NC, 1999: Appendix, p.11)

These developments result in the need for *integers* (positive and negative whole numbers) and an associated arithmetic system.

-4   -3   -2   -1   0   1   2

If we list what we know about the integer system we see that now, the numbers:

- go on to infinity in both directions;
- can be positive or negative;
- must include a zero.

The system is closed for both addition and subtraction, although fractions cannot be accommodated. A further extension to the system is needed and this takes us to a system involving real numbers, which does include fractions and decimals. One of the fascinating aspects of this system is that it can never be physically represented in its entirety.

> If I offer you: 2.0__2.1__2.2__2.3
> you can offer me 2.10__2.11__2.12__
> I can then reply with 2.110__2.111__2.112__2.113__
> but I can not stop you responding with: 2.1110__2.1111__2.1112__

Numbers go on forever, but in a different sense from the meaning that a young child might express, when describing the system of natural numbers. There are as many numbers (or more?) between 2.0 and 2.1 as there are numbers on the number line extending to infinity!

This system of real numbers is closed for addition, multiplication, subtraction and division. Whichever two numbers you choose, and whichever operation you select, the answer to your calculation can be found on this number line.

Using the empty number line to support thinking

Number line fragments are very helpful for supporting children who are developing calculation strategies. Drawing empty number lines and then annotating them has been adopted in British schools from work done in Holland in the 1990s. Empty number lines are a valuable support for mathematical thinking and a powerful image for teachers to employ when focusing learners' attention on calculation strategies. Two useful sources of ideas are; *Mental Arithmetic: Mental Recall or Mental Strategies?* (Beishuizen, 1997) and *Teaching Mental Calculation Strategies* (NNS/QCA, 1999: 16).

Examples of the use of the empty number line

The empty number line and the relevant numbers can be drawn quickly. There are several counting strategies that adults are familiar with. These can be represented on the number line and it is useful to review their use before considering the teaching of calculation to children. They include:

- counting on or back;
- bridging through a decade number;
- finding the difference;
- partitioning;
- shopkeeper's method.

Counting on

Counting on is useful for numbers which have a small difference like 432−425 and it is important to emphasise to children that calculation is not the same as handling objects.

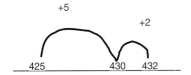

If we were working in a field with 132 sheep and we are intending to sell 125 of them, then the physicality of the situation is likely to prompt a take away activity. When we are calculating, we are working with numbers and they do not need to be thought of as objects. Although we may choose to use a take away response, it is not an imperative. Obviously, people's thinking varies and there is not a one-to-one match between a story and the chosen model.

What we are looking for, with the use of number lines, is to find the most appropriate (i.e. accurate, simple, swift, error free) calculation method. As teachers we help children achieve this by:

- teaching children a selection of strategies but not expecting them to remember them initially;
- teaching children explicitly, through demonstration, a process of writing numbers on a number line and talking out loud, 'How could I do this?' (i.e. which strategy is best here?) followed by experimentation that does not demand perfection at first;
- regularly providing children with opportunities to practise all the strategies;

- encouraging children to internalise the strategies and then call them up from memory as required.

Counting back   37–4

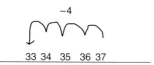

Counting back is a useful strategy for solving problems with a large difference, particularly where one number is small. Counting back requires a search for the shortest fragment of number line necessary to solve the problem.

In number line work, I try to remember to teach a routine of visualisation followed by action. 'Thirty seven minus four. Imagine the pen working by itself. (Pause.) Now show me with your finger where the pen went. (Pause.) Now draw on my flipchart where it went.'

Many younger children will start by finding 37 and then visualising the counting back as jumping back in four single steps. Reward them for this, but ask, 'Can you imagine one big jump?' If they can, then encourage them to *visualise a single jump* whenever possible. If they can not, then leave them without criticising, and allow them to watch you work with another child who can visualise a single jump. Then, if the first child would like to try again, invite them back.

Visualising a single jump may be harder to do if they have to cross a decade as in, $34-7$ because 30 is such a strong psychological feature and may disrupt the visualisation because the decades change from thirties to twenties.

Bridging through a decade   34–7

Bridging through a decade is likely to be needed for a while but may disappear later except in tricky situations, like $604-27$ where it may be invoked again to bridge the 600. Bridging demands very easy access to the results of partition. It requires immediate recall of triads of numbers, like 7, 4 and 3 and how they relate to each other. It demands that we slip easily from one triad to another, 7 goes with 4 and 3, 7 goes with 6 and 1, 7 goes with 5 and 2. Which triad is the one I need right now?

$34-7$
thought of as
$34-(4+3)$

−3   −4

26 27 28 29 30 31 32 33 34 35 36

Finding the difference

Finding the difference is a useful method where counting on can be done smoothly as for example, with $85-58$. The difference is the distance on the number line that separates the two numbers and most people find counting on easier than counting back, so starting with 58 we count to 85 with the minimum of jumps. Initially a child may go to the next decade (60) and then to the decade before 85 (80) before finishing at 85.

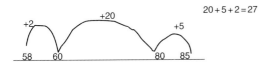

$$20+5+2=27$$

Partitioning

Partitioning is a frequently used strategy. It appeared above in the example of $34-7$ where the 4 in 34 can be matched by a 4 obtained from partitioning 7 into 4 and 3.

In an example like $584-176$ a more sophisticated partitioning can be applied by trying to match the 84 in 584 by conceiving an imagined partition of 176 into 184 and -8. The resulting calculation becomes: start with 584 and subtract 184 to give 400 followed by addition of 8 to compensate for the fact that initially the 176 was increased by 8 to 184.

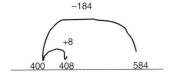

Shopkeeper's method

This is associated with the tendency, prior to the advent of the automatic checkout, to give coins of small value first when giving change. So offering a £5 note for goods worth 93 pence was likely to result in the shopkeeper giving change in a particular order whilst keeping count of the addition from 95 pence to £5. 'Ninety-three and 2p makes ninety-five and 5p makes a pound, and four pounds make £5 altogether.'

Counting on, along the number line, is a modification of the shopkeeper's method of subtraction, modified because the smallest steps are not necessarily the first to be made, as in:

$$43-16$$

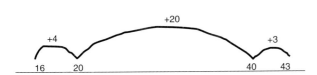

Choosing and discussing strategies

Most children do not develop successful calculation strategies simply through teacher demonstration and practice. These are key elements of successful teaching but are insufficient on their own. With a confident class towards the end of the unit of work or the term, there are two possible review models that will help consolidate effective teaching.

1   *A problem setting approach*, with the teacher choosing a level of difficulty which challenges the children without being too easy or too hard. 'I'm going to show you a number problem. I want you to look at it but, listen to me, I am not interested in the answer. I am interested in finding some different ways of getting started, so I'm hoping that different people will give me some different ways to begin. The problem is'. . . (offer something at a challenge level).

2   *Children identify their own strategies* and set their own level of difficulty so this is easier mathematically, but more difficult to manage in terms of classroom organisation. 'I want to help you to get better at choosing the best way of solving number problems. In a couple of minutes I'm going to ask you to come up to the flipchart and show us some examples. Can you work in pairs or on your own, please, using your wipe boards and make up some different take away (subtraction) sums that you've done recently. Let's just stick with subtraction at the moment. Take a couple of minutes. Get two or three sums ready to show us, that you solve in very different ways. You could choose something like $107 - 73$ but you don't have to. It is your decision and your explanations that I'm interested in.'

With less confident children at the beginning of the year, direct teaching through modelling may be more appropriate. 'I'm going to choose a very easy calculation to look at: something that could probably have done last year. This lesson is about practising giving an explanation – telling me how you would do it. If you can think of two different ways of doing it then that would be really good. The first is really easy, it is'. . . (then write up something chosen carefully from previous year's programme).

The objectives of this activity are:

- improved articulation – smooth, confident explanation from a wide range of children, with the teacher avoiding a competition between children, which might lead to, 'I can do harder sums than you can.'
- improving exposition – children find giving explanations difficult. The teacher can focus on giving a clear exposition of different ways of tackling the same calculation, emphasising the choice between methods. (This is why the calculation itself must be easy and not distracting. Mental energy can then go into learning an alternative method and into learning how to explain methods to others.)

Beyond number lines and number grids

Number grids and 100 squares are extensions of the horizontal number line. They lend themselves to situations where a large set of numbers has to be viewed at once. The 100 square is a powerful device for extending knowledge of the number system. The visual impact is powerful. An interactive whiteboard is ideal for exploring the properties. Use the searchlight to focus on a small cluster of numbers.

1	2	3	4	5	6	7	8	9	10
11	12	13	14	15	16	17	18	19	20
21	22	23	24	25	26	27	28	29	30
31	32	33	34	35	36	37	38	39	40
41	42	43	44	45	46	47	48	49	50
51	52	53	54	55	56	57	58	59	60
61	62	63	64	65	66	67	68	69	70
71	72	73	74	75	76	77	78	79	80
81	82	83	84	85	86	87	88	89	90
91	92	93	94	95	96	97	98	99	100

١٠	٩	٨	٧	٦	٥	٤	٣	٢	١
٢٠	١٩	١٨	١٧	١٦	١٥	١٤	١٣	١٢	١١
٣٠	٢٩	٢٨	٢٧	٢٦	٢٥	٢٤	٢٣	٢٢	٢١
٤٠	٣٩	٣٨	٣٧	٣٦	٣٥	٣٤	٣٣	٣٢	٣١
٥٠	٤٩	٤٨	٤٧	٤٦	٤٥	٤٤	٤٣	٤٢	٤١
٦٠	٥٩	٥٨	٥٧	٥٦	٥٥	٥٤	٥٣	٥٢	٥١
٧٠	٦٩	٦٨	٦٧	٦٦	٦٥	٦٤	٦٣	٦٢	٦١
٨٠	٧٩	٧٨	٧٧	٧٦	٧٥	٧٤	٧٣	٧٢	٧١
٩٠	٨٩	٨٨	٨٧	٨٦	٨٥	٨٤	٨٣	٨٢	٨١
١٠٠	٩٩	٩٨	٩٧	٩٦	٩٥	٩٤	٩٣	٩٢	٩١

Two examples of hundred squares, using Arabic and Urdu numeral systems.

37	37
47	48
57	58

Where are we on the 100 square? (Near the top, the bottom, left hand side, half way down?

Show the class the whole 100 square. 'Just look at it without thinking, but try to look at all of it at the same time with relaxed eyes. Watch while I use the searchlight to focus in on . . . one little bit.'

	24	
	34	

'Close your eyes and imagine you can see the whole square again. When you're ready, use your wipe boards to write down the numbers that surround these two.'

This activity does not require an interactive whiteboard, though they lend themselves to maths work of this kind. An ordinary paper or plastic 100 grid can be covered with a mask made from cut-out paper clouds. An even simpler version for younger children aged four or five, is a washing line of numbers – just remove one number without them noticing and ask what they notice. You can leave the gap, or close it up. The two situations can gives rise to different discussions.

You can show a single row.

61	62	63	64	65	66	67	68	69

'How do the numbers change as we go across this row from 61?' (Increasing by one, counting in ones, they go up one at a time, …)

'Let's look at some more rows. Tell me if they all do the same as this one.'

'Now what about going down a column on the 100 square. Let's say them together.'

1
11
21
31
41
51
61
71
81
91

There is power in rhythmical group chanting (just watch the All Blacks at the start of a rugby match and ask yourself what purpose the Hakka serves and whether it is effective!) Rhythmical chanting in maths lessons was thoroughly disapproved of in many quarters through the 1970s and 1980s because it was associated with children 'not understanding' what they were saying. Chanting however can help put stress on the patterns that exist and some children find this very helpful. We could try counting in ones and stressing the tens. Stressing the fives and the tens, stressing the evens or the odds,

'What's happening here?' (Ten more each time, going down in tens.) Yes. Going down the screen but what about the numbers? (going up in tens).

34	35	36	37
44	45	46	47
54	55	56	57
64	65	66	67

'How much is 45 and 20 more? (It makes 65) OK. If I start at 45 and add 20 where will I finish up? (At 65). OK. I start at 45 and I go down ten to 55 and another ten to 65. That's one way to add 20, but I'm bored with just going down the 100 square from 45, 55 to 65. I want to go another route, a different way. Something that's more interesting. Can you find some interesting ways to go from 45 to 65? Call out your most interesting route.'

'Suppose I wanted to add 20 in the simplest way.' (It is straight down below 45 in two jumps of ten.) 'What's the simplest way of adding 21?' (You could just jump down 20 and along 1) 'What about 45 add 19?' (It's like add 20 then go back one.)

Professor Ruth Merttens creates interest for the children she teaches, by talking about *spider* sums, with the spider using its thread to drop down the grid. The children soon identify what sort of calculation they are faced with, 'It's a spider sum!'

'Is it easy to add 19 to a number? Could it be a spider sum? Try closing your eyes and imagine your spider helping you out. The spider is sitting at 45. You want to add 19. What does the spider do? (Spiders go up and down!) Close your eyes and watch the spider. Then think about finishing the sum off." (The spider goes down to 65 then I go back 1 to 64.)

37	38
47	48

'What's the difference between 37 and 48?' (11). 'Can you please look at some other diagonals and check their difference. Start by looking at 67 and 78. What about a diagonal like 47 and 38, what's the difference there?'

Working with multiples

Using a 100 square, children can put a coloured counter on 4 and all its multiples. They can use a different colour for 5 and its multiples, then see where the collisions occur. It is also a good idea to use short oral question and answer tests in the lesson introduction, to practice number work. If you think about how to ask simple (single fact) and compound (multiple step) questions, then you have a strategy for differentiating between the more and less confident children.

- What is the highest multiple of 6 on the hundred square?
- Tell me the lowest multiple of 5 which is an even number.
- I am thinking of a number which is two more than the third multiple of 4.
- Any multiple of 8 between 60 and 90.

Working with larger numbers

Number lines are less helpful when writing and calculating with very large and very small numbers. Outside the classroom we avoid difficulties by using approximation, and this usually suffices because exact answers to most calculations are not necessary.

Children really enjoy the exploration of large numbers. Hemmings and Tahta (1984) produced an evocative book *Images of Infinity* which provides fertile ground for exploration. Large numbers do of course exist in relation to human experience and children enjoy questions about the number of seconds they have lived, the number of particles in the universe, the number of people in the world, the number of synaptic connections in their brain.

1000	2000	3000	4000	5000	6000	7000	8000	9000
100	200	300	400	500	600	700	800	900
10	20	30	40	50	60	70	80	90
1	2	3	4	5	6	7	8	9

Figure 5.10 We can use a Gattegno chart to say and construct large numbers.

Children can be taught to read and say large numbers through the use of Gattegno number charts (Figure 5.10) which have been used increasingly over the last few years. There is a very useful set of charts which can be photocopied and a report of work with young children, written by Geoff Faux (1998a,b) who worked with Gattegno. In addition, there is a NNS video which shows a teacher using both the paper version and a software version in a very effective lesson.

Reading and saying large numbers is a prerequisite for writing and calculating with them.

Standard form

This is a way of writing large and small numbers in a particular format, which makes use of powers of ten and indices. In order to use standard form successfully, one needs to be very familiar and comfortable with representing numbers as powers of ten and calculating with them. Index notation leads to standard form and on to logarithms.

One million can be written as 10^6 (ten to the power of six) and one-millionth, as 10^{-6} (ten to the power of minus six) Similarly, a thousandth can be written as 10^{-3} and a thousand as 10^3.

5,000,000 divided by 100 (five million divided by one hundred) can be calculated in an interesting way. Five million can be represented as five times one million and this can be written:

$$5 \times 10^6$$

and 100 can be represented by 10^2. The calculation can be written like this:

$$5 \times 10^6 \div 10^2 = 5 \times 10^4 \text{ or } 50,000$$

When calculating the powers of ten it looks as if we have carried out a subtraction with the two index figures (the 6 and the 2) to make the index 4 in the answer.

Similarly, 16,000,000 × 4000 (sixteen million multiplied by 4 thousand) can be written as $(16 \times 10^6) \times (4 \times 10^3)$. We multiply the 16 by 4 and add the indices (6 add 3) to produce the answer

$$64 \times 10^9$$

(16 times 4 = 64 and 10^6 times $10^3 = 10^9$). One final bit of manipulation of numbers. If we divide 1.2 by 100

$$\frac{1.2}{10^2}$$

can be rewritten as

$$1.2 \times 10^{-2}$$

and

$$\frac{1.7}{10^{-3}} \equiv 1.7 \times 10^3$$

but can you see why the indices changed in each case?

Now we are ready to rewrite some numbers in standard form. All numbers can be rewritten as a two-part structure which contains:

1   a number between 1 and 10;
2   an exponent of 10.

For example

$$27,060,000 \text{ becomes } 2.706 \times 10^7$$

(and some people find it easier to work out the exponent by finding how many places we need to move the decimal point when changing 27,060,000 to 2.7060000; answer seven jumps of the decimal point. So the exponent has to be 10 to the 7).

0.00237 becomes 2.37×10^{-3}

And here, there are three moves for the decimal point from 0.00237 to become 2.37. So the exponent has to be 3 as well.

Each time we move the decimal point in a number we have to compensate for moving it. Moving it to the right by three jumps increases the value of the original number by 1000 so the exponent has to be negative three, -3 (a thousandth) to return the number to its original value. Some mathematicians argue that properly, we should imagine the decimal point remaining fixed, and that we should think about moving the numbers. This way of working is easier when working with calculators and computers.

The steps to take are:

1   Rewrite the original number as a number between 1 and 10 retaining all the non-zero digits and any zeros like the one contained in 2706.
2   Calculate the exponent part (always a power of 10) so that it redresses what you have done to the original number.

Standard form has two advantages.

1   It simplifies the way very large or very small numbers are written, making them easier to read and easier to get an accurate sense of the size of the number.
2   It makes calculation easier because the exponential parts can be added or subtracted when one is multiplying or dividing the numbers involved. This is also the basis of the slide rule and logarithms where a multiplication is converted into an addition.

To multiply 0.00000000024 by 120,000,000 we can convert both numbers to standard form and see how that simplifies the way they can be read.

To convert 0.00000000024 to 2.4 we can move the decimal point *ten* places to the right so the exponent must be -10 (minus ten). To convert 120,000,000 to 1.2 we move the decimal point *eight* places to the left so the exponent must be 8 (that is, positive eight).

This gives:

$2.4 \times 10^{-10} \times 1.2 \times 10^{8}$

2.4 times 1.2 gives 2.88

$10^{-10} \times 10^{8}$ gives 10^{-2}

so the result is

2.88×10^{-2}

which can also be written as 0.0288.

How can 1.7 or 12 be represented in standard form? We need to know that 10^0 is equivalent to 1 and 10^1 is equivalent to 10. We can represent 1.7 and 12 as follows.

1.7 already is a number that lies between 1 and 10. So multiplying by 10^0 has the same effect as multiplying by 1.

$1.7 \equiv 1.7 \times 1 \equiv 1.7 \times 10^{0}$

12 has to be reduced by a single power of 10 to become 1.2, so in standard form, 12 becomes

$$1.2 \times 10^1 \text{ (in effect } 1.2 \times 10)$$

To divide 1.7 by 12

$$1.7 \times 10^0 \div 1.2 \times 10^1 \quad \text{or} \quad 1.7/1.2 \times 10^{-1}$$

so the result is approximately 1.416×10^{-1}.

Resources and further reading

http://www.beam.co.uk/ (BEAM – Be A Mathematician) has built up an enviable range of books and resources by a large group of authors. Just to mention a few:

Teaching Mental Strategies

Using Number Lines with 5–8 Year Olds

The Numeracy File

Numeracy Lessons

Number at Key Stage 1

Number at Key Stage 2

Integrating Calculators into the Curriculum

Teaching Primary Mathematics

A Feel for Number

Exploring Place Value

Anghileri, J. (ed.) (1995) *Children's Mathematical Thinking in the Primary Years*. London: Cassell.

Beishuizen, M. (1997) Mental arithmetic: mental recall or mental strategies. *Mathematics Teaching*. MT160, 16–19 September.

Haylock, D. (2001) *Mathematics Explained for Primary Teachers* (second edn). London: Paul Chapman Publishing.

Hemmings, R. and Tahta, D. (1984) *Images of Infinity*. Leapfrogs.

Hopkins, C., Gifford, S. and Pepperell, S. (1999) *Mathematics in the Primary School: A Sense of Progression* (second edn). London: David Fulton.

Koshy, V. (1999) *Effective Teaching of Numeracy*. London: Hodder and Stoughton.

Koshy, V., Ernest, P. and Casey, R. (2000) *Mathematics for Primary Teachers*. London: Routledge.

Mason, J., Burton, L. and Stacey, K. (1982) *Thinking Mathematically*. London: Addison-Wesley.

Menninger, K. (1969) *Number Words and Number Symbols*. Cambridge, MA: MIT Press.

Merttens, R. (ed.) (1996) *Teaching Numeracy*. Leamington Spa: Scholastic Limited.

Mooney, C., Ferrie, L., Fox, S., Hansen, A. and Wrathmell, R. (2002b) *Primary Mathematics: Knowledge and Understanding*. Exeter: Learning Matters.

Montague-Smith, A. (1997) *Mathematics in Nursery Education*. London: David Fulton.

NNS/QCA (1999) *Teaching Mental Calculation Strategies*. London: Qualifications and Curriculum Authority.

Nunes, T. and Bryant, P. (1997) *Learning and Teaching Mathematics*. Hove: Psychology Press.

Orton, A. and Frobisher, L. (1996) *Insights into Teaching Mathematics*. London: Cassell.

Rotman, B. (1987) *Signifying Nothing: the Semiotics of Zero*. New York: St Martins Press.

Stern, C. and Stern, M. B. (1949) *Children Discover Arithmetic*. New York: Harper & Row.

Thompson, I. (ed.) (1997) *Teaching and Learning Early Number*. Buckingham: Open University Press.

Thompson, I. (ed.) (1999) *Issues in Teaching Numeracy*. Buckingham: Open University.

The Logical Journey of the Zoombinis. CD-ROM Published by Brøderbund.

6 Fractions, decimals and percentages

There are two reasons for a separate chapter on fractions, decimals and percentages. The first is that in order to understand these ideas, children need to make a significant shift in their thinking. Pre-school experience of number is mainly about:

- counting objects, often with little reference to a zero;
- numbers as labels (buses, telephone numbers, house numbers);
- fractions as language labels ('I can only eat half this apple' where half is often a very rough approximation, mathematically speaking).

Fractions, decimals and percentages are very different kinds of number from integers, and teachers need to look closely at what mental readjustments are required if children are to use and understand fractional amounts.

The second reason for the chapter relates to the Teacher Training Agency (TTA) Skills Test for trainees. For several years the TTA has imposed an external, computerised test on all trainees, which has to be passed before Qualified Teacher Status (QTS) can be awarded. The focus has been on mental and written calculations which often involve conversion between fractions, decimals and percentages, together with some questions on tables and graphs. The tests can cause some trainees considerable anxiety, partly because they are computer based and partly because the mathematics test involves mental calculations at speed. This chapter guides you through some typical questions and discusses ways in which you can prepare yourself for the tests and reduce your level of anxiety.

Fractions

Fractions are a natural part of young children's speech and thinking, although when they say, 'My half of the cake is bigger than your half,' they are not mathematically correct. Mathematically, half, third, quarter, fifth and so on, are exactly defined terms of division of a whole. When speaking mathematically, two halves have to be thought of as exactly equal, although in practice it is impossible to create two perfect halves using physical objects (or if by chance we managed to, it would be impossible to know). A precise mathematician might never try to make physical fractions, knowing that it is impossible to cut a cake into two exactly equal sized pieces. A technologist might just get on with it, knowing that with care, the halves would be near enough the same size.

Fractions can refer to a sub-area or region of a defined whole: twenty percent of the east coast countryside is at serious risk of flooding. They can refer to a subset of a discrete set of objects: a quarter of the population will need flu' jabs this winter. They can refer to an intermediate point on a number line between two whole numbers. They can be the result of a division say 3 divided by 5. They can be used for comparison of two measures (e.g. length) or between sets: there are 3 apples in set A and 5 apples in set B, so set A has $\frac{3}{5}$ as many as set B. Although originally written in 1984, Dickson, Brown and Gibson not only give a thorough presentation of the different ways in which fractions are used (274), their book also discusses children's errors and misconceptions.

When we write fractions down ($\frac{1}{2}, \frac{5}{16}, \frac{3}{8}$) they represent mathematically perfect fractional parts. And that idea leads us on to equivalence – the idea that two different fractions (e.g. $\frac{3}{4}$ and $\frac{12}{16}$) are equivalent in value because they represent exactly the same proportions or quantities, or perhaps a gradient as shown on road signs.

We use fractions in three main ways:

- to represent part of a whole (half a kilogram, a tenth of a metre, …) with a numerator (how many parts represented here) and a denominator (how many parts the whole was divided into);
- to operate on another number (calculate $\frac{1}{2}$ of 68);
- to show a ratio between different quantities (fat to flour in the ratio of 1:2 can be shown as $\frac{1}{2}$).

Representing fractions with equipment

Cuisenaire rods and Color Factor allow us to build a wall to represent the division of a whole rod into different fractions (Figure 6.1).

Another way of representing equivalent fractions is to use a multiplication grid (Figure 6.2).

Starting with the first two numbers in the first two rows (1 and 2), we can consider them as representing the fraction $\frac{1}{2}$ the succeeding pairs $\frac{2}{4}, \frac{3}{6}, \frac{4}{8}$ provide examples of fractions which are equivalent to the lowest form at the left hand end. Any pairs of rows will provide a

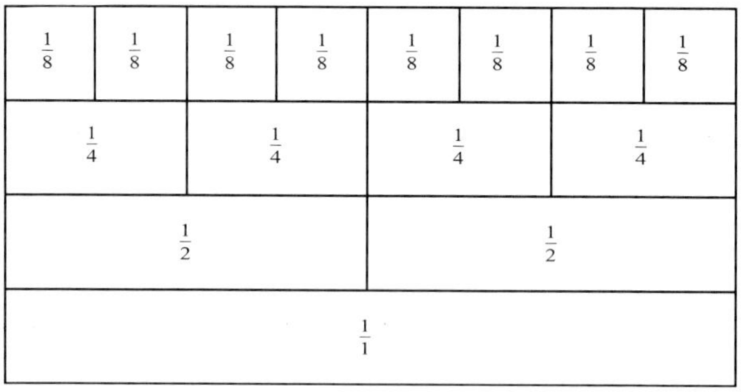

Figure 6.1 Diagram of a wall of rods showing equivalent fractions.

1	2	3	4	5	6	7	8	9	10
2	**4**	**6**	**8**	**10**	**12**	**14**	**16**	**18**	**20**
3	6	9	12	15	18	21	24	27	30
4	8	12	16	20	24	28	32	36	40
5	10	15	20	25	30	35	40	45	50
6	?	?	?	?	?	?	?	?	?
7	**14**	**21**	**28**	**35**	**42**	**49**	**56**	**63**	**70**

Figure 6.2 A multiplication chart can be used to represent equivalent fractions.

similar set of equivalent fractions. Taking the second and the seventh rows we get $\frac{2}{7}$ in its lowest form, followed by $\frac{4}{14}, \frac{6}{21}$ and so on.

Paper strips are a simple but valuable way of identifying different fractions just by folding. One strip of paper folded into halves and quarters, then unfolded to obtain four equal sized quarters as shown here:

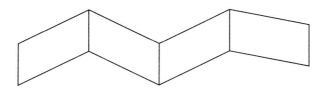

We can represent any of the fractions algebraically as

$$\frac{a}{b}$$

where the value a gives the **num**ber (**num**erator) or pieces we are interested in, in relation to the value b the de**nom**inator, (**nom** ≡ name) of the fractional pieces.

Working with fractions

We often need to do arithmetic on fractions and mixed numbers like $7\frac{3}{4}$ which have a whole and a fractional part. Addition and subtraction of fractions raises problems. It is easy if the fractions have the same denominator. Adding $\frac{3}{4}$ and $\frac{3}{4}$ is straightforward, in the sense that we can think of the activity as collecting quarters giving an answer of $\frac{6}{4}$. The only difficulty here might be in deciding whether to leave the answer in this form or to show that you know $\frac{4}{4}$ is equivalent to a whole and that $\frac{6}{4}$ can therefore be rewritten in an equivalent form as a mixed number, either as $1\frac{2}{4}$ or as $1\frac{1}{2}$.

It is when we try to compare different fractions like $\frac{4}{5}$ and $\frac{5}{6}$ that many people do not have an immediate sense of which is the larger fraction or how the two fractions can be added. The strategy is to make them the same type of fraction by changing one or both denominators so that both are the same number. Finding a *common denominator* is an important skill.

We can just multiply the two denominators (5 and 6 in the example above) to provide a common denominator of 30. Sometimes this method does not produce the lowest common denominator and that can be inconvenient. In this case, the result is 30 and we can then change both $\frac{4}{5}$ and $\frac{5}{6}$ into their corresponding equivalents, both with denominators of 30. Again, we may notice that there is a symmetry to these calculations: we have to multiply the numerator and denominator of $\frac{4}{5}$ by 6 to produce $\frac{24}{30}$. We then multiply the numerator and denominator of $\frac{5}{6}$ by 5 to make $\frac{25}{30}$.

Now it is easy to compare the two original fractions because both the equivalents are thirtieths. We can easily compare them to see which is bigger and we can also add or subtract them.

$$\frac{4}{5} + \frac{5}{6} \text{ is equivalent to } \frac{24}{30} + \frac{25}{30} = \frac{49}{30} \quad \text{or} \quad 1\frac{19}{30}$$

Look at the next example. Let us try to subtract $\frac{7}{10}$ from $\frac{11}{15}$. If we try to find a denominator simply by multiplying the 10 and the 15 we get a common denominator of 150 which is fine – but it is not the lowest common denominator. Finding the lowest common denominator is neater. If we ask ourselves what multiple of 10 is also a multiple of 15 we hit on 30 – the lowest common denominator for tenths and fifteenths is therefore thirtieths.

$$\frac{11}{15} - \frac{7}{10} \text{ can be rewritten as } \frac{22}{30} - \frac{21}{30} = \frac{1}{30}$$

Multiplying and dividing fractions

Multiplying fractions requires less manipulation of numbers than does addition and subtraction. It is easy to do the calculations, but it is not always easy to get a picture (or a story) in your head about what is happening. Lots of experience of multiplying integers may leave us with the belief that multiplying always gives a result where the answer is larger than either of the starting numbers. Multiplication can 'make numbers bigger', but it does not always. A half of 48 (answer 24) is a multiplication ($\frac{1}{2} \times 48$) where the result is smaller than one of the starting numbers. It can be thought of as 48 multiplied by $\frac{1}{2}$ but also as the division of 48 into two equal parts ($48 \div 2$). In spoken form, we often ask this type of question as, 'What's half *of* 48?' We often use the word *of* to signify multiplication by fractions.

In written form, it could look like

$$\frac{1}{2} \times 48 \text{ or } 48 \times \frac{1}{2} \text{ or } 48 \div 2$$

And, a half of a quarter is

$$\frac{1}{2} \times \frac{1}{4} = \frac{1}{8}$$

$\frac{3}{4} \div \frac{1}{8}$ can be thought of as, 'If $\frac{3}{4}$ was divided up into eighths, how many eighths would there be?' One quarter would give 2 (eighths) so,

$$\frac{3}{4} \text{ will give } 3 \times 2 = 6$$

$\frac{3}{4} \div \frac{1}{8}$ is equivalent to multiplying $\frac{3}{4}$ by $\frac{8}{1}$ or $\frac{3}{4} \times 8 = \frac{24}{4} = 6$

This is a very far-fetched and hard-to-believe story, compared to the addition stories of fractions about eating different fractions of chocolate bars and cakes. The rule for division of fractions is 'turn one fraction upside down and multiply'. A better strategy might be to convert both fractions to decimals and use a calculator. There are a couple of useful articles to read. One by Swee Fong Ng discusses PGCE students' reactions to the topic during their training. A second article by Tim Rowland reports a virtuoso performance by a 10-year-old, finding how many $\frac{3}{4}$ there are in a 100, largely by mental methods and producing a generalised method for solving division by fractions as an extra: a stunning performance that is well worth reading.

Representing decimals

One advantage of using decimal numbers is that they are an extension of the Arabic number system. It is a place value system and decimals are easily incorporated into it.

In the Arabic number system, integers are grouped and counted in powers of ten, producing tens, hundreds, thousands and so on, as the columns are extended to the left of the units or singles column, making space for larger and larger numbers. The system can also be made to cope with numbers smaller than 1. Retaining the tenfold relationship between successive places in the system means we can produce tenths, hundredths, thousandths and so on by moving to the right of the units column.

Decimal numbers are also easy to represent using wooden blocks popularised by the Hungarian mathematician, Zoltan Dienes in the mid-1960s (Figure 6.3). The MAB material can also be used in the classroom to represent fractions (Figure 6.4). Blocks are often used to represent units, tens, hundreds and thousands. The large block is scored with lines to represent a thousand of the small single cubes. However, you can hold this large block up in class and then get as far away from the children as possible so that it appears to get smaller. Invite the children to imagine you travelling so far away that the block looks as small as a single cube. 'Let's pretend this block is a single cube and call it one. How much is flat worth now? Remember that the flat is a tenth of the block and we are pretending the block is worth one.'

Teachers can then explore the values of the stick and the small cube using some useful equipment which now represents ones, tenths, hundredths and thousandths. (Incidentally, if we take a single small cube, get the children to roll up a piece of paper and look through it,

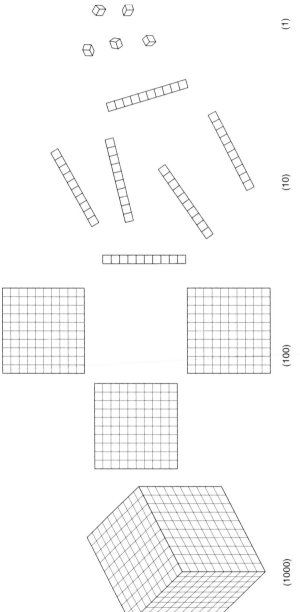

(1000)   (100)   (10)   (1)

Figure 6.3 Dienes MAB material for base 10: five single cubes, six ten-sticks, three-hundred flats and a thousand block, used to represent one thousand, three hundred and sixty-five.

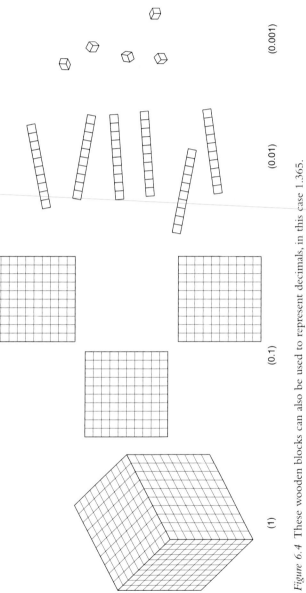

(1)   (0.1)   (0.01)   (0.001)

Figure 6.4 These wooden blocks can also be used to represent decimals, in this case 1.365.

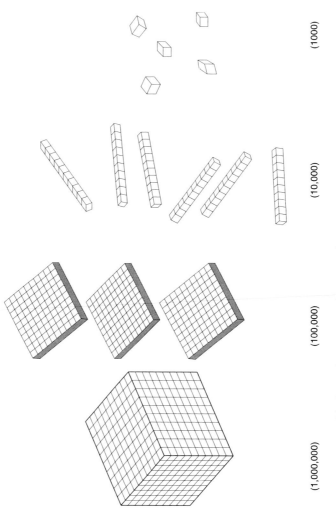

(1000)

(10,000)

(100,000)

(1,000,000)

Figure 6.5 Dienes blocks used to represent larger numbers.

we can pretend that we are using a very powerful telescope to look at it. We can suggest to the children that what we are actually looking at is in fact the thousand block, but a long way off. We then introduce the stick and ask what it might be (10,000), the flat (100,000) and the large block (1,000,000). The children can then write on their wipe boards, what they would see through the telescope when the number 1,365,000 needs to be displayed (Figure 6.5).

Another useful connection is with the metric system of litres and millilitres. We let the large block represent a litre and the small cube, which is 1 cc, represents 1 ml. The definition of a kilogram is a 10 cm by 10 cm by 10 cm cube of water at 25 degrees Celsius (at a pressure of one atmosphere, each millilitre has a mass of one gram). The kilogram has a volume of 1000 cc and contains 1000 ml which is equivalent to one litre.

Working with decimals

Because decimals are located within the Arabic number system, the same general rules of arithmetic apply as for integers, for addition, subtraction, multiplication and division. Multiplication does present problems over the positioning of the final decimal place. It is useful to get an approximate answer by mental calculation as a first step. Take the following calculation for example:

$$1.3 \times 2.5$$

Two and half lots of *one and a bit* is going to give an approximate answer of a little more than 3 (alternatively consider it as just a little more than 1 lot of $2\frac{1}{2}$). The most convenient procedure is to remove the decimal points and proceed as if we had an integer calculation.

1.3	convert	13	The decimal point is removed (multiplied by 10)
×2.5	to	×25	This decimal point has also been removed (multiplied by 10)
———		———	The whole calculation has been increased by $10 \times 10 = 100$. The result will be 100 times larger than the correct answer.
———		———	Put the decimal back when finished (need to divide by 10×10).

13×25 gives an answer of 325. This is 100 times larger than the answer to 1.3×2.5 but the digits are exactly right. Divide 325 by 100 and the answer is 3.25 which fits our original requirement of a 'little more than 3'.

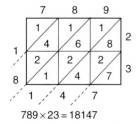

$789 \times 23 = 18147$

Figure 6.6 Gelosia, an alternative long multiplication algorithm.

In 1972 I worked in a first school. We, and the partner middle school did not teach the long multiplication algorithm. It was considered unhelpful and too confusing for many pupils. Instead the schools made use of the Gelosia method, which provides a more helpful structure for pupils than the multiplication algorithm (Figure 6.6).

Division with decimals

This is a similar procedure to the computation with integers except where both numbers involved are decimals.

456.87 ÷ 34

is read as four hundred and fifty six point eight seven (not as point eighty seven) divided by thirty four. The long division and the short division methods are fine for this type of problem.

However, 765.98 ÷ 3.76 does present problems if one is going to use the long or short division written algorithms. Most of us would probably resort to an electronic calculator for this type of calculation. If we are forced to use a pencil and paper method, we need to change both the divisor (3.76) and the dividend (765.98) by the same factor of ten to get rid of the decimal point in the divisor. Multiplying 3.76 by 100 will give us 376. Multiplying 765.98 by 100 keeps the proportion the same and we have an exactly equivalent calculation that can be done using the short or long division method.

765.98 ÷ 3.76 is transformed into the more convenient 76598 ÷ 376

It is useful to encourage children to make a look-up table on a wipe board. Do it quickly by using knowledge of doubling facts.

Multiplier	Multiplicand	How to deduce new facts from knowledge of doubling, halving and multiplying by 10
1	376	Start with 376
2	752	Double 376 to make 752
3		Add 376 and 752
4	1504	Double 2 × 376
5		Find 10 × 376 and halve it
6		?
7		?
8		Double 4 × 376
9		?
10	3760	Find 10 × 376 by adding a zero

The look-up table then makes the division process more accurate and quicker. Try it yourself!

Addition and subtraction with decimals

Addition and subtraction of decimals can be carried out using the same addition and subtraction methods as for integers. Often, a written method is preferable to a mental one because of the number of digits involved, and most people find a vertical layout more helpful when setting out written computations. This is because the vertical methods emphasise the different places (hundreds, tens, units, tenths, hundredths, etc.) and it is easier to keep the digits of same value together.

$$456.12$$
$$+789.54$$

456.12 The same computation method as for integers, and with all decimal
+ 789.54 points lying exactly below each other.

Working with percentages

Percentages are an interesting way of representing fractional parts. Per cent (%) means out of a hundred parts. The process uses the idea that every number can be seen as being divisible into a hundred equal parts. The result is that we can make comparisons between different numbers much more easily. If I run a school of 250 children and 63 children have a day's absence through illness in January, did we suffer a greater rate of absence than a school of 135 children where 44 were absent for one day over the same period?

The answer is not immediately obvious to most people unless we carry out some calculations on the numbers supplied. By converting numbers to percentages it is possible to make direct comparisons. Comparing the percentages produced by converting the numbers is easier than comparing the original numbers.

To compare the percentage absence for January for the two schools means we have to imagine that the numbers 250 and 135 are both transformed into 100 parts. By using skills like doubling and halving we can get a feel for the two situations. It becomes easier to 'see' where 63 might fit if I remember that 63 is approximately a quarter of 250 (4×63 is 252).

So we could place 63 about $\frac{1}{4}$ of the way along the number line running from 0 to 250. We can then do the same with the 44 children in relation to their school's 135 on roll. Four times 44 gives 176, so 44 is more than $\frac{1}{4}$ of 135 and it looks already like that school had a greater proportion of absence. For those people who prefer a visual image, rather than a written description, we can draw the number line to produce an image of the relationship between the numbers.

The number line allows visual comparisons that can support our thinking and provides a check for errors in calculation. Figure 6.7 uses length as a metaphor for the number of children absent from the school. It is easy to find by eye, the mid point, one quarter and three quarters. Halfway ($\frac{1}{2}$) equates to 50%, a quarter of the way ($\frac{1}{4}$) to 25% and ($\frac{3}{4}$) to 75%. A fifth ($\frac{1}{5}$) is represented by 20%.

Calculating percentages often demands that we look at a change in relation to an original or a total amount.

Figure 6.7 The two schools' absences compared as percentages.

Percentage can be thought of as:

$$\frac{\text{change}}{\text{original}} \times 100$$

To create a more accurate picture of the above problem, we can now calculate the absences for the two schools as percentages. To compare 63 with 250 as a percentage we calculate

$$\frac{63}{250} \times 100 = 25.2\%$$

So 63 is 25.2% of 250.

For school 2 the figures are

$$\frac{44}{135} \times 100 = 32.5925925$$

The answer can never be written exactly because the digits 592 recur. This is an example of a recurring, non-terminating decimal but we can approximate it to 32.6 for the purposes of this discussion, and we can now compare the schools' figures directly. The first school had an absence rate of approximately 25% compared with the second school's rate of approximately 33% (rounded up from 32.59%).

QTS skills tests

The calculation of percentages and the conversion between percentages, fractions and decimals is a significant feature of the current version of the skills test you need to pass.

Many trainees find the conversion between fractions, decimals and percentages the worst mathematical aspect of the test. A number line is a strong visual image that can be used to link these three different ways of representing numbers. Some key points are known by heart (50% is a $\frac{1}{2}$ and also 0.5) and they can be drawn on the line. If you know 10% you can deduce 20% and 5% through doubling and halving, so you can gradually add more information to the line (15% can be found by adding 10% and 5%).

Many people find it useful to tie together the key pieces of knowledge they already possess in some visual form, which could be a triangle of information that is like the one shown here. Remember though, there are six conversions here, represented by the six arrows. Some people find moving in one direction easy, but the return along the adjacent arrow is more difficult. Practice until all six routes are easy.

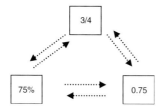

The questions in the skills tests are relatively straightforward, but the speed at which the mental tests are given can be daunting for those who have had little practice of mental calculation at speed for a while. The advice I give trainees is to practise by:

1   Working entirely without time constraints until you achieve more than 90% accuracy with practice questions.
2   Finding your best learning style (e.g. if you are a visual thinker, then practice drawing diagrams until you are fast at jotting information and sketching simple diagrams).
3   Practise doubling and halving strategies, with integers, fractions, decimals and percentages. (Why is it that Customs and Excise has set the VAT rate at $17\frac{1}{2}\%$?)
4   Practise answering tests at speed only when your calculations are regularly error free.

A large proportion of the current questions used in the QTS mental test ask for a conversion of numbers to or from a percentage. Sometimes there is a linguistic catch, where the question gives information about one particular group (e.g. those who have free school meals) but asks for an answer about a different group (those who do not have free school meals). For example:

---

1   Twenty percent of the pupils in a school with three hundred and fifteen pupils have free school meals. How many pupils don't have free school meals?

To solve this numerically, we need to remember that 20% is equivalent to $\frac{20}{100}$ (and also by simplifying), $\frac{2}{10}$ or $\frac{1}{5}$ So if one-fifth do have school meals then four-fifths do not – and this is the information that is being asked for. So, using percentages

$$80\% \text{ of } 315 \text{ is } \frac{80}{100} \times 315 \text{ or}$$

converting to fractions

$$\frac{4}{5} \text{ of } 315 \text{ is calculated as } \frac{4}{5} \times 315 = 252$$

To solve using a visual method, you could draw a number line to represent all 315 pupils, which is 100% of the school population.

```
0_____315
0%    10%    20%                         100%
```

Estimate where 10% will fall on the line, then double to mark 20% (10% of 315 is 31.5 so 20% is double 31.5 which is 63 pupils). These take school meals, so subtract 63 from 315 to find how many do not take them.

$$315 - 63 = 252$$

---

2   In a year group of one hundred and eighty pupils, five per cent were absent. How many pupils were present?

Numerically, you could start by thinking 'absent − present', 5% absent means 95% present. To find 95% of 180

$$\frac{95}{100} \times 180 = 171$$

Visually, you could start by drawing a number line showing 180 (100% of the school population).

```
0      18                                              180
0%     10%                                             100%
```

Estimate where 10% will fall on the line. Mentally calculate 10% (one-tenth) of 180 which is 18. Now halve this to find 5% which is 9. Stop and think. 9 pupils are the 5% who are absent, but we need the numbers who are present, so, we can subtract 9 from 180 which gives 171 (it is easier to take 5% away than to calculate 95%).

---

3   The attendance rate in a school of three hundred children drops from ninety-seven per cent to ninety-five per cent in consecutive weeks. How many more absences were there in the second week?

Numerically, we need to calculate the difference between 97% and 95% of the same original number. In other words, there has been a 2% change over the two weeks. 2% of 300 is $\frac{2}{100} \times 300 = 6$ (the difference in the number of pupils between weeks 1 and 2).

Calculating each stage separately we have 97% of 300 $= \frac{97}{100} \times 300 = 291$

and 95% of 300 $= \frac{95}{100} \times 300 = 285$

The increase over the two weeks was the difference between $291 - 285 = 6$.

Visually, we could start by thinking about the 95% attendance and remembering that if 95% were attending then 5% were not. Mentally calculate the 5% by finding 10% and halving the result (10% of 300 is 30, so 5% is 15 – the number of pupils absent the second week).

```
0    9    15                                           300
0%   3%   5%                                           100%
```

Here we can use the strategy of finding 1% to find the number absent during the first week. We know 97% attendance means 3% absence. We can find 1% of 300 easily, which is 3, so 3% must be $3 \times 3 = 9$ pupils absent in week one). Stop and think. 9 pupils absent in week 1 and the consecutive week the number went up to 15. The question asks 'How many more absences were there in the second week?': Answer 6.

Alternatively, looking at the number line we can see we are looking at a shift from 3% to 5% of the same total of 300. So the shift is 2% change over two weeks. We can mentally calculate 1% of 300 easily, as 3, so 2% must be 6.

4 A supplier offered schools a five per cent discount on sports equipment they had purchased. How much was saved on a furniture order of nine hundred pounds?

Numerically, the school can cut the cost of their £900 order by 5% which is $\frac{5}{100} \times 900 = £45$.

Visually, draw a number line to represent the full cost of £900. Mentally calculate the 5% reduction by calculating 10% (90) then halve the answer, to get the 5% reduction (45). Estimate where 10% and 5% would go on the line. Mark the answers on the number line and inspect it to see whether the answers fit the visual picture.

Alternatively, calculate 1% of 900 (9) and multiply by 5 to get 5% ($5 \times 9 = 45$). Stop and think. What does the question ask? 'How much was *saved* . . . ?' Answer £45.

```
0__ 45_____90_____900
0%   5%      10%                                           100%
```

Gradually, as confidence increases, try to visualise a number line in your head without drawing, then try to place the relevant percentages and numbers on it as a visualisation. To do this successfully, you need to be relaxed, and in a quiet environment, rather than stressed and under time pressure. Try it at home in the bath first, if this is a relaxing time. Try to move the visual images around, get some control over them, change the numbers, try thinking in different colours. Once you have gained control, introduce this way of working into a more pressured environment, such as during a practice test available from the TTA website (http://www.canteach.gov.uk). In many problems, it is useful to find 10% or 1% of a number or an amount. This quickly gives access to 2%, 4%, 8%, 5%, 20%. Doubling and halving is a valuable strategy to develop.

Do not try to visualise and draw diagrams if this is unnecessary for you, or if it slows you down. Visualisation has been introduced here as a strategy for 'trying to see' how to start. Once you become proficient, it is likely that you would not need to rely on visualising so much.

Using equipment to represent percentages

Because Cuisenaire rods and Color Factor use the length of a coloured wooden rod to represent a number as so many centimetres of length, they employ the same metaphor as the

Fractions	Decimals	Percentages
0	0	0
1/4	0.25	25
1/2	0.5	50
3/4	0.75	75
1	1.0	100

Figure 6.8 Make your own look-up table for converting common fractions.

National expectations about current classroom routines are not always conducive to effective learning and some classrooms are not particularly healthy places for thinking mathematically. Where this is the case, there may be too much demand on immediate understanding. Instead of deep mathematical thinking, what we demand is shallow and immediate mathematical explanation from learners. One further result, too often, is that children worry about their response for fear that it will be wrong. They may not contribute at all and certainly do not feel encouraged to mull over ideas between lessons.

Most adults rarely understand new ideas first time round, but we can easily give children the impression (deliberately or unconsciously) that they should. Thoughts and ideas do become clearer over time, but for most of us, this clarification takes effort and work, and often requires the active participation of others. Creating a climate where we feel inadequate in such situations is counter productive for any learner, adult or child.

In mathematics lessons in particular, there are many learners who would prefer not to communicate openly about their mathematical thinking. This places a serious limitation on the education process and on the work of the teacher. The most challenging environments to create in school are those where the mathematics is taught at a good pace, with plenty of discussion involving the vast majority and where children are invited to speak and know that their ideas are valued.

Culturally, we have much to learn from Hungarian, Polish and German class teachers. Research findings suggest that in several European countries, teachers use children's mistakes as a focus for classroom discussion without the child who produced the mistake experiencing a sense of embarrassment. In Britain, this is difficult to achieve. We are culturally disposed to perceive mistakes in lessons as opportunities for criticism, punishment and evidence of a lack of intelligence. We need to find ways to increase the robustness of learners and change the classroom environment so that errors and misconceptions can be talked about more easily in open classroom discussions without embarrassment, and used as points for exploration and further learning.

Resources and further reading

Dickson, L., Brown, M. and Gibson, O. (1984) *Children Learning Mathematics: Teacher's Guide to Recent Research*. London: Holt Education.

Haylock, D. (2001) *Mathematics Explained for Primary Teachers* (second edn). London: Paul Chapman Publishing.

Hopkins, C., Gifford, S. and Pepperell, S. (1999) *Mathematics in the Primary School: a Sense of Progression* (second edn). London: David Fulton.

Koshy, V., Ernest, P. and Casey, R. (2000) *Mathematics for Primary Teachers*. London: Routledge.

Menninger, K. (1969) *Number Words and Number Symbols*. Cambridge, MA: MIT Press.

Mooney, C., Ferrie, L., Fox, S., Hansen, A. and Wrathmell, R. (2002b) *Primary Mathematics: Knowledge and Understanding*. Exeter: Learning Matters.

Nunes, T. and Bryant, P. (1997) *Learning and Teaching Mathematics*. Hove: Psychology Press.

Orton, A. and Frobisher, L. (1996) *Insights into Teaching Mathematics*. London: Cassell.

Parsons, E. (ed.) (1999) *GCSE Mathematics Revision Guide* (Higher Level). Coordination Group Publications.

Rowland, T. (1997) Dividing by three quarters: what Susie saw. *Mathematics Teaching* MT 160 September 1997, pp. 30–33.

Swee Fong, N. (1998) Can you please help us see what is a fraction divided by another fraction? *Mathematics Teaching* MT 165 December 1998, pp. 28–29.

7 Algebra

The primary teacher who has a specialist interest in mathematics has an advantage when it comes to teaching other curriculum subjects and responding to multicultural issues, PSME and citizenship. Mathematics can be used and explored in three distinct and powerful ways in primary schools.

1   To develop knowledge, thinking skills and techniques in this distinctive area of the curriculum (studying the beauty of mathematics for its own sake).
2   For understanding the world. By explicitly relating mathematics to subjects like science, geography, music, technology, etc. maths can be applied to other activities, for example, to represent a dance sequence in PE (maths as a tool for learning other things).
3   For exploring social, cultural and historical themes in support of multicultural teaching, PSME and citizenship. We can do this by exploring children's games from around the world, for example, Five Stones, Mancala, Cat's Cradle, and by looking at the origins of the mathematics we use today (maths as a social and historical artefact).

I am not suggesting that we teach the history of number to ten-year-olds. I am suggesting that if we know something of the history of counting, and the origin of subjects like algebra, we can use them to promote a wider understanding and appreciation of culture. Meeting the Standards – particularly in the area of Professional Values, can be done more effectively through a broad knowledge of mathematics as a social and historical artefact.

David Pimm describes algebra as being:

> … about form and about transformation. Algebra, right back to its origins, seems to be fundamentally dynamic, operating on or transforming forms. It is also about equivalence: something is preserved despite apparent change.
>
> (Pimm, 1995: 88)

Algebra offers one of the most useful opportunities to connect mathematics and multicultural education, and to explore history from a non-Eurocentric position. The expansion of the seventh century Arab empire created the conditions for an astonishing series of mathematical developments; including the introduction of Arabic numerals, the development of a place value arithmetic system by Arab scholars and traders and the systematic teaching of arithmetic and algebra throughout the known world.

The Arab commitment to the expansion of knowledge

It is hard to overestimate the influence of the burgeoning Arab empire. It had a huge impact on the development of mathematics in Western Europe. It created and sustained one of the Ages of Enlightenment, by spreading eastwards through Byzantium and Persia, and in the same development of influence, westward through Egypt along the North African coast, eventually through Spain and into France. It was the Arab commander, *Djibel-al-Tariq* who in 711, crossed what are now known as the Straits of Gibraltar.

The empire was a significant preserver and developer of culture, architecture, the arts, music and literature. It established a dynamic cultural centre in Damascus in 635 under Caliph Omar the successor to the prophet Mohammad; where Jews, Christians and Muslims enjoyed religious freedom. As world traders, the empire generated and sustained contacts with India and China via international trade routes, and communicated contemporary ideas to Western Europe. The empire created a powerful climate for the communication of ideas on astronomy, number, philosophy and technological advances such as paper making from China, which supported the communication of mathematical and other ideas.

The Arabs published theoretical and practical texts which helped develop the skills of computation using Indian numerals. Arab scholars were enthusiastic translators of Greek philosophy and science, the mathematics of Euclid, and Ptolemy's astronomy. The impact of the Greek mathematicians did not arrive in Western Europe in a westwards movement from Greece, but was brought, adapted and reinvented, by Arab thinkers through North Africa and into Spanish centres of learning in Cordoba and elsewhere. It was not until 1258 that Baghdad finally fell to the Mongols. Granada survived until 1492 as a Moorish enclave.

The Arabs needed an effective system of numerals with which to run their huge world empire. The indigenous systems in conquered countries were allowed to continue because initially, the Arabs had no useful way of managing figures. Edicts were communicated initially in Greek and Arabic, but Arabic numbers were communicated in words and appeared in translation in Greek texts using the Greek alphabetical numeral system. In 706, in some administrative offices, Greek was finally suppressed in favour of Arabic except for the writing of numerals which continued to use the Greek system. This does suggest that by this date, Indian numerals had not penetrated far into the Arab empire – at least not as far as Damascus.

In 773 everything changed. A book written by Brahmagupta was brought from India to Baghdad. The book, known in Arabic as the Sindhind, was translated from Sanskrit into Arabic and allowed Arabic scholars to develop their studies of astronomy. In approximately 820 Al-Khwarizmi the most significant mathematician of his day (and who was also known by his Latin name, Algorismus), produced a small arithmetic textbook in which he demonstrated the use of the Indian numerals. There followed another book on solving equations and problems from everyday life. Its twelfth century Latin translation was called *Algebra et Almucabala*. The arithmetic book ended up in Spain at the beginning of the twelfth century and was translated by Robert of Chester, an English student of mathematics.[1]

The introduction of the Indian numerals together with Arab developments and guidance on their use in calculation, allowed an alternative to the contemporary practice in Europe, of using a counting board for managing financial and business transactions. The two methods survived side by side for some time each with their advocates. One group supported the use of counting boards and abacus methods, whilst the other group promoted the newly developed algorithmic methods based on the place value system which used what are now called the Arabic numerals (Tahta, 1998: 4–11).

One way to emphasise personal wealth and status at that time was to commission a portrait painter. Many paintings and woodcuts of successful European traders and business people dating from the sixteenth century attest to the existence of counting boards: some even show both abacists and algorists at work as in the Gregor Reisch woodcut of 1503 (Tahta, 1998: 4). Robert Recorde,[2] shows a dispute between abacist and algorist on the relative advantages of counting boards and place value numerals. Recorde was born in Tenby in 1510. He studied at All Souls College, Oxford and later graduated as an MD from Cambridge and was personal physician to King Edward VI. He was also comptroller of the Bristol Mint and in charge of the silver mines at Wexford. Recorde's influence is apparent behind Edward's decision to introduce a new silver five-shilling piece; the first English coin to have a date written in Arabic numerals rather than Roman numerals. Recorde is attributed as establishing the English school of mathematics and introducing algebra into England. He wrote a number of books on mathematics and sought to provide a complete course of mathematical instruction for students. He also deliberately published in English rather than Latin or Greek in order to be more widely read.

A three page spread of interesting visual images is provided in *Mathematics Teaching* (MT 115: 19–21) entitled Ethnomathematical Origins of Algebra.

Teaching and learning algebra

The early versions of the National Curriculum in England and Wales made explicit links between algebra and pattern making activities that many teachers at KS1 include in the mathematics curriculum for young children. In his article on an algebraic approach to arithmetic, Hewitt (1998) contrasts a quotation from Vygotsky, '…algebra is harder than arithmetic' with his own view that 'arithmetic is impossible without algebra'(p. 19).

It is worth remembering that all the work we do with the associative and commutative laws is fundamentally algebraic work. We can also include the long multiplication algorithm because that too requires us to work algebraically.

$$\begin{array}{r} ab \\ \times cd \\ \hline \end{array}$$

What we actually do when using this long multiplication algorithm can be written in expanded form as:

$$(10a + b)\ (10c + d)$$

which generates four products.

The definition of algebra as the exploration of structural relationships challenges many people's assumptions that the defining role of algebra is the manipulation of equations in secondary school. One result of a redefining of algebra was that an algebra curriculum in primary schools could be conceived from the Foundation Stage through KS1 and KS2, feeding into work at KS3 and beyond. A further benefit is the potential for unification that algebra brings. Children's understanding of mathematics is developed more effectively when we teach algebraic understanding alongside number. Algebra provides opportunities to develop logic, reasoning and proof through such activities as prediction, inverse operation, looking for equivalence, disproving by counter-example, proving by induction, solving equations (Mooney, 2002b, *Primary Mathematics: Knowledge and Understanding* has a useful chapter on reasoning and proof).

Logic and reasoning can be supported, for example, by investigating odd and even numbers. Suppose we use click cubes. We can see the patterns as we snap a stick to make two towers.

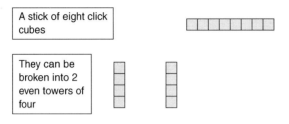

Eight cubes can be broken into two equal towers. Can we do the same with nine? What about ten? Suppose we say that eight makes two even towers (four high) and nine makes two odd towers (a four and a five). Can you find some more even numbers? Can you guess which numbers will be odd before you break the stick into two pieces? Can you tell me about 999, 1000 and 1001? Talk to me about your thinking? (What's your reasoning?)

$$(m + 1) + (n + 1) = m + n + 2$$

if m and n are even, then, $m + n$ is even and therefore $(m + 1) + (n + 1)$ is also even. Why must $n + (n + 1)$ always be odd for real integers? What kind of algebra is useful for children during the three Key Stages of primary education? How can appropriate activities create a personal fluency in algebra? One example is to move children beyond a specific knowledge of the results of arithmetic ($3 + 7 = 10$) to a more general understanding (e.g. that the result of adding two odd numbers will always be even). The benefit to young children of working algebraically lies in the opportunity it gives to make generalisations, to explore lots of arithmetic examples (thereby providing opportunity for practice and consolidation of number facts) and to look for relationships within the number system so that children develop their ability to spot patterns and make predictions, based on problem solving activities.

It is useful then to look at the distinction between algebra and arithmetic. Understanding the algebra of any situation involves an understanding of the rules that apply within that world. For instance, we might remember that when we add $3 + 7$ we get 10. This is arithmetic knowledge. Shifting our attention away from practising computation for its own sake and towards a study of the properties of numbers is a shift away from arithmetic to algebra.

Teachers may continue to ensure that their children's addition facts are recalled efficiently but at the same time, draw their attention to some patterns, for example that although three and seven are odd numbers, the result of adding them generates an even number. The way is now open for an investigation. Children can then check other pairs of odd numbers, and invent ways of recording their results efficiently. They will begin to see a pattern emerging when they find that the same result occurs with other pairs. The teacher has shifted the focus of their awareness from the recall of number facts and onto the algebra of arithmetic – the structure and rules that govern the addition of integers. This is not at the expense of practising computation because in order to explore the proposition that odd + odd = even, children have to carry out large numbers of calculations in the search for a pair that might break the rule.

It is important to develop a conceptual framework for the teaching of algebra in primary school, so that we can see how to provide effective contexts for learning from the Foundation Stage through to KS2. As teachers, there are three points to bear in mind when thinking about developing conceptual teaching frameworks. These apply to all teaching of mathematics, not just to algebra teaching.

1   Humans have an extraordinarily powerful ability to recognise, generate and use patterns. We can recall and recognise patterns far more easily than random events and pieces of disconnected knowledge that we have to memorise. Teaching strategies that harness pattern and pattern recognition are more effective for supporting learning than those which rely on memorisation.
2   Humans are fundamentally social creatures and collaborative problem solvers with enormous linguistic powers: language and discourse are fundamental to the development and application of mathematical thinking strategies. Mathematics classrooms should be noisy places, and the voices that should predominate should be those of the learners, rather than that of the teacher.
3   Humans use written language to communicate initial thoughts, as an aid to further thinking and as a signifier of personal worth and self-esteem. All pupils gain self-esteem from seeing their mathematical ideas in written form. Teachers intuitively scribe for young children as a way of celebrating their ideas and opinions. As children develop their writing skills, they are increasingly able to write concise statements: their writing should provide examples of reasoning, logic and proof together with an increasing ability to use mathematical symbols and conventions.
4   There is great value in using spoken language, written language, written numerical symbols and pictures, and diagrams and graphs, in the same lesson, to represent the same ideas in different ways.

In brief, young children can demonstrate their skills as powerful problem solvers provided the teacher creates appropriate classroom contexts for learning. Dialogue needs to pervade all mathematics teaching – the teacher should create an active web of language and discussion that envelops teacher, learners and context. This discourse should feature both teacher and children as protagonists. It is not the teacher's remit to be the only leader of discussion. Children too, must take the lead during discussions, didactical instruction, questioning, explaining, the naming of parts, the describing of actions, explanation, the teaching of inductive and deductive method and logical reasoning. Indeed a useful maxim for effective teaching is to provide regular opportunities in classrooms when those who know the most, say the least, in order that children get used to developing half-baked ideas and presenting them publicly for discussion.

One example of progression for developing algebraic thinking and skills

Sorting and grouping common objects by different criteria, both given and chosen. Responding to teacher's questions with simple explanations and reasons.	Grouping all the seashells and separating them from the conkers. Putting all the jigsaws in the correct cupboard, putting other games elsewhere. All these words are names of animals, … Games such as *My Granny Likes…apples* but she doesn't like *pears*…
Recognising patterns in a collection of objects, words, music, dance, etc. being able to follow them, and then invent your own examples. Working to improve different memory types, pattern, spatial, recognition and semantic – facts, definitions, classifications and episodic – filmic, narrative, procedural. Offering and inviting explanations of the rules, explaining why a rule has been broken, and what is needed to put things right again.	Red lorry, yellow lorry, red lorry, yellow lorry, … Apple, plum, peach, cherry, apple, plum, peach, cherry… Loud, soft, soft, loud, soft, soft, … Jump, crouch, hop, hop, step, jump, crouch, hop, hop, step, … Pellmanism, Snap, Kim's Game, Happy Families (but beware the stereotypes, e.g. all white, all married – Mr and Mrs, etc.)
Predicting the next item in the sequence. Providing reasoned arguments for your predictions. 'I think the next one's got to be 3 because…'	Square, triangle, square, triangle, … 1, 2, 3, 4, 5, … 7, 6, 5, … 1, 2, 1, 2, 1, 2, … 2, 4, 6, 8, … 1, 1, 2, 3, 5, 8, 13, … And then, what about: apple, elephant, tie, egg, buffalo, orange, … (could it possibly be a sequence? How will you know?)
Using symbols and boxes to represent possible solutions to simple number sentences. Forming equalities and inequalities in written number sentences. Finding solutions in a variety of contexts. Learning to write and read number sentences and interpret their meaning.	$5 > \square$ $5 + 2 = \square + \square$ $7 + 3 \neq \square$ $3 \, \square \, 2 = \Delta$ (no operator given) Working on inverses. If I double 6 – how can you undo what I've done? (I can get back again by halving 12) Introduce division as 'undoing' multiplication $54 \div 6 = \square$ Let's try $6 \times \square = 54$
Playing computer games like 'Blocks' which can also be played as table-top game with 3 dice, paper and pencil, number cards or fans. ($\star$ means any operator)	$\square + \square = 24$ $\square \star \square \star \square = 24$
Interpreting and solving number problems. Offering explanations and reasons.	'I'm thinking of a rod that is as long as two red rods plus a white rod. Which rod am I thinking of?' 'I'm thinking of a whole number that's one less than half of 26. Tell me my number.' 'I tried taking one away from 26 but that didn't really help.' 'Try doing the halving first.'

	'Let's play there and back again. I start at 11, add 3 multiply by 2 and arrive at 28. Can you take me back again by undoing what I did?'
Verbally expressing relationships.	We found out that every minute, the temperature went down by 4 degrees.
Writing problems and solutions to number problems in words and pictures. Identifying and following written rules of procedure.	'I'm going to invent a rule then write it out in steps for my partner to try.' (1) Think of a number. (2) Halve it. (3) Then add one.
Distinguishing between discrete counts and continuous measures.	Measures like temperature, height, weight are continuous. They are never exact and measurement is only ever an approximation. Shoe size, dress size, days of week, months are discrete. You can't have 'Wednesday and a tenth'
Writing algebraic sentences accompanied by evidence of reasoning and explanation	'If everyone in my family kissed each other once, we'd all get 5 kisses and there'd be 15 kisses all together. Guess how many are there in my family. I think it's, $\dfrac{f(f-1)}{2} = 15$ so $f = 6$. I think you've got 6 people in your family and everyone gets 5 kisses, because they don't kiss themselves!
Developing logical thinking that makes it possible to argue the value of the 100th term in a series, without generating all 100 terms.	

Thinking and working algebraically[3]

Research suggests that the teaching of algebra remains problematic. In her paper to the International Group for the Psychology of Mathematics Education (PME, 1999), Ainley discusses some of the evidence that shows why children in the upper end of the primary school find it difficult to get a sense of what algebra is. She discusses young children's early learning experiences and makes the point that young children are very familiar with learning in social settings where they occupy peripheral positions, but that when algebra is introduced at KS2 it is often done in such a way that children cannot occupy this familiar and comfortable peripheral position.

Children learn better when they have had the chance to learn from a peripheral perspective, where they can begin by observing others engaged in tasks that they will later take up themselves. This is a typical position occupied by young children in family contexts and is one reason why families can create such effective learning environments. Ainley (1999) refers to the term peripheral participants to describe learning as an activity carried out on the edge. Learning on the edge allows a broader viewpoint and provides a greater chance that the learner will see the activity in relation to the broader enterprise. KS2 teaching of mathematics is by contrast, often very direct, very focused. All centre and no edge (metaphorically rather than geometrically speaking).

One way to retain room for the peripheral learner is to engage in brief discussion with one small group, perhaps following work on a differentiated task by a target group of more able children, which is more difficult than most of the children can cope with. We are not demanding that the others will learn here and now, how to solve the problem given to the more able group. We are trying to provide an opportunity to listen in, to learn edgewise. 'I'm going to do something fairly difficult with the green group now for a couple of minutes. Don't worry if you don't follow it all. Join in if you can, I'd like that! Listen carefully and see what you think.'

'Green group: can one of you explain your ideas? I'll write them down. Then we'll move on to the next person. Hopefully you'll give me different words and different ways of thinking.'

An interactive whiteboard is an ideal way of capturing each child's thinking. You can move backwards and forwards between each 'flipchart sheet' to compare and contrast thinking. Keep it brief – otherwise you will lose the audience.

The problem in many classrooms is that children have to learn things first time round, and this is particularly challenging and unrealistic when studying some algebraic topics for the first time.

Ainley also points out that many KS2 attempts at developing algebra start with number patterns. The teacher's lesson objective may well be to get children to generate a general algebraic expression, following some iterative calculations that will produce a number of terms in a series. Many children do enjoy the search for successive terms, the application of a generative rule, the activities of prediction and confirmation, and the exploratory nature of such investigations. But, Ainley argues:

> …if you already have a rule for finding any term in the sequence, what is the point of expressing it again algebraically? An alternative approach often proposed as a way of providing meaningful contexts for algebra is the use of word problems [but] … in practice, such problems can often be solved by arithmetic approaches, … so the usefulness of algebraic notation remains unclear for pupils.
>
> (PME, 1999: 2–10)

The teacher may be very comfortable with the context for learning, but this does not necessarily cut the mustard as far as the children are concerned. The move to producing an algebraic solution does not always appear relevant.[4] So what is to be done? Ainley (1996) is well known as an enthusiast of electronic environments for teaching. She has explored the use of spreadsheets as vehicles for teaching algebra. She argues that because algebra is embedded within spreadsheet functions and procedures, using algebra within a spreadsheet environment provides children with greater opportunities to grasp the point of the algebraic activities they undertake: they are more likely to see the point of the activity because the algebra is partly a consequence of the computer software.

Ainley argues that spreadsheets are useful because one has to input the algebra in accordance with the spreadsheet's procedural rules, to get the spreadsheet to do what one wants. There is plenty of research and anecdotal evidence which shows that children are highly tolerant of receiving feedback from computers about their errors. Children know that they can only input data in a particular format. The computer's refusal to accept 'illegal' inputs is tolerated as part of the computer environment.

Children are very likely to experience such feedback as a challenge and a non-judgemental response to their errors or thinking. They respond less positively to human criticism and are more easily deterred by human feedback: which they more frequently perceive as critical of them as learners.

Ainley argues that spreadsheets provide useful opportunities for

- generating formulae for 'function machine' activities and games of guess the rule;
- for collecting and graphing data;
- for entering and copying formulae.

Much of this work could be described as pre-algebra, in the sense that it involves the interpretation of symbols, the reading of formulae where values change and the expression of general relationships. Resources include graphs, grids and mappings, number squares, multiplication tables, Cuisenaire or Color Factor rods and function machines.

Children enjoy making physical 'function machines'. The activity lends itself to cross curriculum work. Mathematically, the important feature of the work is that it requires children to think at, and be aware of, two different levels of knowledge. The first level is arithmetic. Function machines and mapping activities are useful activities for learning arithmetic and for using and applying known number facts. The second level is a meta-level that allows children to glimpse the structures and rules of arithmetic, in other words helping them to gain access to the algebra. Increasingly complex machines can be designed and their operations can be reversed – supporting an important algebraic idea (e.g. that multiplication can be 'reversed' by division) (Figure 7.1).

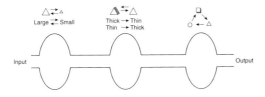

A useful resource are Logic Blocks, commercially produced closed sets of plastic coloured regular shapes of two thicknesses, two sizes and three colours. Function machines can be designed around changes to the attributes of the Logic Blocks.

Children start by working with shapes. They might design and make a function machine and label it to show it carrying out three functions in a strict order: (i) it changes size, (ii) it changes thickness, (iii) it changes all four-sided shapes into three-sided shapes and it also changes three-sided shapes into circles. Children select a single shape from the set of Logic Blocks (which contained a specific set). They name all its attributes (e.g. they might take a large, red, thin square) and put it into the machine, changing it at each of the three stages where it is changed by the machine's function. They can then name and find from the set of Logic Blocks, the resulting shape produced by sending the selected shape through the 'function machine': in this

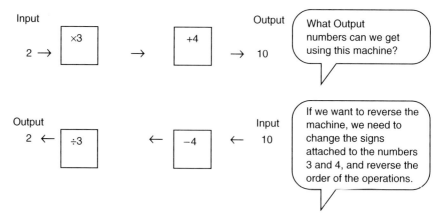

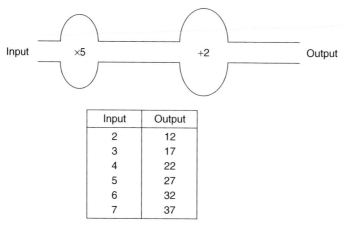

Figure 7.1 Some examples of function machines.

case (small, red, thick triangle). By working on shapes in this way at an early age, with teachers who emphasise the connections with number, children can develop meta-level ideas about the rules by which numbers can change when functions are applied to them. Children can also design and use different characters in the software game, *The Logical Journey of the Zoombinis*.

Children learn that the four rules of number (addition, subtraction, multiplication and division) can be thought of as operations that are carried out using a machine: there is an input, an operation and a result or output. A similar activity can be set up using a calculator with a function key, or using a computer. A useful teaching resource is the TTA booklet *Using ICT to Meet Teaching Objectives in Mathematics*.

Algebraic activity in primary school needs to be seen as promoting mathematical thinking. In some classrooms where mathematics is seen as content to be passed onto students, algebra may be seen only as learning how to manipulate symbols and expressions according to rules of syntax: you can do certain things and you can't do other things. This is not a helpful view. We need to avoid presenting algebra as just a rule learning activity because this runs the risk of

1   creating a climate of dependency in learners – they learn to copy the teacher but do not learn how to think mathematically;

2　limiting opportunities to see the interconnectedness of mathematical ideas, skills and problem-solving approaches – learners' problem-solving strategies can be undermined by this approach.

The teacher's focus needs to be the development of children's mathematical reasoning and not just their ability to answer factual questions accurately. LOGO provides a strong visual and kinaesthetic context that captures many learners in a powerful way. LOGO allows for the building of procedures. I can define a procedure rectangle but I can also use the definition as a procedural name to create some more interesting action. The following example of LOGO programming code is conceptually within children's grasp in primary school if it is taught effectively.

```
To rectangle        :length   :height
                    Repeat 2      [FD: length RT 90°
                                  FD: height RT 90°]
                    end
```

Having created rectangle I can use it in future code.

Mathematical reasoning is an important part of the NC Programme of Study (Ma1, for KS2).

Using and Applying Number
1. Pupils should be taught to:
   – understand and investigate general statements
   – search for pattern in their results; develop logical thinking and explain their reasoning
   (NC Using and Applying, KS2 online at http://www.qca.org.uk)

The teacher's role is twofold: the teaching of strategies for effective mathematical thinking and the explicit teaching of algebraic techniques in a classroom context where promotion of discussion allows learners to use, describe and express algebraic relationships.

Unknowns and variables

The use of symbols in algebra needs some discussion. Teachers and children are well used to seeing unknowns in number sentences although few teachers of primary children currently use the word when they write a number sentence like: $17 + \square = 20$. What teachers say is something along the lines of: 'Seventeen and something make twenty,' or, 'Seventeen plus box equals twenty, what must we put in the box?'

This method may be useful for children who can store number facts quite economically (little mathematical mental 'effort' and no affective 'effort' or panic about remembering). For others it may be more useful to use a function machine approach and to investigate what happens when the problem is represented in a slightly modified way on a whiteboard as:

$$\square + 17 = \square$$

The function machine adds 17 to any number that is entered and then outputs the answer.

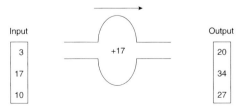

A calculator with a constant function can be programmed to do the calculation. Recording results on a whiteboard is dynamic enough to get the feel of a calculating machine.

A list of inputs and outputs can be found by the children in response to the question, 'What numbers will come out of the machine if we input numbers like, 1, 2, 3, and so on?' Children can then make a list of inputs and their corresponding outputs.

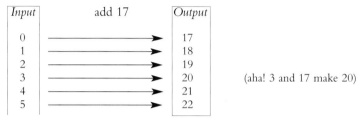

There are several alternative images that engage children. One Reception class teacher used the image of a train coming out of a tunnel. Numbers were stuck on the carriages and she engaged the children in a lot of discussion about the next number that might come out into the open from inside the tunnel. Sometimes she revealed the answer during the discussion, but on occasions children had to wait until the next day, when pulling the carriages from the tunnel became the first activity of the morning, with a considerable build up of tension and excitement.

Another teacher uses clouds to obscure parts of wall displays, and on a smaller scale, pretend ink blots are useful to hide parts of equations in books. I was fortunate to work in a school which had a piano delivered in a cardboard box – which I kept for putting children in. One hole for the input, one for the output and a mad scramble between pairs of children inside with a calculator and a paper till roll. There was never any shortage of volunteers.

Using a box □ to represent an unknown was introduced into primary textbooks in the 1970s. It is an image that teachers have found useful. Employing a number sentence with an unknown is an example of an algebraic statement and introduces children to the idea of a single symbol that can contain a range of values according to the rules defined by the rest of the equation.

Using the word box to describe the shape is a powerful strategy because the word box has strong associations for children with the idea of container. Children readily associate with the real or virtual activity of putting or thinking a single numerical value into the box and testing the number sentence for validity. It is interesting to note that conceptually, $17 + \square \neq 20$ is much more difficult for many young children to respond to, although the function machine approach makes it easier to generate possible solutions. Here, we are no longer looking for a single unknown and the notion of what values are permissible is harder to grasp, as is the apparent change in meaning of the equals sign, from carry out an action and produce a single result, to carry out several actions, each with its own result.

Reading and forming equations

The position of the box in the number sentence also affects the level of difficulty of reading and interpretation. Where the box follows an equals sign, as in $17 + 3 = \square$ many children and teachers conceptualise the box in terms of action and result, rather than as a variable. So in $17 + 3 = \square$ some children may read the box as equivalent to a question mark. To answer the question, they then carry out the action implied on the left-hand side.

The idea of a variable is more problematic in a function like

$$\square = \Delta + 25$$

The boxes no longer represent a single unknown. The idea that an endless succession of values can be put into the square and the triangle can pose conceptual and recording difficulties. Rewriting the function using symbols may make it more familiar for some people

$$y = x + 25$$

but this may not help others. Working with algebraic statements requires a different conceptualisation of the '=' sign. Algebraically, the equals sign is used to signify balance or 'the same on each side' of an equation. This is usefully demonstrated with a number balance, a practical piece of equipment for building up equations. Plastic bars can be hung on at different points along its length, either side of a pivot, allowing children to explore ways of achieving a balance.

The problem is that the two sides of an algebraic expression can look very different. But then, so can 100 single one pence coins compared with a shiny golden one-pound coin. Yes, the two are equivalent – but only in one particular sense – their value. There are also lots of ways in which the two are different. When working with an algebraic expression, often the challenge is to prove that the two parts on either side of the equals sign are equivalent. If we use the example:

$$a^2 + 2ab + b^2 = (a + b)(a + b)$$

Or, more visually

	a	$+$	b
a	a^2		ab
$+$			
b	ab		b^2

we are likely to run into difficulties when faced with checking to see if the expression on the left hand side is equivalent to that on the right, because the left- and right-hand sides look so very different.

Also, if we think that the equals sign means do something with the left-hand side to make the right-hand side, then we are not going to be successful. In the above example, there are clearly many ways in which the two sides of the equation are different, and it is not a trivial task to respond to the question, 'In what algebraic sense are they equivalent?' Talking about the equivalence of the two sides only makes sense if one accepts the following:

1   The task is to check whether one side can be made to look exactly like the other.
2   There are rules of algebraic manipulation that must be strictly followed when changing the appearance of an algebraic expression.

Working with an algebraic statement requires us to know whether we are working with a single unknown or a variable. In the case of $y = x + 5$, y can be given an infinite number of

Values of y (domain)..........and corresponding values of x (range)
−5 ⟶ −10
−4 ⟶ −9
−3 ⟶ −8
−2 ⟶ −7
−1 ⟶ −6
0 ⟶ −5
1 ⟶ −4
2 ⟶ −3
3 ⟶ −2
4 ⟶ −1
5 ⟶ 0
6 ⟶ 1

Figure 7.2 Table of values for $y = x + 5$.

different values and for each one, there will be a single value for x that satisfies the equation (Figure 7.2). When y is given the value -5, x takes the value -10. When y takes the value 0, x is -5. Just like the example above with the function machine, it is easier to see what is going on if we write what we know about the function (rule) and what it does. We can write a table of values to show how the function maps (changes) one number into another.

Williams and Shuard (1997) provide a selection of different mappings. In the above function each number in the domain maps to a single unique number in the range: it is a one-to-one relation. This is not always true and functions can have many-to-one relations. A good example is a function that contains squared values,

$$m = n^2$$

When we draw a diagram to show some numbers in the domain and their corresponding range we get a mapping which can be spoken and written in several ways:

$(f: x \rightarrow x^2$ 'x maps onto x squared'$)$, $(f(x) = x^2$ 'f of x is x squared'$)$

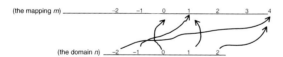

Graphs are diagrams which powerfully represent the relationships between two sets of numbers in a very visual way. The graph shows the line $y = x + 3$.

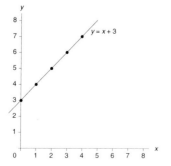

Children in primary schools need plenty of practice in

- comparing sets of numbers;
- describing and explaining the relationships between sets of numbers;
- drawing lists and tables of data;
- creating their own graphs;
- using graphing software and hand-held computers;
- interpreting graphs from newspapers and other sources;
- recognising graphs which are designed to give incorrect impressions, to distort and to falsify data.

Towards generalisation in algebra

The move from spoken language, via written longhand English expressions, through to the use of mathematical symbols, is a steady move away from ambiguity of English expressions, towards a terse, economical and unambiguous symbolic representation of mathematical ideas and calculations. A generalised form like

$$y = mx + c$$

is intended to represent all cases of a straight line, where y, m, x and c can take any value. This provides mathematics with great power, but at the same time it is contrary to the accumulated experience of young children whose reactions to school mathematics are revealed by Martin Hughes (1986) in his book *Children and Number*.

Hughes discusses children's grasp of mathematical ideas and argues that even at the pre-school stage, children possess considerable mathematical skills and understanding. However many find generalised mathematical statements difficult to understand, precisely because they do not stand for something specific and are not embedded in children's experience.

> …the abilities of young children are most likely to be elicited by problems that arise naturally in a context which the children find interesting, and where the rationale for working out an answer, using a symbol or writing something down is clearly spelt out. As Margaret Donaldson has pointed out, their difficulties frequently start when they are required to move 'beyond the bounds of human sense'.
>
> (Hughes, 1986: 168)

The Cockcroft Report (1982) signalled one particular difficulty that learners and teachers face. It is difficult to avoid classroom contexts where learners perceive that: *mathematics lessons are very often not about anything. You collect terms, or learn the laws of indices, with no perception of why anyone needs to do such things (para 462).*

One of Hughes' suggestions was to encourage children to make and use their own invented symbols and this idea was taken up by people like Sue Atkinson and the Emergent Mathematics Group (Huyton *et al.*, 1998). Hughes argues, '… that children have a striking capacity for written symbolism even before they start school' (p. 177).

The essential differences between arithmetic and algebra are that whilst both can be seen as procedural, much of what has to be done in algebra is structural. We can see that a numerical statement like $17 - 8 = 9$ requires us to follow a procedure. The same is true when we try to find the value of an algebraic example like $4m + n$ by substituting m with 3 and n with 2 and calculating the resulting answer of 14.

Working with an expression like $3x - 5y + 6x = y - 3x$ requires an algebraic answer, not a numerical one.

The differences between … [arithmetic and algebra] lie in the fact that in algebra
(a) the objects that are operated on are algebraic expressions and not numerical as in the case with arithmetic;
(b) the operations are not computational as in arithmetic;
(c) the results are other algebraic expressions, not numbers.

(Nickson, 2000: 114)

Nickson's book contains valuable discussions about recent research and how it can be used to develop effective teaching strategies throughout mathematics.

Children do not necessarily see the connections that the teacher sees between arithmetic and algebra. They may tend to see arithmetic and algebra as closed systems of mathematics and as separate activities. It is helpful if teachers model explicit activities that show children how to move, not only from arithmetic to algebra and geometry but also how to move from algebra and geometry to arithmetic.

Children should become accustomed to working back and forth between algebra and arithmetic and be able to identify the advantages of each, depending on the nature of the task… It is considered that in this cyclical interchange between the two, a better understanding of the structural nature of algebra will emerge.

(Nickson, 2000: 117)

Dialogue between children and with their teacher has also been the subject of research in relation to algebra teaching. (Saenz-Ludlow and Waldgrave, 1998). The research discusses a similar process to that advocated by Hughes. The children's discussion helps the teacher's understanding of the children's cognitive progress. The children have to construct meaning from the conventional symbols and they do this with two parallel processes, they have to invest equality with arithmetical meaning whilst also learning to incorporate symbolic language into their discussions. They do this by means of a transitional step whereby they write their 'spoken symbolisation' using conventional symbols to demonstrate what they have done.

The importance of verbalisation in coming to understand symbolic meaning in the transition from arithmetic to the algebraic level is further evidence of the general importance of language in constructing meaning for mathematical concepts generally,

(Nickson, 2000: 119)

Having internalised the notion of unknown and variable, and interpreted the equals sign in terms of the equivalence of two sides of a balance, we can now look at some uses to which algebra can be put when studying number sequences. When learning multiplication facts from a multiplication table, many children enjoy the symmetry of the diagonal, and the appearance and qualities of the square numbers (Figure 7.3).

1	2	3	4	5	6
2	4	6	8	10	12
3	6	9	12	15	18
4	8	12	16	20	24
5	10	15	20	25	30
6	12	18	24	30	36

Figure 7.3 Children enjoy the symmetry of the square numbers located on the diagonal.

Instead of making lists of the square numbers, algebra offers a short hand code to represent the fact that multiplying a number by itself generates the square of that number. If we let the letter n represent any number we care to think about; then the square of the number can be represented by n^2.

We can then explore other sequences of numbers built up from this starting point. For example, what do the first nine numbers in the sequence $n^2 + 1$ look like? The most organised way is to make a table and build up the results so that any errors can be spotted more easily (Figure 7.4). Simple spreadsheets can also be used to produce this type of data.

The last term in the sequence is known as the nth term. In this table the last term (nth term) is the ninth one. The nth term of any length of sequence is given by the general expression $n^2 + 1$. Try using it to calculate the value of the nth term when $n = 100$. That is, find $n^2 + 1$ when n is the 100th square number.

N	1	2	3	4	5	6	7	8	9
n^2	1	4	9	16	25	36	49	64	81
$n^2 + 1$	2	5	10	17	26	37	50	65	82

Figure 7.4 Calculating terms for the expression $n^2 + 1$.

Some more complex examples

We can produce sequences from much more complex expressions. If all that we are given is the first few terms, we can try to work out the general expression that will give the nth term.

Suppose we start with the sequence

9, 24, 47, 78, 117, 164, 219, …

This looks fairly impenetrable at first glance! However, a useful starting point is to look at the numerical difference between each term and the next. Where the differences are constant, as for example, in a series like, 3, 6, 9, 12, 15 (and we recognise the terms as belonging to the three-times table) the difference between one term and the next is always 3. When this first set of differences is constant, there will only be terms involving n in the general expression and no terms involving higher terms like n^2 or n^3.

The term is given by the position of the number in the sequence multiplied by 3. When $n = 2$ (the second position) the term is 6 (3×2). When the position is 5 the term is 15 (3×5). When the position is n the term is $3n$.

Since this is the general term, it gives the nth term for any number n we care to invent. So, the general expression for the three-times table is $3n$, which is not very surprising. It could be useful practice to plot

$$y = 3x$$

In the sequence, 9, 24, 47, 78, 117, ... however, the first set of differences is not a constant and so we need to look at the differences between the differences. If these second set of differences are constant then there will be an n^2 in the general expression. Putting information in a table is a helpful way of displaying things more clearly (Figure 7.5).

As we had to go to the second set of differences before we got a constant value, we know that the expression will contain values of n^2 as well as values of n. It will look something like

$$pn^2 + qn + r$$

That is, some multiple of n^2 (the value of p could be either, 1, 2, 3, 4, 5, ...etc.) together with some multiple of n and possibly some constant number (r) as well.

The next stage is to reproduce the table of differences, this time using the expression $pn^2 + qn + r$ and replacing the values of n^2 and n with the actual numbers. We will just do the first four, i.e. $n = 1, 2, 3$ and 4.

When we substitute $n = 1$ into the expression,

$$pn^2 + qn + r$$

we get

$$p + q + r$$

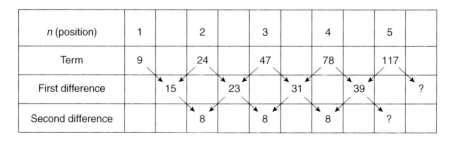

n (position)	1		2		3		4		5	
Term	9		24		47		78		117	
First difference		15		23		31		39		?
Second difference			8		8		8		?	

Figure 7.5 Calculating first and second order differences.

When we substitute $n = 2$ into the expression, we get

$4p + 2q + r$

For $n = 3$, we get

$9p + 3q + r$

For $n = 4$,

$16p + 4q + r$

We can now put these into the table and recalculate the differences using these expressions rather than numbers. The first difference will be $(4p + 2q + r)$ subtract $(p + q + r)$ which leaves $3p + q$ and we can put this into the table as the first difference.

n (position)	1		2		3		4
Term	$p+q+r$		$4p+2q+r$		$9p+3q+r$		$16p+4q+r$
First difference		$3p+q$		$5p+q$		$7p+q$	
Second difference			$2p$		$2p$		

Figure 7.6 Calculating differences using the expression $pn^2 + qn + r$.

So, after calculating all the first differences, we can continue by calculating the second differences, where we discover there is a constant difference of $2p$. We need to combine the information from Figures 7.5 and 7.6. Figure 7.5 used the actual numbers provided by the original sequence and gave us a value for the second difference of 8. Figure 7.6 produced a value of $2p$, so we can combine this information.

$2p = 8 \therefore p = 4.$

We can now use this value of p to find the values of q and r. If we start by looking at the row of first differences in Figure 7.6 we have the term $3p + q$, which corresponds to a value of 15 in table. So, $3p + q = 15$ and substituting for p we have $(3 \times 4) + q = 15$ which gives a value for q of 3. Similarly, if we look at the first term in Figure 7.6 we have $p + q + r$ and a value of 9 in Figure 7.5. Substituting for p and q in $p + q + r = 9$ gives us $4 + 3 + r = 9$ and therefore $r = 2$.

We can now use this information to build up the general expression.

$pn^2 + qn + r$ becomes:
$4n^2 + 3n + 2$

We need to check for errors, so let us try for $n = 4$ and see if we produce the fourth term of 78 that we were originally given.

$4n^2 + 3n + 2$

becomes $(4 \times 4^2) + (3 \times 4) + 2$ which is,

$64 + 12 + 2$

which equals 78.

Building up a sequence from an expression

In the last section we started from a sequence and deduced the expression. If instead, we already knew the expression and we wanted to produce the first few terms of the corresponding sequence, then we can begin by building up the data in a table.

If we start with the expression $4x^2 + 3x + 2$ and want to produce the first few terms then a table is a clear and organised way to work, which minimises errors. We know that for each position or value of x we need to calculate a value for, $3x$, x^2 and $4x^2$, and finally combine these to produce the whole expression. So we use these various parts of the expression to name the different rows of Figure 7.7. This allows us to build up the values step by step. Try filling the empty boxes.

x	1	2	3	4	5	6	7
$3x$	3	6	9	12			
x^2	1	4	9	16	25	36	49
$4x^2$	4	16			100	144	196
$4x^2+3x+2$	9	24	47	78	117		

Figure 7.7 Starting from the expression and producing the sequence for the first n terms.

The strong link between algebra and geometry can be emphasised by drawing a graph. We can argue that for each value of x there will be a value to the expression which we could label as y. We can then find values of y for a few values of x (Figure 7.8) and draw part of the graph of y against x (Figure 7.9).

Try calculating the missing values of y and plotting the values of y against x on the graph as shown in Figure 7.9.

Values of x	−3	−2	−1	0	1	2	3
Corresponding values of y calculated from $y=4x^2+3x+2$	29	?	3	2	?	24	?

Figure 7.8 Corresponding values of x and y for $y = 4x^2 + 3x + 2$.

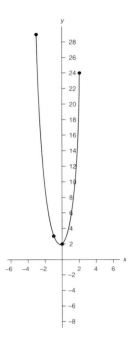

Figure 7.9 Graph of y against x for $4x^2 + 3x + 2$.

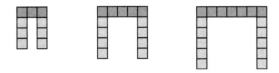

Figure 7.10 Making growth patterns with click cubes and saying what you see.

Using algebra to explore growth patterns

Many children and adults enjoy construction activities with clicking cubes. These are ideal for introducing work on algebra through posing mathematical questions about growth patterns. The National Curriculum (NC) for KS1 requires that children are taught to 'create and describe number patterns', and at KS2 they are taught to 'understand and investigate general statements' and 'search for patterns in their results, develop logical thinking and explain their reasoning'. If we combine the use of click cubes with these NC requirements, we can create some interesting activities that support algebraic work (Figure 7.10). The children can make simple growth patterns which follow a rule. The teacher asks everyone; 'Say what you see'.

'I see a doorway that grows taller and wider by two and by one.'

'I can see two towers and a stick across the top. The towers get bigger by one each side. The stick across the top gets bigger by two each time.'

'The first one is two lots of 3 plus 3 on the top. Then two lots of 3 add two ones, plus one lot of three add two more. Then it's two lots of one more on the bottom and another two across the top.'

Different ways of seeing are important and can give rise to different spoken descriptions and mathematical statements. Later, the work can be formalised further with the inclusion of a table of information to follow the verbal descriptions (Figure 7.11).

Since the first difference produces a constant value, we know that the expression will contain no more than first order values of n (no n^2 or n^3 values). So, what will the expression look like? Something like $an + b$.

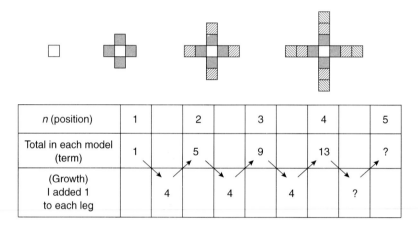

n (position)	1		2		3		4		5
Total in each model (term)	1		5		9		13		?
(Growth) I added 1 to each leg			4		4		4		?

Figure 7.11 Building up a table to show growth patterns based on construction with click cubes.

We can develop a second table as we did in the previous problem. Substituting as we did before, this time knowing that the constant difference is 4 in Figure 7.11 and a in Figure 7.12. Therefore, $a = 4$.

We can use this to find the value of b. We know that when $n = 2$ we have $2a + b$ and a value of 5. Therefore,

$2a + b = 5$ where $a = 4$

So,

$2 \times 4 + b = 5 \therefore b = 5 - 8$ or -3.

Substituting in our original expression of $an + b$, we get

$4n - 3$

as the general expression. Testing this out on model number 5 produces $4(5) - 3$ or 17 as the number of cubes needed to make the fifth model in the sequence.

A really useful and popular resource is Cards for Cubes. There are several sets with each set containing a large number of A4 activity sheets printed on durable laminated card, together with a book containing black and white versions for teachers to use for planning.

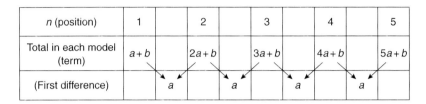

n (position)	1		2		3		4		5
Total in each model (term)	$a+b$		$2a+b$		$3a+b$		$4a+b$		$5a+b$
(First difference)		a		a		a		a	

Figure 7.12 Building up a table to show the results algebraically.

Cards for cubes cover a wide range of activities including pre-algebraic activities, much easier than these above.

Resources and further reading

http://www-groups.dcs.st-and.ac.uk/~history/Mathematicians/Recorde.html

http://www.988.com/scientists/recorde_robert.php (Information on Robert Recorde).

Ainley, J. (1996) Enriching Primary Mathematics with IT. London: Hodder and Stoughton.

Ainley (1999) *Doing Algebra Type Stuff: Emergent Algebra in the Primary School*. Paper given at Psychology of Mathematics Education 1999, published in Proceedings of the 23rd Conference of PME Vol. 2 1999: (2-9–2-16).

BEAM (Be a Mathematician: Exploring Series) *Exploring Number Patterns*.

BEAM (Starting from Scratch series) *Starting from Scratch: Algebra*.

Cockcroft, W. H. (1982) Mathematics Counts: Report of the Committee of Enquiry into the Teaching of Mathematics in Schools. London: HMSO.

Dickson, L., Brown, M. and Gibson, O. (1984) *Children Learning Mathematics: Teacher's Guide to Recent Research*. London: Holt Education.

Donaldson (1978) *Children's Minds*. London: Fontana.

Faux, G. (1998a) What are the big ideas in Mathematics? *Mathematics Teaching* MT163 June pp. 12–18.

Hewitt, D. (1998) Approaching Arithmetic Algebraically. *Mathematics Teaching* 163 June pp. 19–29.

Hughes, M. (1986) *Children and Number: Difficulties in Learning Mathematics*. London: Basil Blackwell.

Huyton, M., Carruthers, E. and Wilkinson, M. (1998) Emergent Mathematics. *Mathematics Teaching* 162 March pp. 11–23.

Menninger, K. (1969) *Number Words and Number Symbols*. Cambridge, MA: MIT Press.

MultiLink *Cards for Cubes* (E. J. Arnold) Available from: www.nesarnold.co.uk

Nickson, M. (2000) A Teacher's Guide to Recent Research and its Application. London: Cassell Education.

Pimm (ed.) (1992) *Mathematics: Symbols and Meanings*. Open University Monograph (Course EM236). Milton Keynes: Open University.

Saenz-Ludlow, A. and Waldgrave, C. (1998) Third Graders' Interpretations of Equality and the Equal Symbol. *Educational Studies in Mathematics*. **35**, 153–187.

Williams and Shuard, H. (1997) *Primary Mathematics Today*. Harlow: Longman.

8   Shape, space and measures

The National Numeracy Strategy (NNS) has one strand devoted to 'Shape, space and measures' (see NNS Framework section 1: 39–40). This is a rich area with plenty of opportunities for teaching mathematics and for emphasising the human response to the environment. Humans are opportunists and technologists, many of whom have an innate desire to decorate themselves, and everyday objects such as jewellery, pottery, walls and floors. Teachers need to cultivate those children who have an ability to visualise, and who can describe what they see with precise detail. Most children go through phases of spatial exploration, although much of it is done before formal school. They get involved in space filling, tidying shelves and cupboards, fitting objects into others (cramming lunch boxes with small toys), connecting large pieces of furniture with adhesive tape or string. Linda Pound gives a good account of these activities as *schema* in her book about mathematics and Early Years. For children with a passion for shape, art and spatial activities, this part of the mathematics curriculum can be crucial in gaining access to the rest of mathematics.

In all cultures there are marvellous examples of the celebration of nature and the appreciation of natural form. There are many starting points for classroom activity. Young children's curiosity about symmetry and asymmetry is easily exploited through play with large floor construction materials and table-top activities with Poleidoblocs, Play People, Duplo, Pattern blocks, large cloths and blankets and so on. This provides for a response to the materials, an exploration of inner feelings about symmetry and the beginnings of notions of aesthetics in relation to architecture, art and technology.

Visual learners in particular benefit from the shape and space curriculum. Currently the mathematics curriculum overemphasises the place of number. It is important to begin moves to redress this imbalance by re-establishing the importance of shape and space work. Children live in a highly stimulating world of movement, shape and colour much of it provided by television and computer software. Children do not need to remain passive recipients in a visual electronic world. Both electronic and traditional classroom activities can link art, mathematics and technology in ways that provide opportunities for aesthetic involvement and discrimination.

Visual learners are good at seeing how to solve spatial mathematical problems. They have a preference for using the visual to promote the intellectual. They are adept at using visual and spatial means to think, explore their immediate mathematical world including number, record their knowledge and express their ideas.

An important part of the pedagogy of mathematics is to find ways of working visually with children. Visualisation and imagining are powerful tools for the teacher to develop.

The ability to visualise has benefits not only in shape and space work but in all areas of mathematics including number and particularly in the use of number lines.

Under *Knowledge Skills and Understanding* relating to Shape and Space the National Curriculum (NC) emphasises the teaching of connections:

> *Teaching* should ensure that appropriate connections are made between the sections on **number** and **shape, space and measure**.
>
> (QCA, 1999)

In Ma1 using and applying, teachers are expected to provide opportunities for problem solving, communicating and reasoning.

Problem solving
(a) try different approaches and find ways of overcoming difficulties when solving shape and space problems
(b) select and use appropriate mathematical equipment when solving problems involving measures or measurement
(c) select and use appropriate equipment and materials when solving shape and space problems

Communicating
(d) use the correct language and vocabulary for shape, space and measures

Reasoning
(e) recognise simple spatial patterns and relationships and make predictions about them
(f) use mathematical communication and explanation skills.

> (QCA, 1999)

In *Understanding Patterns and Properties of Shape*, in Key Stage 1 (KS1) children are expected to describe properties of shape that they can visualise and see and develop the appropriate vocabulary. They need plenty of opportunities to handle, draw and use 2-D and 3-D shapes. They should be able to describe and name some common mathematical features (side (2-D), face (3-D), vertex or corner, edge, rectangle, triangle, square, oblong, circle, cube, cuboid, etc.). It is an area that many trainees also need to work on, so it is a useful activity to do in school early on in the training.

Children need opportunities to create all kinds of shapes and recognise reflective symmetry. They should experience different kinds of movements and be able to visualise and describe positions, directions and movements. They should be able to combine a sequence of straight line and rotational movements and recognise the special features of right angles (they can do this in Physical Education (PE) for example and when using programmable toys like Roamer and software packages like LOGO).

At KS2 Ma1 using and applying requires:

Problem solving
(a) recognise the need for standard units of measurement
(b) select and use appropriate calculation skills to solve geometrical problems
(c) approach spatial problems flexibly, including trying alternative approaches to overcome difficulties
(d) use checking procedures to confirm that their results of geometrical problems are reasonable

Communicating
(e)　organise work and record or represent it in a variety of ways when presenting solutions to geometrical problems
(f)　use geometrical notation and symbols correctly
(g)　present and interpret solutions to problems

Reasoning
(h)　use mathematical reasoning to explain features of shape and space.

(QCA, 1999)

Children at KS1 who use LOGO or programmable robots like Roamer, discover that 90° is a magic number. At KS2 children show their increased sophistication and understanding by recognising right angles, perpendicular and parallel lines. They know that angles are measured in degrees and that a whole turn is 360°. They learn that the sum of the angles on a straight line, and the sum of the internal angles of a triangle add to 180° and they realise that the movements of programmable robots like Roamer equate to exterior rather than interior angles and that the exterior angle sum of a polygon is 360°. Children develop their knowledge of 2-D and 3-D shapes and strengthen their ability to visualise and describe shapes. They begin to learn about the properties of triangles, quadrilaterals, prisms and pyramids. They can draw with increasing accuracy. They use and recognise patterns to explore tessellations and symmetry. They learn to group and classify shapes by their properties. They use practical activities including ICT to transform shapes and create movement. They can visualise and describe more complex movements. They can apply rules of translation, reflection and rotation to predict the final position of simple shapes undergoing transformations. They begin to use grids, and coordinates.

Once again, the activities that are provided are crucial for children's understanding. Activities need to be challenging. Often, the most interesting way is to set them within a problem solving context. It is far more motivating to search for the 'odd one out' in a set of shapes than to learn the properties of a series of shapes for no apparent purpose.

The skilled teacher works subtly with this kind of activity, searching for the most appropriate shapes and resources. They find examples of shapes which are only just within or beyond the boundary of the given rules, or are positioned in such a way that children are challenged to close down their use of a broad definition, or widen their understanding to include something they had not previously considered.

For example, for many young children looking at Figure 8.1, (a) is a square and (b) is not. Diamonds have so many more associations with excitement, treasure and mystery than do squares: it would be a pity to miss an opportunity to identify a diamond when you see one. There are likely to be perceptual factors too – in that we have to develop a Gestalt of square, built up from all the different orientations derived from experience, before we can recognise squareness when we see it from a new or different perspective. A third factor is that book publishers tend to like neat pages, so a child may have been exposed to book images like diagram (a) on lots of occasions when looking at print, but hardly ever to images that are referred to as squares and which look like (b).

When we make careful choices about the shapes to work with and the problems to solve, we push children's powers of discrimination and force them to work carefully at the edge of their abilities.

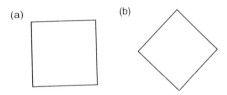

Figure 8.1 When is a square not a square? When it is a diamond of course!

Combining mathematics with stories is always a useful strategy. A story about a journey that requires the careful transportation of magic powder through dangerous regions, to the safety of a castle, carries all the archetypal imagery of our own precarious life journey from childhood through to adolescence and adulthood. We do not need to spell out the literal interpretation of a good story with them: children absorb the metaphor and potential meaning without explanation. What we do need is a good story and some maths resources.

The problem which I set a class of 10-year-olds and some student teachers actually hooked both groups (not surprising perhaps, because student teachers are also on a potentially dangerous journey during their training period). The problem for the children was to design and make a square based pyramid that could be filled exactly with a certain quantity of the appropriate magic powder (sand in our case, suitably enriched with a spell), together with a wish, a charm, and a talisman that would see them through the difficult journey.

For the trainees, the task was the same, but the pyramid had to be skewed with its apex not over the centre of the base. Both groups had to calculate lengths and volumes, before designing and making appropriate shapes. They also had to think about filling and sealing their pyramids so that the magic dust was held securely.

The story prompts the activity. The teacher defines the boundaries and tries to find a level of difficulty for the task which relates well to mystery and the imaginary, whilst at the same time forces a level of precision and accuracy appropriate for the group: not too easy to allow carelessness, not too difficult to be frustrating.

For young children especially, guessing what is contained in a bag is an enjoyable task. What does the shape feel like? What does it sound like? Put several shapes in a bag and pass it round. There are various options which develop visualisation, language and discrimination:

- name the single shape in the bag today (it is a square shape. No it is not, I think it is a little bit oblong);
- name any one of the shapes before taking it out of the bag;
- find the shape that someone else has named;
- find the shape when only its qualities are described (it has a round base, one edge, two faces, and it's pointed);
- find the two shapes that have something in common;
- find the yellow shape (they know they cannot, but they still try?).

Large square, rectangular and circular blankets are very useful. They can be laid on the floor. Children like to lie, sit or stand on them. You can fold the cloth in half in different ways and compare how many can lie on it now. How many can stand around the perimeter? Fold and fold again. How many bottoms can fit this time? Without using the children, you can

detailed work. They enjoy designing and making things like my perfect bedroom (all built to scale inside a shoebox), with miniature objects, self-designed wallpaper, lights and light switches. Many schools have gardens that are well used throughout most of the year.

Mathematical activities and language

What makes an activity mathematical is the way in which problems are conceptualised, thought about, explored and discussed. Appropriate intervention is essential, but so are children's self-directed explorations. Foundation and Key Stage 1 activities need to recognise and promote children's curiosity, dexterity and sociability, by blending mathematical activity with high levels of language use. A rich mathematical environment requires access to outdoor as well as indoor activities, toys, flexible media such as play dough, sand, water, physical shapes, drawing materials, large equipment and opportunities for discussion. Material and resources are effective only when children have plenty of opportunities:

- for free exploration without adult intervention;
- to collaborate with other children and adults in relatively undirected play;
- to interact singly and in small groups, with adults working in 'teaching mode' who can skilfully, direct children's attention, force awareness through the careful choice of resources (e.g. by including heavy objects that float and light objects that sink among the resources made available in a water tray), and who can use discussion to significantly raise the level of linguistic interaction without 'talking over children's heads'.

For all subjects, but especially maths and science, it is important to encourage children to theorise the phenomena they observe and make predictions. 'What do you think is happening here? Why? What might happen next?' As children move through the Foundation Stage and into KS1, measures and measurement work should revolve around the support of children's linguistic development, so that they are increasingly able to explain, interrogate and explore their surroundings. They will need to do the following:

- to use comparative language terms, *more, less, the same as*, *lighter, heavier*, in a rich and continuing variety of situations where they describe their explorations and interests;
- to compare objects, animals and people, using language and ideas associated with length, area, volume and capacity, weight, time, using mainly direct comparisons. For example, *this pencil is longer than that one, my lunch box is smaller than yours, this is a heavy ball – that one is lighter, I'm five now so I'm older than him*;
- to estimate, with opportunities for trial and improvement, immediately prior to direct experience for checking purposes, *I think there are more biscuits in the jar because the packet is smaller than the jar, I think Goldilocks' bowl is too small to hold as much porridge as mummy bear's bowl*;
- to practise putting events in chronological order, learning the names of the days, comparing and measuring objects by using non-standard uniform units (e.g. Multilink cubes, straws, …) *this pencil is as long as eight cubes*;
- to use standard units of length (centimetres and metres), weight (kilograms), capacity (litres), time, angle (as a measure of turn);
- to choose appropriate equipment to help solve problems and carry out tasks.

At KS1 and KS2 the NC is a useful descriptive source of the mathematics to be taught and learned, though it gives only limited guidance about how to teach. The NNS Framework is very useful for planning related number work but guidance for measures teaching is less developed, and you will probably need other sources of practical suggestions for activities.

Using fantastic and everyday contexts for mathematical activity

The NC and NNS contain several references to using real world examples to support mathematical thinking. Too narrow a definition of what constitutes the 'real world' for children is as unhelpful as it is unproductive. Children's fantasy worlds are powerful and motivating, so let us use them. Work in measures and measurement can provide the task, whilst fantasy can provide the storyline or context.

Young children are particularly drawn to fantasy, myths and legends and their imaginative powers are at their height during the primary years. Several writers (Jung, 1964; Steiner, 1973; Bettelheim, 1976) point to the fact that non-rational, spiritual and mystical experiences are essential for healthy development and well-being. The study of myths and legends is a particular feature of Steiner education. The continued success of pantomime and sales of the books of traditional Fairy Tales and the Harry Potter stories are very obvious signs of continuing interest. Fantasy is not the sole province of the language and drama curriculum. Teachers should not become confused between characters and contexts that are imaginary, and children's interest, excitement and creativity, which are very real components of their development. Mathematics can both nurture, as well as draw on primary children's motivation and interest in myth, legend and fantasy.

Giants and tiny people is a theme around which to build a series of activities. At the simplest level perhaps, is the opportunity to ask questions about height, weight, shoe size, etc. of giants and tiny people. Next is to compare their vital statistics with those of humans. A link with forensic science is possible too. If we only have a footprint or a handprint, can we accurately calculate height or weight? Roald Dahl's BFG could have left a palm print on Sophie's window as he listened for the sound of sleeping children. Could we calculate his height from such data?

At KS2, there is a series of useful activities that can develop from a set of questions about proportions in the human body. Is it true that:

- people are as tall as nine of their hands?
- people's neck measurement is twice their wrist measurement?
- people's waist measurement is twice their neck measurement?
- the human foot is as long as the ulna?
- Our reach from finger tip to finger tip is the same as our height?

In order to promote an investigational approach we can pose children the following questions.

1   Do you think these are true claims?
2   Can you think of a way of testing the claims?

3   Do you think the results will be the same for babies, children and adults?

4   Do you think that just measuring one person will give you enough information?

5   Can you plan a way of checking out whether these claims are true?

6   Can you find any more ratios like these?

My experience is that children find these hugely interesting. There is a problem to solve, accurate measurement for a purpose, statistical issues to decide upon and plenty of physical activity. It is also a popular ice-breaker for trainees in the first couple of mathematics sessions.

If we establish the truth of some of these claims, we can then set about designing clothes for giants and tiny people – assuming the ratios between the different parts of a giant's body are the same as ours. Knowing how tall a giant is, we can confidently make a belt, a pair of socks, a hat, a scarf.

Tree planting and wish-making

In a semi-urban school in S. E. Bristol, on the edge of an established housing estate, the children had very little experience of seeing how a managed woodland environment could be created to their benefit. The locality contained badly degraded paths, litter, broken vegetation, bramble, dog faeces, and areas of privately owned and inaccessible, fenced-off woodland.

The head teacher decided to involve the children in a programme to improve the school grounds and the immediate environment. To do this meant collaborating with parents and local residents and landowners. A thousand trees were obtained for planting in and around the school grounds, and everyone, children and adults who worked at the school, were given their own tree to plant, study and research. Factual knowledge of the requirements of trees for healthy growth can be woven into such a project, alongside the symbolic use of trees to represent, growth, regeneration solidity and mystery. Writers like Frazer (1890) and Graves (1962) provide a rich source of historical information for teachers.

Mathematical problem solving was built into the project. Children had to follow a plan created by specialists in arboretum work. Children had to consider several factors.

- The final height of the different types of tree will partly determine where they should be planted.
- The density of tree planting is important, this gives a figure for the number of trees needed per hectare.
- The correct spacing between the different types of tree is important for successful growth.

Teachers built opportunities for maths into their medium term plans and then developed activities that were appropriate for the children in their class. This type of project is much more likely to succeed educationally if the following three things are borne in mind:

1   Children should be expected to take responsibility and to make real decisions.

2   Work should involve precise calculations, including estimation and approximation activities, which extend and develop children's mathematical knowledge and skills.

3   Opportunities should be created for children to make emotional responses to their work.

The example given was part of a series of millennium celebrations. Teachers and children all shared and wrote about their personal hopes for the new millennium, in the context of the symbolism that relates to trees. The planting ceremony included the opportunity for everyone to write a personal wish or prayer and a poem. As each class took part in the planting ceremony, poems and wishes were read out in public before being buried beneath each person's tree.

Planning lessons for measures development

One of the most challenging features of lessons involving measures and measurement is that in addition to considering the relevant subject knowledge, planning needs to ensure a single focus to the lesson, to which all children can be directed. It is very difficult for beginning teachers to maintain good control and classroom management if the lesson is not focused on a precise outcome. Your lesson plan is there to help you teach, but a practical lesson involving measures and measurement is more complex to plan and teach. Some of the more important issues that arise in teaching measures include the following:

- keeping the focus of the lesson alive in the children's minds (this is much easier to do if you use a story that poses a problem which can be explored or solved through measures lessons (e.g. *The Light House Keeper's Lunch*);
- developing subject knowledge through practical activity;
- teaching the technical skills of measurement, estimation of quantities, reading of scales, collection of data, recording of results and discussion of findings;
- ensuring that resources, time for practical activity and formal discussion are appropriate;
- clear planning that recognises the sequential and developmental nature of technical skills (counting, reading a scale, estimating, approximating), and children's use of resources such as tape measures, protractors, weighing scales;
- ensuring that only a few technical skills are demanded in each part of a lesson so that children who lack skills will not be excluded from taking part;
- direct instruction of essential skills (to a single child, small group or class) so that everyone can benefit from the lesson by acquiring the necessary skills;
- organising children to distribute and collect equipment as part of the lesson so that they can eventually do it with the minimum of instruction and disruption;
- finding and arranging suitable, safe and efficient resources in a safe, organised space so that children can get 'hands-on' experience without disruption.

It is useful to have a few very simple activities available that can be left for a week so that children can work quietly between lessons. A collection of beautiful bottles could be started, with children bringing them in (but remind them of safety issues involving glass objects, and objects picked up in the street, etc.). When you have an interesting collection, they can be numbered. Children can be given a sheet and asked to put them in estimated order of capacity. When everyone has completed their competition sheet, you and they can carry out a test to find the actual capacity.

Not just at Christmas, it is useful to have some parcels wrapped in interesting paper (preferably designed and made by the children). What might a parcel contain? What can't this parcel contain? The children can estimate volumes, surface areas, weights, cost of posting (if you know the cost per 100 g). These can be in a puzzle corner, for children who finish other work unexpectedly quickly.

One particularly useful book is *Lines of Development in Primary Mathematics* (Deboys and Pitt, 1992). The authors look in detail at the hierarchy of technical and conceptual steps involved in measures and measurement. In order to teach measures work successfully, teachers need practical knowledge of a hierarchy of development in children's conceptual understanding and the technical skills required for using equipment. This is best achieved by observing an effective teacher and reviewing her planning and her current knowledge of the children.

To teach measures effectively requires knowledge of the stages of development of both technical skills and conceptual understanding. Most trainee teachers are at the disadvantage when teaching measures because:

- trainees generally know very little about the practical skills of the children they are preparing to teach;
- it is hard for us to build up our understanding of stages of development from our own experience, because we find it difficult to recall how we achieved proficiency with resources like a ruler or weighing scales.

A useful start is to work alongside an experienced teacher initially and to team teach with them, sharing responsibility for planning, organising resources, teaching and managing a group of children, then reviewing the session with the teacher afterwards to see what you learned.

Resources and further reading

BEAM Exploring Series which includes for example *Exploring Weight, Exploring Volume and Capacity*.
Bettelheim, B. (1976) *The Uses of Enchantment: the Meaning and Importance of Fairy Tales*. Harmondsworth: Penguin.
Blinko, J. and Slater, S. (1996) *Teaching Measures*. London: Hodder and Stoughton.
Deboys, M. and Pitt, E. (1992) *Lines of Development in Primary Mathematics*. Belfast: Blackstaff Press.
Frazer, J.G. (1890) *The Golden Bough: A Study in Comparative Religion*. London: Macmillan.
Graves, R. (1997) *The White Goddess: A Historical Grammar of Poetic Myth*. Manchester: Carcanet.
Hopkins, C., Gifford, S. and Pepperell, S. (eds) (1999) *Mathematics in the Primary School: A Sense of Progression* (second edn). London: David Fulton Publishers.
Jung, C.G. (1964) *Man and his Symbols*. London: Pan Books.
Mooney, C., Briggs, M., Fletcher, M. and McCulloch, J. (2002a) *Primary Mathematics: Teaching Theory and Practice*. Exeter: Learning Matters.
MultiLink *Action Mats*. (E. J. Arnold).
Rhydderch-Evans, Z. (1993) *Maths in the School Grounds: Learning Through Landscapes*. Southgate.
Steiner, R. (1973) *Theosophy: An Introduction to the Supersensible Knowledge of the World and the Destination of Man* (fourth edn). London: Rudolf Steiner Press.
Williams, E. and Shuard, H. (1997) *Primary Mathematics Today*. Harlow: Longman.

9 Statistics and probability

We use statistics:

- when we have a lot of data which we want to reduce to make life easier, but without losing the information that the data contains;
- to organise data to reveal and extract information;
- to compare sets of data;
- to find trends in a data set;
- when we need to predict what might happen in the future, based on current information;
- to show changes over time;
- to persuade people and to argue about ideas.

Statistics can help us simplify information so that we can have a better picture about what is going on in the world. Statistics can also be used to represent ideas in a particular way in order to convey values, attitudes and beliefs. Children need to see how data is used to present biased arguments.

Probability is a way of expressing our responses to events in the world around us. In practical situations, planners need to know how many people are likely to use roads, buses, rail and air services. Buildings insurance has to be based on the risk of damage assessed by collecting large amounts of data and spotting trends. Weather forecasters need to be able to make the best guess possible about future weather patterns. Probability can make use of data that is derived from statistical sources. The language of probability is very familiar to children and is derived from social settings like trying to win the lottery, a horse race, or a card or table-top game.

National Curriculum

The *Handling Data* Programme of Study begins at Key Stage 2 (KS2) and there is no corresponding Programme at KS1. The early ideas associated with statistics actually appear in the *Number* Programme of Study under the sub-heading Processing, representing and interpreting data.

Pupils should be taught to:
(a) solve a relevant problem by using simple lists, tables and charts to sort, classify and organise information
(b) discuss what they have done and explain their results.

(QCA, 1999)

Most children are taught quite a range of activities and ideas, much of it to do with collecting and counting objects, and then representing them. They get to use pictograms and simple block graphs. There is a lot of opportunity here for using ICT and children generally find this area of the curriculum enjoyable because teachers often use the children's interests as raw data. (Food preferences, favourite colours, pets, birthdays and so on, all provide opportunities for children to express their own preferences, learn about each other, collect information and display it, often using computers and software packages.) Venn, Carroll and binary tree diagrams are really useful ways of organising information.

If there is any weakness in this curriculum area, it is that in some classrooms, there is not enough opportunity to interrogate and interpret data from other sources. When you are intending to provide some data for children, you need to put yourself in the children's shoes. Think about data that really interests them and consider their answers to the questions given here. Next, find some interesting data sources for them to work on. During the lesson time, you can put the same questions directly to them. This will help them think about efficient ways of organising themselves and the data. The following questions need to be part of the lesson whether you provide the data sources or whether the children produce their own data.

- What do you want to find out?
- What might be a good way of finding out?
- What's the best way of collecting the data?
- How will you organise the data?
- How will you display the data?

When they have had the opportunity to work on data collection, display and analysis, you can ask them the following.

- Were you able to answer your initial questions?
- What did you discover?
- What new information did you find that surprised you?
- What new questions do you have now?

At KS2, using and applying (Ma1) identifies the following that children should be taught.

Problem solving
(a) select and use handling data skills when solving problems in other areas of the curriculum, in particular science
(b) approach problems flexibly, including trying alternative approaches to overcome any difficulties
(c) identify the data necessary to solve a given problem
(d) select and use appropriate calculation skills to solve problems involving data

Communicating
(e) check results and ensure that solutions are reasonable in the context of the problem
(f) decide how best to organise and present findings
(g) use the precise mathematical language and vocabulary for handling data

Reasoning
(h) explain and justify their methods and reasoning.

(QCA, 1999)

At KS2 children are taught to process, represent and interpret data. They learn to solve problems involving data. They can interpret data in a range of different formats including tables, list and charts which can be found in everyday settings in and out of school. They learn to construct and interpret frequency tables, including tables with grouped discrete data, for example by finding the children with shoe size in the ranges 3–5, 6–8 or 9–11.

They have opportunities to collect a wide range of data from different sources including the Internet and from software packages. They learn to represent and interpret data by using graphs and diagrams. They use pictograms, bar charts and line graphs.

They know that mode is a measure of popularity (à la mode) and that range is a measure of spread of data and they can use these two ideas to discuss different data sets. They learn to tell the difference between discrete data like shoe size and continuous data like hair length in centimetres. They can draw conclusions from statistics and graphs and they can recognise when data is being used to mislead.

They can discuss and explore ideas of certainty and they develop an understanding of probability through classroom situations. They learn to discuss events using a vocabulary that includes words and phrases such as, equally likely, fair, unfair, certain, unlikely. Young children enjoy sweets and many successful maths lessons are built around coloured sweets like Smarties. For a healthier option, buy some green peas in their pods, broad beans, small grapes in bunches or raisins which are sold in tiny boxes.

The small boxes of Smarties contain a range of sweets and the first activity can be to shake your box and try to guess how many Smarties the box contains. This can be represented by a simple mapping of child's name to their estimate using post-it notes on a flipchart. This allows a simple consideration of range (the lowest and the highest guesses). The whole exercise can be repeated with the boxes open and the Smarties tipped onto a paper plate. The actual number can be written on a second note and stuck beside the first for comparison. How many children guessed correctly? The sweets can then be sorted by colour and children can simply move them around on a paper plate and compare results. They can talk about preferences and the teacher can scribe some the simplest data onto the flipchart to support discussion. I have seen this done by a very skilful teacher working with small groups of six Reception children at a time, repeated throughout the day.

With older children, Janine Blinko devised an activity to develop the statistics further. One simple way is to stick masking tape along the classroom wall to represent the horizontal line of a block graph. Post-it notes are very good representations of blocks. If the teacher asks for guesses about how many sweets the boxes might contain, older children are more likely to know there is likely to be a spread of results. They usually over-estimate the range. The children can write their estimate on a post-it and then come out to the block graph on the wall and post their guess. There needs to be some discussion about how to proceed (maybe from lowest guesses to highest) and a further discussion when the children discover that several people have made the same estimate.

The block graph of estimates begins to emerge as children bring out their notes with their written estimate writ large. The resulting block graph will give you range, opportunity to discuss spread and find a modal value. If the activity is repeated with the actual results, a second batch of notes can be brought out and put underneath the horizontal line. The result is seldom a mirror image because the actual variation between boxes is surprisingly little. This can give rise to discussions about how the factory is organised to ensure this. The two graphs can then be compared and the mode of the second set found.

It is a dynamic lesson, with opportunities for all children to take part. There are good opportunities for prediction, analysis, interpretation and statistical calculation. At the same time as finding the *mode*, it can be useful to look at other statistics like the *median*, which is the point which divides the data exactly into halves, with 50% of the cases above and 50% below the median or median value. The same technique can be used with the upper half of the data, to find the upper quartile (the 'median' so to speak, of the upper 50% of cases) and the lower quartile (the 'median' of the lower 50%). The average or arithmetic mean is the most complicated to calculate, requiring the addition of all the values and then dividing this total by the number of cases to obtain the mean value.

As with all lessons which involve activity, and the steady development of mathematical ideas throughout the lesson, it is difficult to be fully successful until one has the basic teaching skills in place. Asking good questions and teasing out children's ideas from their (sometimes) inarticulate answers is a crucial skill.

Children need to make plenty of use of physical objects like stacking cubes, to represent counts, before they move to direct recording using tables and charts on paper. They need to experience the full range of modes of representation.

- Tally marks can be used against a picture or a label (jam sandwich, packet of crisps) to show how many like each type of food.
- Physical objects can be organised in some way (stacking cubes in a tower).
- Block graphs are used to display discrete data. To begin with, one block represents one item. Later, one block can represent more than one item (but a key is needed).
- Pictographs are used to display discrete data with a symbol like a car or a face (again a key is needed to show the 'value' of each symbol, e.g. a plate to represent every ten people eating lunch, half a plate to represent five).
- Bar charts are used to represent discrete data like shoe size, but the length of the bar represents the number of items and a scale is useful to show the length of the bar. Each bar is kept separate. A single line can replace the bar.
- Pie charts represent data divided into different sectors. If software is used, then pie charts can be employed with quite young children. The pencil and paper calculation is difficult for many children though. The task requires ability to use a protractor, familiarity with fractions or percentages, knowledge of 360° and the ability to calculate, for example, how many degrees to use to represent data such as the sixth of the class who like goldfish. The visual result is powerful of course and pie charts are very useful for data comparison.
- Scatter graphs and line graphs require the use of axes and the ability to plan a scale that matches the paper. They demand the comparison of two data sets and the reading of both the horizontal and vertical axes at the same time. Children with dyslexia can find the mental processing involved too stressful and frustrating unless the activity is carefully managed.

The activity of producing graphical representations of data is only valuable if it is complemented by activities where children are faced with interpreting data that they have not produced. The questioning process is a key activity too. At first, the teacher can pose questions and invite children to seek answers. Gradually though, at the upper end of KS2 the teacher can introduce data from various sources like newspapers and ask children to develop their own questions. This then allows children to be much less vulnerable to misleading data.

Probability

There are several areas of activity that I like to promote in the KS2 classroom including

- the language of chance;
- sorting the language to convey moods, feelings and ideas from impossible to certain;
- using a probability scale with words;
- converting to a numerical scale from 0 to 1;
- using theoretical and empirical approaches to chance events to illustrate the difference between the two processes.

A useful start is to get children to collect phrases used at home and heard on the television. You could include superstitions. Collecting this data illustrates just how pervasive the language of chance is and the degree of concern we express about chance, luck and risk in our lives. The children could then provide a drawing to go with a phrase. These can be used as a display

- chance would be a fine thing;
- the luck of the draw;
- what are the odds of . . . ;
- no chance;
- even Stevens;
- fifty-fifty;
- odds on;
- iffy;
- dead cert;
- a definite maybe;
- very likely (which often means the opposite);
- no way José (not so familiar now, but others appear from time to time on TV and elsewhere).

Some but not all these phrases can be placed at some point along a horizontal line from impossible to certain. Later, these phrases can be reduced until a standard scale remains, as shown in Figures 9.1 and 9.2. The idea is to use the scale to evaluate future events, like, 'I will have tea when I get home.' However, at the top end of KS2 the children seem to enjoy exploring pessimistic viewpoints and it becomes difficult to ascribe anything to do with human behaviour that can be placed further along the line than *likely*. 'Your house might burn down and you'll have to get your tea at your auntie's house.' Many children seem to enjoy exploring the idea that nothing is certain except death. This can lead to interesting cross curriculum issues.

Some debate is needed and the children's attention can be drawn to the variability and inconsistency with which language is used and the richness of language which is a

Impossible	Unlikely	Even	Likely	Certain

Figure 9.1 A conventional probability scale.

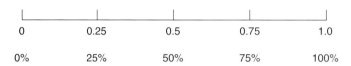

0	0.25	0.5	0.75	1.0
0%	25%	50%	75%	100%

Figure 9.2 A numerical probability scale.

consequence of the varied usage. In mathematics we need something less inconsistent. The children can look at coins and drawing pins and other objects which can produce statistical results. A drawing pin will either land point up or point resting on the table surface – but are the two outcomes equally likely? Pass The Pigs is a useful game with which to explore six different positional possibilities! Coin tossing is easier to predict as two equally likely results. Drawing cards from a pack gives the chance of a picture card, a heart, an ace, a black, and so on. More results mean greater accuracy in relation to theoretical predictions.

We can deduce theoretical probabilities by reason and logic alone. When we start to toss coins, the empirical results may be very varied for a few tosses (e.g. 7 heads and 3 tails in 10 tosses). The children can then observe how the empirical results tend towards (a correct) theoretical prediction as the number of events increases. It is important to explore children's views of the probability of the next event, so that you are aware of their thinking: many young children believe that adults are 'better' at throwing a six than children are.

Resources and further reading

Blinko, J. and Graham, N. (1994) *Mathematical Beginnings: Problem Solving for Young Children*. Claire Publications.

Nickson, M. (2000) Probability and Statistics. In: Marilyn Nickson (ed.) *Teaching and Learning Mathematics: A Teacher's Guide to Recent Research and its Application*. London: Cassell.

Williams and Shuard (1997) *Primary Mathematics Today*. Harlow: Longman.

PART III

Developing the pedagogy for effective teaching and learning

10 Managing teaching and learning

Managing teaching and children's learning forms a cycle of activity throughout each year and feeds into the school's management system. For most trainees and Newly Qualified Teachers (NQTs) the focus is naturally on the children in your own class. To meet the Standards however, you need a broader knowledge of the management of teaching and learning.

Management needs to be seen to be taking place at three broad levels:

- the class
- the key stage
- the school.

Looking at teaching and learning systematically allows you to assess standards and provide evidence of your effectiveness as a teacher. The main purpose for trainees and NQTs is to become better teachers by studying what is happening in your classroom in a systematic way, so that you know on a day-to-day basis, how to improve your classroom effectiveness and your next lesson.

Put simply, we need a way of checking that our teaching is as effective as possible and that the learning opportunities we provide are having the greatest possible impact on the children. Since none of us is perfect, the management of teaching and learning is about getting the best possible blend of all the different components. Being very good at providing practical mathematical investigations is not much use if we remain poor at giving feedback, assessing children and marking their work. We need to maximise our effectiveness by being as good as possible across a range of key activities.

The components of the management cycle are usually taken to include:

- *monitoring* (this includes *observing, noticing, being alert* to what is going on at an individual, group and class level, during lessons, as well as more formal planned activities, such as choosing to monitor a target group of children for a specific purpose for five consecutive lessons);
- *assessing* (this should be mostly through informal, in-your-head judgements about individuals, groups and the whole class, guided by the monitoring process you have put in place. It will rely to a great extent on your oral questioning of children within each lesson and your assessment of their responses, but will include asking children for their

self-assessment, and more formal assessment such as quick five-minute tests, the marking of books and the work in special groups such as Booster classes);

- *recording* (this will cover *attainment* and *progress* of individual children and groups, but should also include children's interest and response to topics, their special qualities and abilities. Recording is often a weak point with teachers. It is very easy to be pressured into recording too much superfluous data of little value. Good assessment data means something significant to you and others, it can be interpreted easily and gives you clear guidance about what to do next in your teaching);

- *reporting* (this is a legal requirement and schools have their own policies for ensuring they meet the requirements for reporting to parents and other external agencies. Reporting includes the publicising of the school's assessment results and involves such activities as Parent Meetings, writing School Reports and maintaining Progress Files);

- *accountability* (this is the means by which the standards achieved by the school are publicly scrutinised and justified. Each teacher has a significant contribution to make to the effectiveness of the school through the achievements they secure for their children and through meeting other targets. Accountability is managed internally by head teachers, the senior management team and the governors, against targets set for and by the school. Most schools also use visiting head teachers and other professionals including Local Education Authority (LEA) inspectors to carry out audits. Office for Standards in Education (OFSTED) and Her Majesty's Inspectors (HMI) provide national accountability data and published school league tables are one source of public evidence about standards).

Mathematics is a significant subject in the curriculum and occupies a special place. It is important to become familiar with the way mathematics is taught, learnt, monitored, assessed and reported on in the schools in which you train. You can gain valuable insight into the school by looking at the most recent OFSTED report available on line from the OFSTED website.

Within the context of the Monitoring, Assessment, Recording, Reporting and Accountability (MARRA) cycle, your immediate concern as a trainee is to provide effective teaching that leads to the best possible learning in your classroom. In addition, you need to understand your school's procedures in relation to the MARRA cycle.

Lesson planning

The planning process is one aspect of teachers' work influenced by recent changes. The original National Numeracy Strategy (NNS) Framework contains schemes of work for each term and half term, for each year group from Reception through to Year 6 (Y6). Significantly, the mathematics curriculum provided in the Framework does not follow a linear pathway. The schemes of work are modelled on a cyclic pattern whereby teachers can return to many topics at least twice each term. Each of the three terms contains broadly similar content, allowing regular revisiting over the year of the most important areas of knowledge and skills.

The suggestion in the NNS *Framework* is that each revisit should be at a higher pitch, with increasingly challenging content used to explore the same mathematical ideas. In the supplementary materials published at the same time were simple examples of a five-day planner (now available electronically from the Department for Education and Skills (DfES) standards website) for the class teacher to use with the expectation that there would be five daily maths lessons (DML) each week. The time given over to each mathematics topic is referred to in the Framework termly plans, as Units of work. These original suggestions have now been strengthened by the publication of very detailed Unit Plans. An alternative source of teacher's planning has been produced by the Hamilton Maths and Reading Projects (www.hamilton-trust.org.uk). As a trainee teaching plans allow you to:

- identify the topic and the time to be allocated from the Framework, and review the key vocabulary and your grasp of the mathematical concepts;
- review notes about the previous visit to this topic and decide on the level of difficulty (pitch) for this visit to the topic;
- use the examples section of the Framework to choose activities for up to three ability groups within the class, consider any children with SEN and the more able;
- prepare a five-day plan to help you manage the focus and the pitch of the work throughout a week of sustained teaching;
- use the *Unit Plans* to help you prepare the *lesson introduction* (including mental warm-up activities), the *main activity* and the *plenary* (including homework if appropriate);
- identify a target group of children for special attention (this could be just light monitoring during lessons, or it might be that you will work with this group during the main activity part of each lesson);
- use your five-day planner as the basis for *detailed lesson plans* for each day, to include, the lesson focus, groupings of children, various reminders to yourself, the timing of each stage of the lesson, key questions to pose, resources and their deployment, opportunities for assessment;
- annotate and change the five-day planner as the week progresses, in response to the real events in each lesson (no one should teach exactly what is planned each day because we need to respond to children's interests and follow up opportunities as they arise).

There has always been a tension between teachers' planning and commercial schemes. Some commercial schemes were restrictive in the sense that it was difficult to integrate other materials into them, and OFSTED frequently criticises schools that rely too much on one narrow resource base.

The NNS has its weaknesses. One is that the examples of activities for children are too variable in quality. When you are planning, you need to look at the wealth of resources available for teaching. Start your planning from the Unit Plans, the Hamilton Maths Plans or the NNS Framework. Look at the examples provided for you to teach and for children to learn. Then recall the National Curriculum (NC) *using and applying* requirements and search the available commercial and other resources for material that supports not only the content you plan to teach, but also *problem solving, communication* and *reasoning*.

You then need to integrate the references to commercial materials into your planning and prepare the materials for teaching.

Advice on planning is steadily becoming much more detailed and there is a lot of supportive material on the DfES Standards website which includes a healthy comment about the need for planning, from a management expert, especially apt for someone like me who is always resistant to detailed planning of anything:

> Planning is an unnatural process. It is much more fun to do something. The nicest thing about not planning is that failure comes as a complete surprise rather than being preceded by a period of worry and depression.
>
> (John Harvey-Jones)

planning and organisation. The availability of the Unit Plans, means that trainees can spend a greater proportion of their preparation time on other key areas that require their attention, for example, as shown in Table 10.1.

In discussion with the class teacher and mentor, the trainee will be made aware of the way the school has decided to adapt the Unit Plans. The following page is an example taken from Unit 10 *Shape and space*: intended for the Autumn Term of Y6 and shows the plan for Day 1 of a five-day block of teaching. Part of the process of annotating and adapting the basic plans is to consider, in consultation with the class teacher and school-based mentor:

- the actual time available for the lesson;
- the way the children will be grouped and the number of groups required;
- the arrangements needed for the support of children with SEN;
- the guidance to be given to teaching assistants (TA) or other supporting adults.

Table 10.1 Key areas for preparation when working in school

	Examples
Updating curriculum knowledge to ensure you are familiar with what you are to teach	By revising knowledge of 2-D and 3-D shapes including their mathematical names
Developing pedagogical knowledge related to general issues of class management and organisation	By thinking about *when* and *how* to change your working focus from the whole class to a group, to a pair of children and back to whole class
Developing pedagogical-content knowledge related to the effective teaching of the mathematics topics you are preparing	By planning to incorporate large-scale *floor* work, *tabletop* resources and *visualising* activities with eyes closed, within a single lesson, to teach the relationship between 2-D and 3-D properties of shapes
Acquiring knowledge of learners and their characteristics, to ensure appropriate support for learning, especially for those with SEN and the more able	By using the fact that many 8 year-olds love making collections of objects when planning interesting lessons around the latest collecting craze
	By ensuring that you position children with hearing or sight difficulties for maximal learning
Acquiring knowledge of practical contexts for learning	By planning for children to use today's mathematics within the English lesson
	By giving children the opportunity to discuss in pairs, or play a game together, to consolidate some new knowledge
	By asking children to bring in something from home to use in a lesson, or going on a visit

Planning sheet	Day One	Unit 10 Shape and space: Position, movement and scales, and solve problems	Term: Autumn	Year Group: 6

Oral and Mental

Main Teaching

Plenary

Objectives and Vocabulary	Teaching Activities	Objectives and Vocabulary	Teaching Activities	Teaching Activities	Teaching Activities/ Focus Questions

Oral and Mental

Objectives and Vocabulary

Order a set of positive and negative integers.

Teaching Activities

- Hold a counting stick horizontally and count from negative five through zero to positive five in steps of one.

  Remind the children of the symmetry involved. Ask them to identify the biggest number on the stick and the smallest. Quickly point to various divisions on the stick asking which numbers lie there. (It is helpful to keep your thumb on zero.)

- Repeat holding the counting stick vertically so that negative five is at the bottom.

- Explain that the stick now represents the range −25 to 25. Repeat the counting activity from −25 to 25 in steps of 5, first with the counting stick horizontally and then with the counting stick vertically.

- Remind the children that so far the zero has been in the middle. Ask them to identify the zero on the stick for different ranges of numbers, e.g. −10 to 40, −40 to 10, −20 to 30, −30 to 20, −15 to 35 etc. For each range get the children to identify the step size for the divisions and as a whole class count forwards and backwards to confirm this and the position of zero.

VOCABULARY
positive
negative

RESOURCES
Counting stick

Main Teaching

Objectives and Vocabulary

Read and plot co-ordinates in all four quadrants.

VOCABULARY
quadrant
x-axis
y-axis
origin
vertex
vertices

RESOURCES
OHT 10.1
Squared paper

Teaching Activities

- Show the first quadrant on OHT 10.1 (cover the other 3 quadrants). Remind children that both axes begin at zero and identify the x-axis and the y-axis. Say that if they forget, it might help to remember that the x-axis goes across.

  Mark a point on the grid.

  Q What are the co-ordinates of this point?

  Discuss and remind children about the notation, e.g. (3, 2).

  Q If I move the cross 2 squares down what will the co-ordinates be?

  Record the co-ordinates on the board.

  Q What if I move it 5 squares down?

  Establish that the cross would be off the grid.

- Uncover the other 3 quadrants.

  Refer to the use of negative numbers on the counting sticks in the oral/mental session. Explain that this is like two counting sticks crossing at zero which form four sections, or quarters. Say that these are called quadrants.

- Plot points in each quadrant of the grid, stress the (x, y) convention. Say that if they forget that x comes before y in the alphabet and so they should read along the x-axis first. Label each quadrant (first, second, third and fourth) pointing out that the order is anti-clockwise around the origin (0, 0).

Teaching Activities

- Draw the diagram:

The Four Quadrants

Ask the children to give you instructions to plot (2, 5) (−2, 5), (−2, −5) and (2, −5), start from (0, 0) each time. Ensure that they are confident with this.

Tell the children to draw axes (each from −10 to 10) on the squared paper and plot the following co-ordinates (−1, 1), (2, 5) and (5, 2). Tell the children that these are 3 of the 4 vertices of a square. Ask them to plot the fourth vertex and check this with a partner.

Give the children other groups of co-ordinates to plot which are vertices of triangles and different quadrilaterals e.g. parallelogram. Get the children to identify and plot the missing vertices. Explain that there may be more than one answer if only two vertices are given.

Collect children's results and correct any mistakes and misunderstandings.

Q A square has vertices at (−1, 0) and (1, −2). What are the positions of the other two vertices?

On the board or OHT show the 3 possible squares that have vertices at (−1, 0) and (1, −2).

Plenary

Teaching Activities/ Focus Questions

- Write (4, 2), (8, 2), (−2, 4), (−2, 8) on the board. Explain that these should be the vertices of a square. Plot the points on OHT 10.1. Ask the children to suggest where mistakes have been made in the co-ordinate notation.

  Q What must we remember when we plot co-ordinates?

  Establish that the first number in a pair of co-ordinates always refers to the x-axis, the second to the y-axis.

HOMEWORK – Give the children squared paper on which to plot points that make up 4 different shapes. For each shape the children are to name the shape.

Shape 1 – (−4, 6), (−3, 10), (5, 8), (4, 4)
Shape 2 – (−8, −4), (−8, 1), (−5, 4), (0, 4)
Shape 3 – (−5, −5), (−2, 1), (−2, −8), (−1, 0)

Shape 4 – (2, 4), (9, 1), (3, −3).

By the end of the lesson children should be able to:

- **Read and plot points beyond the first quadrant;**
- **Identify the co-ordinates of the 4th vertex of a square.**

(Refer to supplement of examples, section 6, page 109.)

Figure 10.1 NNS Unit Plans can be adapted for individual use.

If you are working in a Foundation Stage setting you will need to understand how and what the practitioners do in terms of keeping records on children's mathematical development and the progress they make in relation to the stepping-stones and the Early Learning Goals.

If you are working in a Reception class then you will need the Curriculum Guidance for the Foundation Stage in addition to NC documents and the NNS documents. You will need to discuss with practitioners how they are preparing for the changes to the end of the Foundation Key Stage assessment.

You may find that the setting you are working in has chosen to continue the use of baseline assessment on entry, though this is not a statutory requirement. Take the opportunity to observe the process if you can.

For those working in Reception and KS1, your day-to-day assessment decisions are related to your lesson plan and your teaching intentions. Assessment opportunities in lessons can be planned for by using the NNS Framework and support materials. Most assessment will be informal, especially at the start of training. Assessment opportunities need to be built into your lesson plan as a simple check to see if:

1   what you planned for your lesson is appropriate for the children;
2   the children learned what you intended;
3   any of the planned work was too easy, too difficult or unclear;
4   you taught well.

When you plan lessons you can base the mathematical content and skills on the NNS Framework examples. If, for example, your lesson objective is written for the children as: 'I can use a protractor to measure angles to the nearest degree', then the simplest level of assessment will be to ask them at the end of the lesson, 'Well, can you?' (Later on, when you are well established in a classroom, you will be more able to assess accurately the extent to which they could use protractors *before* your lesson!)

Mathematics is hierarchical in the sense that much of what we learn is strongly connected to, and dependent upon earlier learning, (e.g. expertise in multiplication demands knowledge of addition and the associated skills). This means that we often need to plan and teach a sequence of lessons that will help children build up a number of interconnected ideas over time. The King's Study (Askew *et al.*, 1997) demonstrated the importance of teaching using a *connectionist* approach. Teachers who explicitly taught children to look for and make links between different areas of knowledge, helped them achieve greater understanding than teachers who used other styles of teaching.

Until you have been based in a school for a while, you are unlikely to have the opportunity to develop the skill of planning and teaching a sequence of lessons. Obviously, the assessment opportunities become more complex and interrelated when this happens. The NNS written and video support materials for Assessment and Review are useful in thinking about how assessment can fit within your lesson planning.

When you start training, the immediate results of informal assessment will probably be of more use to you than to the children. By assessing individuals and small groups through *observation* you will get immediate feedback about how successful you are at communicating what you want them to do. Only later, when you are more adept at teaching, know the children well and can create a range of learning opportunities, will your assessments begin to truly reflect what children can actually do.

Two sources of guidance are Brown (1998) which has a chapter on assessment in mathematics, and Shirley Clarke who published two books in 1995 on formative assessment in primary mathematics at KS1 and KS2, and several generic books on assessment in primary schools (Clarke, 1998).

Most assessment in the primary school is carried out as you teach, and its purpose is to monitor how well the children are able to understand you and the lesson content. There is a wide range of different types of assessment available to teachers with which you need to be familiar. It is vitally important that you realise that assessment does not have to be a separate activity for you and the children. Most assessment is best carried out within the normal activities that you provide. The forms of assessment included here are examples. They are not meant to be read as exclusive. Most can be carried out informally, and can be the result of another activity such as Circle Time discussion, concept mapping, children's self-assessment or a simple activity where children use their thumbs 👍 👎 to show their level of confidence and understanding following part of a lesson. You need to be familiar with the ideas behind these forms of assessment:

- *Informal* – examples include, verbal and written feedback, short activities during the plenary to ensure that what was introduced at the start of the lesson can now be done;
- *Formative* – part way through a lesson or a series of lessons, giving simple verbal feedback, marking a book with a written comment rather than a grade, being *explicit* with children about what they need to do next, to improve and develop;
- *Diagnostic* – for the child who is facing difficulty, this is finding out what exactly their problem is;
- *Ipsative* – comparing what the child can do now, with what the child achieved earlier, looking back through a child's book at earlier work and reviewing progress, using a portfolio or record of achievement with snapshots of achievement taken over a term or half term, with children selecting what *they* consider to be their best work and providing a reason why;
- *Target setting* – negotiated between teacher and individual child or group as something to achieve within a short space of time (I want to learn to write my numbers the right way round before the next holiday);
- *Formal* – a five-minute test within a lesson, an activity with less than usual level of support to see if children can tackle a problem unaided, some homework that sets out something to learn which will be assessed during the next lesson;
- *Summative* – a concluding assessment following a sequence of lessons on a topic, an assessment that does not offer any further opportunity to develop, typically SAT tests with no feedback to suggest how to improve.

You need to find during your lessons, the lightest touch possible and the most motivating ways of providing yourself with the feedback you need. For example, concept mapping is very flexible. It can be part of a lesson with children working on maps individually or in pairs. The observations you make as you monitor them could provide you with a range of assessment data including *informal, formative, diagnostic* and *ipsative* – by asking the children during a review lesson, to show new learning using a different coloured pen or a better grasp of information by adding to an earlier map made at the start of the topic.

Identifying an assessment opportunity during planning

This is a difficult skill to perfect. It requires a knowledge of the outcomes that are likely to occur when an activity is planned, which itself depends on previous experience of using the activity. Planning for likely outcomes is easier when we have tried an activity a few times,

A good question:

- is sufficiently *open* that most if not all children can offer a relevant response which helps sustain and continue the dialogue;
- is sufficiently *closed* and unambiguous that children can understand how it relates to the lesson;
- is an effective *bridge*, that is to say, the question contains explicit and implicit links which provide children with a conceptual bridge that connects what they *already securely know*, and the *new knowledge* that is being developed in the lesson.

There is some evidence to suggest that the longer the question, the longer the response. Short questions are essential if we are to give every child opportunity to respond, but a long question that allows an elaborate, lengthy response from an individual child can also be invaluable.

The first few pages of the *National Numeracy Vocabulary Book* originally published and distributed with the NNS Framework contains really valuable guidance on questioning. When questioning is really effective, there can be some unanticipated responses from children. They are much more likely to feel that you are generally interested in their opinions. They come to believe that you are trying to teach them *answering techniques* because you want to teach them how to engage with a wide variety of questions in broad, accurate, informative ways. They come to believe that you are not just interested in who does or does not know the answer to any single question. A pedagogically good question can perhaps only come when the teacher ceases to imagine that 'the cultural identities, desires and, perhaps, the learning difficulties of their students [are] unrelated to themselves' and their own learning. (Britzman and Pitt, 1996: 120). We need then to have at least considered how *we* might respond to our own questions; if we were pupils, rather than teachers in our class.

2. *Review the way you give and mark homework. Compare what you do, with the class and school policy documents and take a critical stance to see whether homework actually leads to learning.* When teachers give marks or grades for homework, the numbers are what the children focus on: they do not pay much attention to comments or internalise suggestions for improvement. If children are given *only* comments (these may be largely oral at KS1 and may include both oral and written statements at KS2) they tend to respond to comments which ask for action which will lead to improvement. Comments need to be truthful: children know a trivial or patronising comment when they find one. It is not helpful to say something is wonderful when it is not. Better to make an honest judgement about the good points, followed by only one or two specific suggestions on exactly what to do to improve.

3. *Try to create regular opportunities for children to take part in the assessment process and to assess each other.* Your assessment responsibilities are a blend of monitoring and providing accurate diagnosis. It is not a good use of your time to mark every piece of children's work, this just trivialises assessment, reducing it to marking, which is an activity of a lower order. Children should mark their own work and each other's in class. They can do this in a number of ways. As pairs, they can sign their name when they have checked a friend's work. Where you use target setting and children have a simple target written on a piece of card, a friend can corroborate the fact that a target has been reached. Not all teacher-led group work should be the introduction of a new topic: a group of children can discuss their work and talk about errors with you. Being part of the assessment process gives them insight into your assessment criteria and the source of their errors. They can then mark and sign their books

at the end of the session. This is much more efficient than you collecting the books in and marking with each individual child in the group. Children gain very little when you mark books away from them, so this should be avoided. You do need to monitor every child's book, for neatness and coverage, but this is not the same as *marking* and needs to be done quickly and purposefully as part of monitoring. Try to avoid focusing on errors: if there is a single purpose to education, it is to celebrate success, so look for quality in children's work. (cf. Pirsig, 1974).

One of the most enjoyable tasks for my class of Y3 children was to mark my homework. I would photocopy a sheet of calculations (usually around a particular mathematical theme) and get a few calculations wrong. They marked them, and of course needed to double check their answers if they differed from mine. They then had to say what my problem was (maybe I was making the same error in crossing a decade, so my wrong answers were all ten out). They had to identify my error and explain how it could be corrected. This was much better for their learning and we all found this an enjoyable alternative to me marking their work.

Creative and varied strategies for *assessing* children's work with them are what is needed, and this is not easy to achieve. Strategies include, carrying out assessment with children in groups and letting them mark their own work under your guidance, and in whole-class situations getting children to swap books while you give answers. The focus is to make sure that the result of assessment is an *improvement in understanding*. Children should have a greater awareness of errors and be shown what they must do to become more successful in future.

4. *When you are planning assessment and review lessons, involve the children in choosing the questions and activities.* Tell them what you will be looking for and ask them what questions they would like to be asked, to show you they know the work they have just covered. Invite them to suggest a variety of ways of demonstrating their new knowledge and understanding. They can learn to set their own criteria for success.

Children really do feel the pressure to succeed in tests. The stress of even short, simple classroom tests can lead to very poor performance by some children. By including the children in the design and construction of tests, by discussing what sort of tests they like and dislike, by involving them in marking, by following tests with very practical discussions and advice on *how to do better*, the purpose of tests can be recast as something *to learn from* rather than something *to measure them with*.

As Black and Wiliam explain about their research findings on the King's College website:

> These improvements in test scores convince us that, by focusing on teachers' professionalism, and involving pupils more in their learning, you can raise standards of achievement without teaching to the test.

Their main research findings show that:

- There are practicable ways to raise standards which do not involve 'teaching to the test'. Teachers welcome these new ways because they enrich rather than narrow the learning of their pupils.
- Emphasis on competition and competitive testing, which inevitably creates losers as well as winners, can damage learning. What is needed is emphasis on helping all to achieve their best – it is not enough to set targets, pupils must also be helped to reach them.

Liebling, H. (1999) *Getting Started: An Induction Guide for Newly Qualified Teachers*. School Effectiveness Series. Stafford: Network Educational Press.

Pirsig, R.M. (1974) *Zen and the Art of Motorcycle Maintenance*. London: Bodley Head. Chapter 24.

Torrance, H. and Pryor, J. (1998) *Investigating Formative Assessment: Teaching, Learning and Assessment in the Classroom*. Buckingham: Open University Press.

TTA (2000) Using ICT to meet Teaching Objectives in Mathematics.

Wright, R., Martland, J. and Stafford, A. (2000) *Early Numeracy: Assessment for Teaching and Intervention*. London: Paul Chapman.

11 Progress and progression in mathematics

Children's progress can be thought of in terms of personal development over time. We all make progress in our lives as we learn to talk, walk, tolerate frustration, learn a second language, ski, cook, windsurf, snowboard, write poetry or start to play a new musical instrument.

Children's progress needs to be considered from a wide perspective, and our professional interest should include children's moral and spiritual, emotional, physical and academic development. Mathematics lessons should contribute to children's overall development and not be seen as something separate from it.

Children's progress in mathematics

As a trainee or a newly qualified teacher (NQT), the main focus of interest will be the class you are working with. You can quickly see from children's responses, over a series of lessons, whether the children:

- make use of the ideas you have taught;
- choose for themselves to apply their new knowledge and skills to solve new problems;
- show increasing understanding, confidence in you as a teacher and enthusiasm for the subject.

By talking with different people including the children, the class teacher and your mentor, you will soon be able to make sound judgements about the progress that individual children are making in their mathematics. You will be able to judge the extent to which they are acquiring new knowledge and skills, working confidently, seeing connections between current work and earlier work with a previous teacher and whether they are aware of the relevance of prior knowledge when trying to solve new problems.

After teaching for several weeks in the same class, you will begin to get sufficient evidence to make more subtle judgements, based on the children's responses to three or four different mathematics topics which you have planned, taught and evaluated. You will be able to judge individual children's progress and ask more general questions about the progress that the class is making and what the school's performance is like in relation to expectations. You might choose to look at Statutory Assessment Tasks (SAT) scores and inspection reports to improve your understanding of the school's context and its role within the community.

There are a number of ways in which we can consider progress. For example:

1   We can take several samples of one child's work and match them to the assessment criteria in the National Curriculum (NC) so as to ascertain the level that best describes the child's attainment. By looking back at earlier data on the child, we can draw conclusions about the child's progress over time.
2   We can compare the difference between SAT scores in Year 2 and Year 6 (Y2 and Y6). Progress can then be expressed in terms of changes of level for the majority of children from Key Stage 1 to Key Stage 2 (KS1 to KS2).
3   We can compare the difference between a collection of individual children's attainment levels at a single point (say, in Y6, using a selection of KS2 SAT questions) and the notional average attainment for all pupils, which has been set at Level 4 at the end of KS2 (Table 11.1).

Table 11.1 Making general judgements about children's progress

Making general judgements about progress	Commentary
Are you teaching the children what is generally expected for the age group, based on NC content and NNS Framework guidance?	There can be good reasons for not teaching the NC or the NNS content that is generally recommended for an age group at a particular stage in the year. But do you *know* whether your planning matches, and if not, do you have a good reason for doing what you are doing?
Are most of the children making sense of what is being taught, getting an opportunity to practise and consolidate new learning and showing confidence in tackling work?	The difficulty here is making a judgement about whether you and they are coasting, rather than working hard. Again, it is often necessary to take more time as a new teacher with a new group, and to speed up as you settle in. This is where a mentor who knows the school is invaluable, in helping you make this difficult judgement.
Are the most able being challenged by differentiated questioning during whole-class introductions, plenary sessions and during group work?	Until you can get the whole class off to a quick, purposeful start, you cannot free yourself to address this issue. This happens when too many children are unsure about what to do. Generally, that is down to the teacher. We need to be precise, clear and encouraging, so that children can make a good start at least for 5–10 minutes before they seek further guidance. During that time, we can then provide extra guidance to an able group, maybe by giving a harder task that will make a greater intellectual demand on them. We can also visit a less able group to reassure them that they are doing well and we are pleased with their efforts. Over the years, British teaching styles have created a greater spread of performance within a class, than one would see in classes of similar age and ability in other countries. There has been a long 'tail of underachievement' in many classes, absorbing most of the teacher's attention, with a consequent lack of time being devoted to more able children. One of the objectives of the NNS model is to improve on this situation.

(Continued)

Table 11.1 Continued

Making general judgements about progress	Commentary
Are the least able getting work at an appropriately challenging level, the support they need, and the encouragement to work independently as often and for as long as possible?	Students and new teachers can easily get drawn into spending most of their time with the least able. Usually, things improve when we can provide strategies for children so that *they know what to do when they do not know what to do.* At first, the only strategy may be to call on you. 'You can introduce classroom rules that reduce this dependence on you. If you are stuck, you are allowed to stop and think. You can ask a friend. You need to ask three friends before you come to see me.' For older children, try to write down the problem. One danger of being too eager to help them, is that you end up doing the mathematics and they just copy it down. You need to find ways to help them become less vulnerable to anxiety, more resilient to the uncomfortable feeling of not knowing. If you feel the way many trainees do about maths – not quite sure if you are teaching well, not sure if you *like* teaching maths, then your sympathies are likely to be with anxious children. It is not unusual for us to be too sympathetic, reduce the cognitive demand, be too helpful, and consequently cause them to be even more dependent on an adult to do the work. Some of us avoid being critical, lest we destroy their confidence, some of us tend to over-criticise, nagging them rather than giving positive encouragement. Few of us provide learners with enough thinking time or sufficient choice in how to proceed.

As an Office for Standards in Education (OFSTED) inspector, I was required to judge *children's progress* in mathematics by looking for evidence of *changes in attainment* achieved between two measurement points. This could be across a week or two within a single class, or across a school over a term or more. When looking across the school, I could examine children's written work, and within a class over a week or two; I could observe a lesson and follow this up by talking to a small group of children about their current maths topic.

To get a sense of progress over the past year, I could look through samples of children's written work taken from every class in the school (made available during inspection). From this I could make an impressionistic judgement about the performance of children in each class or year group, against what I know is generally expected. I could then use the National Curriculum (NC) attainment level statements to help me. I needed to test these impressionistic judgements to decide what questions to ask, in order to confirm what I had found out. I needed to develop a series of further questions to be taken up with a class teacher, the maths coordinator or the head, and of course with the children themselves wherever possible. I could then make a judgement about how quickly and successfully children are introduced to the various parts of the mathematics curriculum.

One difficulty that teachers face is the language of the inspection. If everything is fine, and children are successfully learning new topics, as one would expect, then because everything is on target, the children's progress in OFSTED speak, is *satisfactory*, typical or average. *Good progress*, in contrast (in OFSTED speak) means making progress faster than normal, faster than is expected, and this would logically lead to SAT scores which are higher than the national average. In contrast to the language of OFSTED inspections, teachers tend to describe children's progress as *good*, when the children are enthusiastic, they learn what is taught, and face few difficulties with current or new topics. Children are described as making *satisfactory progress* (i.e. typical and expected) if they achieve Level 2 in the KS1 SATs and Level 4 in the KS2 SATs. They are then judged to be making progress in line with the national expectations.

Curriculum progression in mathematics

> The introduction of the National Curriculum increased the importance of progression, since it assumes that it is possible to organise and sequence learning and therefore assign levels to children's achievements.
>
> (Connor, 1999a: 141)

An OFSTED inspector does not just look at children's progress. It is also necessary to look at what the school is teaching in each year and the extent to which this is delivered at an appropriate pace and matches what the children actually need.

- Does the school teach the curriculum topics or units in a sensible order, helping children to build up their knowledge and skills efficiently?
- Does the school make good use of the spiral curriculum embedded in the NNS Framework to revisit topics over sensible periods of time and to help children consolidate their knowledge and skills?
- Is good use being made of Assessment and Review lessons to support children's learning and to help the teacher confirm her judgements about the progress of individual children and groups?

Traditionally, the syllabus was a list of topics to be taught and schools chose their own path through it. Over the years, the emphasis has shifted dramatically. Teachers are no longer expected to devise a complete mathematics curriculum for primary schools. It is now realised that this is something that is better done at national and local levels. The focus of the teacher's professional skill and judgement is on turning dry ideas on paper into active lessons through highly effective teaching.

The emphasis in the NNS Framework is on mental and oral calculation as a *first resort*. This means that children are taught to develop ways of inventing their own *informal jottings* as an aid to thinking. This is done prior to teaching the use of formal written calculation methods and requires us to re-interpret mathematical progression in number, to incorporate progression in mental calculation strategies: something that most teachers will have to learn from scratch because their own learning experiences in school is likely to have been very different. Most teachers will need to acquire and then internalise, a model of appropriate progression of mathematical knowledge and skills that incorporates mental calculation strategies.

The NNS Framework attempts to provide a coherent, sequential list of topics that invite greater intellectual challenge at each turn of the spiral: the teacher revisits the topic but increases the intellectual challenge each time, as appropriate. Also, the NNS Framework ideas are supported by guidance booklets and video material and trainers generally make extensive use of these resources.

One way to get a sense of progression is to look at the NNS support materials, *Teaching Mental Calculation Strategies* (QCA, 1999: 21–36). If we take addition and subtraction strategies as an example, the booklet identifies the strategies children need to develop and then shows for each, a progression in knowledge and skills fromY1 toY6.The strategies are:

- counting forwards and backwards;
- reordering calculations;
- partitioning by using multiples of 10 and 100;
- partitioning by bridging through multiples of 10;
- partitioning by compensating;
- partitioning by using near doubles;
- partitioning by bridging through numbers other than 10.

The challenge is to begin to internalise the progression for each of these, so that you are able to introduce children to increasingly sophisticated methods as their knowledge and skills develop.

One of the key characteristics of mental calculation strategies is that they are idiosyncratic: we develop our own strategies for mental calculation. We often change the methods we use to suit the numbers we are faced with. We want children to develop these same flexible skills and this means we cannot just teach a single method to children and expect them to adopt it. What we can do is to explore different strategies with children over time and gradually encourage them to be selective.This can work successfully *provided*:

1   We explain to children *why* we are teaching a variety of methods.
2   As a key part of subsequent lessons, we involve the children in discussion about how they choose which method to use.
3   We work with them to improve their choice of method, and to make the methods they prefer as efficient as possible.
4   We teach children to take responsibility for themselves for *changing the calculation* into something more manageable for them.

They must be encouraged and supported so that they learn to decide how to tackle calculations in different ways.This should not be seen as negating the teacher's role: rather, teachers should incorporate into their lessons over time, a range of ways of working, and should invite children to try different ways and discuss their preferences as part of the lesson.

Developing mathematical thinking: the power of the number line

We have explored the number line as part of the number curriculum. It is worth exploring the pedagogy further in this section because for most of us, using number lines is not something we experienced in school, and using them with children requires a complex set of skills.

a consistency of approach throughout the school particularly in the area of *using and applying* so that children learn to be mathematicians from an early age and build up their enthusiasm and skills as they move through the school. This does not mean teachers should be clones, they should teach to their strengths and give children a unique experience, but as members of the school team, they do need to share ideas about teaching methods and provide a consistent approach especially to *problem solving, communicating* and *reasoning.*

Resources and further reading

Anghileri, J. (ed.) (1995) *Children's Mathematical Thinking in the Primary Years.* London: Cassell.

Beishuizen, M. (1997) Mental Arithmetic: Mental Recall or Mental Strategies? *Mathematics Teaching,* MT 160, September, pp. 16–19.

Black, P. and Wiliam, D. (2002) *Inside the Black Box: Raising Standards Through Classroom Assessment.* London: King's College (Department of Education and Professional Studies).

Brown, T. (1998) *Coordinating Mathematics Across the Primary School.* London: Falmer Press.

Clarke, S. (1998) *Targeting Assessment in the Primary Classroom: Strategies for Planning, Assessment, Pupil Feedback and Target Setting.* London: Hodder & Stoughton.

Clarke, S. and Atkinson, S. (1996) *Tracking Significant Achievement in Primary Mathematics.* London: Hodder & Stoughton.

Cockburn, A.D. (1999) *Teaching Mathematics with Insight: The Identification, Diagnosis and Remediation of Young Children's Mathematical Errors.* London: Falmer Press.

Connor, C. (1999) Two steps forward, one step back: progression in children's learning. *Primary File,* 36, pp. 141–144.

Connor, C. (ed.) (1999) *Assessment in Action in the Primary School.* London: Falmer Press.

Cooper, B. and Dunne, M. (2000) *Assessing Children's Mathematical Knowledge.* Buckingham: Open University Press.

DfES (2001) *Guidance to Support Pupils with Specific Needs in the Daily Mathematics Lesson.* London: DfES.

DfES (2001) *Assessment and Review Lessons.* London: DfES.

Gipps, C. (1997) *Assessment in Primary Schools: Past, Present and Future.* London: British Curriculum Foundation.

Headington, R. (2000) *Monitoring, Assessment, Recording and Accountability: Meeting the Standards.* London: David Fulton.

Hopkins C., Gifford, S. and Pepperell, S. (1999) (eds) (second edn) *Mathematics in the Primary School: A Sense of Progression.* London: David Fulton Publishers

Hughes, M. (1999) *Closing the Learning Gap.* Stafford: Network Educational Press.

Hughes, M., Desforges, C., Mitchell, C. and Carré C. (2000) *Numeracy and Beyond: Applying Mathematics in the Primary School.* Buckingham: Open University Press.

NNS (1999) *Teaching Mental Calculation Strategies.* London: QCA.

QCA (1999) *Teaching Written Calculation Strategies.* London: QCA.

SCAA (1997) *The Teaching and Assessment of Number at Key Stages 1–3.* London: SCAA.

Torrance, H. and Pryor, J. (1998) *Investigating Formative Assessment: Teaching, Learning and Assessment in the Classroom.* Buckingham: Open University Press.

Wright, R., Martland, J. and Stafford, A. (2000) *Early Numeracy: Assessment for Teaching and Intervention.* London: Paul Chapman.

12 Teaching for understanding

Through the 1950s and 1960s it was fairly commonplace to see practical equipment in nursery and infant classrooms. Equipment was much less in evidence in junior classrooms. In 1952, Caleb Gattegno made the first English translation of Piaget's *The Child's Conception of Number*. Piaget's theories that learning takes place through interaction with the environment, led to some bizarre classroom practices, which continued for a while, and which Piaget himself might well have disowned. Gattegno had met George Cuisenaire in a Belgian school, encouraging him to publicise the use of the little coloured wooden rods that he had developed for his children, to support the study of number. Attention to the learning process led to the development of what we now know as *constructivist theories of learning*. Piaget's biological perspective of the individual's learning process was later challenged by the translation of Vygotsky's work into English, the promotion of Vygotsky's social constructivist ideas by Jerome Bruner and others and by important theoretical and observational research by Margaret Donaldson, Martin Hughes and others at Edinburgh University.

Learning through concrete experience

An interest in constructivism has been sustained in British education for more than half a century, derived in considerable part from Piaget's early studies of children's reasoning. Piaget conducted wide-ranging studies of children's reasoning, including studies on number, space and geometry, fractions, proportionality, functions and probabilities. His work led to the identification of two different types of mathematical understanding, *procedural* and *conceptual*, though the influence on teaching was slow to develop. The teaching of procedural knowledge dominated work in classrooms for a considerable time before later interest in conceptual knowledge shaped classroom practice.

Skemp (1986, 1989) made important contributions to a theoretical perspective on effective teaching. He drew an important distinction between *Instrumental* or rule-based learning and *Relational* or intelligent learning and conducted many classroom-based research studies that led to structured activities for children. Mathematical understanding can be thought of in terms of the acquisition and use of concepts and conceptual frameworks, routines and procedures, and insightful ways of tackling and solving problems. In a short article written in 1985, Caleb Gattegno makes the point about deep and surface learning that still needs to be stressed:

> In this 'age of information' there is no doubt a place in our minds for knowledge, but it is much smaller than is usually assumed. ... We all know how to count. We were taught

how to count in classroom lessons, so counting might therefore be called knowledge, because it is normally transmitted by society. But in my daily use it is no longer knowledge, it does not feel capable of being forgotten. It is in my flesh; it is a skill which does not need to be recalled, … When we teach the multiplication tables we teach them as knowledge which can only be retained by memory; … The fact that some older students are placed in remedial classes because of their inability to retain products does not seem to generate in the public at large any doubts about the value of memorising tables. But if knowledge in this field is replaced by know-how, then these same students make sense of the challenge which defeated them and in a very short time master multiplication. … Once the stress is shifted from knowledge to experience it becomes clear that education can change…

(Gattegno, 1985: 35–37)

From the 1950s onwards, Cuisenaire and Color Factor rods could be found in many Reception and Key Stage 1 (KS1) classrooms to support the development of addition skills, but they were in less evidence in classrooms for older children. From the 1960s there were Logic Blocks and Dienes base 10 apparatus.

In many Key Stage 2 (KS2) classes, mathematics was confined to arithmetic, and arithmetic was limited to practising calculations. Children worked in many different bases. Despite a curriculum that was often rich in music and art, work in English was often arid and in maths it was mechanical – with children in the summer term of Reception classes being given tens and units addition sums to perform as their main if not entire mathematics curriculum experience, in preparation for transfer to the juniors. Children were often not allowed to *calculate* mentally, and the beginning of calculation was often based on the cardinal counting of objects. Children were taught to transcribe results based on using counters, into vertical tens and units 'sums'.

The cardinal approach fitted Piagetian theory, in that Piaget's biological basis for understanding argues for interaction with the environment – with physical or concrete objects. It was argued that children could not think in the abstract and number was argued to be an abstract concept, so therefore concrete objects were essential for counting and computation.

One consequence of the misinterpretation of Piaget's ideas was the way it affected the role of the teacher. Teachers were trained to believe that until children reached an appropriate 'maturational level' through natural development, (relating in some vague way to Piaget's stages of development), it was impossible to teach them certain concepts.

Individualised learning and its effect on teaching styles

In the 1970s whole-class teaching declined in mathematics classrooms, influenced mainly by the introduction of individualised work books and work cards for children. Teachers were encouraged to let children 'work through books and cards at their own pace'. It was almost impossible within this pedagogical framework to draw together children with the same mathematical difficulty because they would only meet the problem when they tackled the particular page or card. We really were in a mess! The individualised programmes were presented by publishers, psychologists and educationists as a response to psychological ideas that 'children progressed at their own rate', and that the rate was biologically determined and part of the process of maturation.

The result in many schools was that bright and able children who could cope with textual based learning moved rapidly ahead, but not necessarily consolidating what they were learning. Slow, less able children lagged further and further behind, producing a long tail of underachieving children who struggled daily.

Interaction with children – teachers and children talking mathematics together – became an almost completely forgotten experience. Whole-class discussion led by teachers was almost impossible, as the children in a class of thirty, could be ploughing through five or six different work books, each with a completely different content.

Teachers could give explanations to individual children on a one-to-one basis, no bad thing in itself, but most explanations were about what the author wanted the child to do, rather than about mathematical ideas. When pages were badly designed, one found oneself saying, over and over again, 'Colour the elephants red, colour the buses blue, and draw a line from each elephant to each bus'.

The mathematics was lost in the detail of managing the author's intentions on each of the pages, and managing the children, managing the work cards and work books. The irony is that this demise was brought about through a poor interpretation of the works of a theorist whose personal goal was that children should be helped to understand the world in which they live. Instead, curiously bizarre worlds of pictures and diagrams were invented for children to colour, and the power of discourse and spoken language relegated to daily explanations of trivia.

There was never a golden age of teaching for understanding, or certainly not in the case of mathematics. Certainly there was an expectation throughout the 1950s and 1960s that children should be taught as a class, with the teacher introducing new ideas to the class as a whole, and modelling techniques through the medium of the chalkboard. Children were expected to be able to readily recall a considerable repertoire of arithmetic factual knowledge – children in school in the 1950s were more likely to be taught their tables than children in school in the 1970s, but in the 1950s, the teaching of written procedures and algorithms dominated, and understanding was assumed to develop from regular practice of routine procedures. Many children failed to understand what they were taught and the school diet was almost exclusively arithmetic.

The importance of contexts for learning

A key turning point was the work of Margaret Donaldson and others, in the early 1970s, who involved children in tasks that were similar to the ones that Piaget had devised in the 1930s and 1940s. Their evidence contradicted Piaget's, in two ways. First, the language and status of the adult was found to have an enormous impact on children's performance and second, where the context was familiar to the child, the problem was more likely to be solved than when the problem involved unfamiliar contexts and requests.

A social and linguistic theory of classroom interaction began to emerge, significantly influenced by writers like Jerome Bruner who promulgated Vygotsky's work and its emphasis on language and the power of the social group. Valerie Walkerdine looked closely at teacher's language and power relationships in the mathematics classroom and produced a book,

The Mastery of Reason, which was very influential in mathematics education and teacher training, though less directly influential on primary teachers. Walkderdine's theme had similarities with Donaldson's, but with a greater emphasis on the need to deconstruct the language of instruction within the classroom.

Children were seen as active and capable linguists; social experts, motivated to search for ways of making sense of the contexts in which they find themselves. Walkderdine agued that children search for reason, that their intellectual skills are significant, and their perception of social and power relationships in the classroom profoundly influences their decisions about 'what they are supposed to do'. Walkderdine's research clearly showed that children's interpretations were often logical and sound, within their own thinking framework, but that their perceptions of the classroom were often very different from the teacher's.

The National Curriculum (NC) and more recently the National Numeracy Strategy (NNS), has continued to shape teachers' thinking about mathematics teaching and learning. The Teacher Training Agency (TTA) and more recently the Department for Education and Skills (DfES) has encouraged teachers to research their own classrooms and grant money is available to teachers who wish to do this.

Teachers as experts

In a curious and unforeseen way, it was the introduction of the Office for Standards in Education (OFSTED) inspections which brought about some major changes to the way the mathematics curriculum is organised and taught. When OFSTED inspections began, relatively few primary schools had coordinators for mathematics. Inspectors quickly found themselves overloaded with disjointed information and unable to make whole-school judgements about the quality of mathematics teaching and learning. What they needed was a single person to talk to. Head teachers were too distant from the everyday detail of the NC across ten subjects, and the very cumbersome assessment processes that went with the NC.

Schools quickly invented mathematics coordinators and they quickly became designated as experts. OFSTED inspectors began to talk directly to them about mathematics. Early OFSTED reports identified very patchy planning: excellent in some schools, but unsatisfactory in a large minority. Where planning was good, it was being done in teams. Teachers in large schools were meeting in year groups and many small schools held weekly whole-school meetings. Teaching was often much better where planning was being done jointly.

Prior to this period in the early 1990s, many teachers did all their planning alone. What they taught in the classroom was not well known to anyone else. This meant that good ideas did not circulate very well, and poor quality teaching could not easily be improved. Even more crucial, the NC for mathematics requires more than most other subjects *continuity* and *progression*. Continuity of the subject is needed so that children are taught efficiently, topic by topic across each year, with teachers introducing topics in a conceptual hierarchy; with less difficult concepts introduced first and more complex topics taught later. Good progression ensures that the increase in difficulty is right, that as children move from one classroom to another, they do not have to ignore what they were told in an earlier class, in order to do well in a subsequent one. Consistency of approaches to teaching and learning between classes is crucial for children's progress.

The transformation from individual planning to teamwork has been dramatic and this, more than anything else, has improved dialogue between teachers, not only on *what* but also *how* they teach. This has resulted in a much more open approach to discussions about effective teaching and learning and how to solve the particular problems that a school constantly finds itself with.

Until quite recently, much of the research output about learning has not been directly helpful to teachers who were seeking to improve their practice. Teachers often found research was something that was done to them and their children rather than with, and by them.

Increasingly it is teachers who carry out research in their classrooms, often as part of higher degree work. They research their teaching and their children's learning, frequently in collaboration with colleagues in other schools and in HE. The TTA and DfES research grants have supported much of this change.

The philosophy of the Numeracy Strategy

Members of the NNS Task Force who created the Numeracy Strategy, see the underlying philosophy of the NNS initiative as:

1   Encouraging interactive whole-class teaching.
2   Helping children to make sense of the mathematics they are learning.
3   Providing just the right amount of practice and consolidation, but no more, so that children become secure in their mathematical knowledge and skills.
4   Making language, and particularly discourse, central to the strategy.

The key to structuring and applying conceptual and procedural knowledge, especially in social settings such as classrooms, is through language. Effective language use helps us:

● construct, manipulate and label the objects of thought;
● organise our thinking and current knowledge;
● develop new structures and classifications so that old knowledge becomes accessible through meta structures;
● revisit and review previous learning so that nothing is seen as essentially new, rather, a new experience is viewed as a novel instance in which to apply previously gained knowledge;
● collaborate and communicate with others so that learning is acquired from and tested through collaboration;
● hear, speak, read and finally write the language of mathematics.

We expect children to read mathematics quite early in their lives. We give considerable attention to the stages of learning to read English, but give less attention than is warranted, to teaching children how to read mathematics. In fact the assumption that children could easily draw from classroom routines is that reading a number sentence is not much different from reading a sentence of English text.

The reading of a simple number sentence such as $8 + 3$ needs to be taught explicitly by the teacher. Embedded within the meaning of the reading are two quite different concepts.

First, we can read $8 + 3$ at a procedural level: an instructional code defining the particular action of adding three more to eight and announcing the result of eleven. Alternatively, we can read the sentence in terms of conceptual knowledge: the knowledge of the relationship between 8 and 3, which can be illustrated by recalling that the commutative law applies and so $3 + 8$ will give the same answer. The associative law applies, and so we know that the original statement is equivalent $8 + 2 + 1$. Thus, we can now read the sentence in terms of related concepts.

> We have suggested that maths, rather than being conceived as a body of knowledge (a bundle of facts and procedures), can be described as being like a language. Many of the techniques that children apply to the learning of language can equally well be applied to their learning of mathematics. In place of the vexed notion of mathematical under-standing, we have suggested that children are required to produce plausible *readings* of mathematical statements.
>
> (Merttens, 1996: 59)

Toys are useful in reading mathematical situations. Two play people sitting at different points on a number line can all too easily be read as 'me and my sister playing in a park'. We cannot expect children to achieve a mathematical reading without some modelling from us.

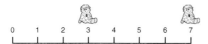

'I've got two children. One is aged 3 and the other is aged 7. How can I use the number line to show how old they are? … Can you see they are different ages? Can you tell me what the *difference* is between their ages?'

I could use a number track and some cubes to show the problem in a different way.

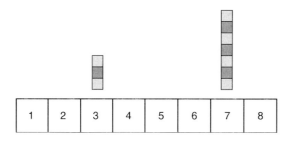

There are problems with illustrating *difference* and *take away* contexts appropriately. Dienes blocks are powerful for illustrating difference but are problematic when trying to show take away. Get some blocks and try! Remember, what the teacher is trying to do is to make a *connection* between an oral explanation that accompanies the physical manipulation of the equipment. The two need to be in harmony if the children are to learn how to make a mathematical reading of the context.

The child's problem is that when we teach, we constantly move between different readings, but usually without realising what we are doing, and often without warning children that we are expecting them to read different contexts at different times for a range of different purposes. For teachers who particularly enjoy teaching English and early reading, it can be liberating to recognise that the skills they need for textual analysis in English lessons, are needed in maths lessons too.

Procedural and conceptual knowledge

I have already sketched in general terms (see page 169), some features of the historical development of mathematics teaching during the second half of the last century. The emphasis that teachers placed on children's *procedural* knowledge gradually declined from the 1970s, while interest in children's *conceptual* knowledge increased. One of the driving forces for the shift came from research that showed that many children were either unwilling or unable to transfer procedures learned in mathematics lessons to solve problems in other contexts outside the classroom.

The Cockcroft Report, *Mathematics Counts* (Cockcroft, 1982) collected substantial research data which showed that many adults have forgotten the written arithmetical procedures learnt in school as children. When one considers the length of time children in school spent practising procedures like long multiplication, it is important to consider why adults find it so hard to retain the procedures learnt in childhood.

Research evidence from the APU (Assessment of Performance Unit, a small team of researchers at the Department for Education and Science) showed that many children never learned classroom-taught procedures for written calculations sufficiently accurately. For many, the procedures they learned contained errors which limited their effectiveness: they never learned an error-free method and most children were never able to remove the bugs.

When we lose our way in a procedure, or fail to remember a small but significant part of the routine, we do not get consistently right answers. Our interest in the procedure declines, as does our confidence in our ability to obtain right answers. This is similar to the argument made by Richard Skemp that relational learning (which tends to be judgement-based) is a more productive and secure approach than instrumental learning (which tends to be rule-based), where one mistake in applying the rule leads to failure. Relational learning relies on general familiarity, making connections, knowing the territory, having a range of strategies, being allowed to exercise choice, knowing where you need to get. This is very much the current philosophy behind the design of the NNS.

The formal written procedures for computation like long division are highly condensed and contain several concepts within a single routine. They contain many sub routines but few internal checking processes that might allow us to monitor for procedural errors.

Evidence has shown that many children fail to retain taught written computation algorithms into adulthood. Many adults do however, develop idiosyncratic self-taught mental methods that give sufficiently reliable and accurate answers and in consequence, inspire self-confidence (Figure 12.1).

What is difficult to convey to the reader who is currently in training, is how naïve and ignorant we teachers were of children's and adults' mental methods of calculation, prior to the last decade. Many of us who taught mathematics, knew a colleague in business or

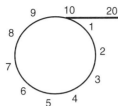

Figure 12.1 Mental image for addition and subtraction revealed by a grandparent during a school Open Evening.

commerce whose mental mathematical skills were superb, but who clearly did not derive their skills from applying the written procedures taught in school.

As teachers searching for a solution to unsatisfactory learning outcomes to our maths teaching, we were unable for a long time, to transfer our own streetwise knowledge, to our work in the mathematics classroom. What many of us knew tacitly, was made explicit through the publication of fascinating and detailed studies of Brazilian street children (Nunes *et al.*, 1993), whose very survival on city streets depended on them being able to carry out complex mental calculations in bartering and street-trading situations. However, these very adept children failed to perform in a school context and could not solve the problems when they were presented to them in a formal way. A very revealing book *Children's Mistakes* by Herbert Ginsburg opened up considerable discussion. Ginsburg sought to explain the problems from a constructivist point of view but did not really engage very much in how to shift pedagogy away from procedural knowledge.

Instead of recognising that we could appropriate some of the efficient mental methods used by Brazilian street children, for use in our teaching, we still tended to see self-taught people as somehow differently gifted. Our attitude towards the school curriculum was to continue to be immersed within it and be regulated by it, working with it as though it was fixed and immutable. Many individual teachers continued to regard the most likely solution as working even harder on teaching the same curriculum.

Occasional voices were heard (Plunkett, 1979) but too many of us could not see how to substitute unhelpful written computation methods with something more useful. It was clear that some children and adults developed a level of *conceptual understanding* that was sufficient to:

1   Free them from over-dependence on procedural methods.
2   Help them to detect and eliminate bugs in faulty procedures.
3   Help them acquire rapid, accurate mental computational skills.
4   Allow them to develop a meta-knowledge of problem solving, so that for any given problem, they were able to move fluently between conceptual and procedural strategies.

For many teachers and teacher educators, the publication of the Cockcroft Report played a significant part in helping to free up thinking. The PRiME project (Shuard *et al.*, 1990) and its associated curriculum experiments played a powerful role in creating a new dialogue for exploring problems in primary mathematics education. The project provided research findings, which addressed issues related to procedural and conceptual knowledge.

During the 1990s, there was a big increase in interest in the way teachers outside Britain tackle the teaching of calculation in primary school, and more than just a little surprise that European and Asian classrooms are not copies of British ones. The work of Dutch teachers and teacher educators had a particularly strong impact, and visits to Russia, Hungary and Japan featured in several discussions about pedagogy and number. A series of discussions and articles opened opportunities for British teachers to explore alternative teaching strategies (Beishuizen, 1993; Watson, 1993; Andrews, 1997; Beishuizen, 1997; Harries, 1997; Thompson, 1997a,b; Beishuizen, 1998; Stokoe and Illushin, 1998; Foxman and Beishuizen, 1999; Thompson, 1999). Useful research about the social factors that influence mathematical performance in classrooms (Brousseau, 1997) illustrated what some people had tacitly thought for several years, that children's behaviour in mathematics lessons is often shaped by the social context of the lesson and not just by the children's mathematical knowledge.

There are still many gaps in our understanding, both as researchers and as teachers.

> Research on the development of additive reasoning as assessed by children's performance in problems of different types has become incorporated in textbooks for teaching primary teachers and may already have an impact on the design of lessons and assessments. What is not clear is to what extent teachers may be able to support children's learning beyond providing them with a variety of problems and discussing variations in the solutions provided by children. Although there is some research on possible developmental mechanisms, this research so far has not been considered in teacher education texts.
>
> The research on children's understanding of multiplicative reasoning and the properties of the four operations does not seem to have had a noticeable impact yet although its relevance to teaching is undeniable. The current focus on the teaching of mental calculation without considering how the moves made in mental calculation relate to the children's understanding of the properties of operations is cause for concern. Recommendations to teach multiplication as repeated addition and division as repeated subtraction are also cause for concern. Research suggests that such teaching may be at the root of later misconceptions.
>
> (Nunes, 2001: 13)

Studies of children's *conceptual knowledge* have given rise to recommendations to teachers to teach certain strategies in order to better support understanding. Not withstanding the concerns expressed above by Nunes it is worth looking at some of the results of studies into children's conceptual development. In early addition for example:

> …for the operation of addition with numbers to 20 the following strategies represent increasing levels of sophistication: count all, count on from first number, count on from larger number, use known number facts to derive a number fact…
>
> (Thompson, 2001: 15)

For additions between 20 and 100 Thompson identifies the following:

- 'partitioning', where $56 + 38$ is calculated as $50 + 30 = 80$, $6 + 8 = 14$, $80 + 14 = 94$;
- 'sequencing', where $94 - 56$ is calculated as $94 - 50 = 44$ then $44 - 6 = 38$.

Thompson identifies variations of these two strategies. Partitioning is extended through a mixed method, where:

- $73 - 35$ is calculated as $70 - 30 = 40$, $40 + 3 = 43$, $43 - 5 = 38$.

Sequencing can be extended using a compensation method:

- $38 + 43$ is calculated by starting the calculation as $40 + 43 = 83$ and $83 - 2 = 81$.

Complementary addition is often used where *difference* rather than *subtraction* or *take away* is implied. So

- $81 - 43$ when read as the *difference* between 43 and 81, prompts, $43 + 7 = 50$, $50 + 30 = 80$, $80 + 1 = 81$, so, $30 + 7 + 1 = 38$.

In fact, the spoken command to *take away* often triggers a subtraction response in children, even when they have a preferred alternative method. ('But the teacher said it was a take-away!'). Many children when faced with $81 - 43$ as a *takeaway* will adopt subtraction rather than a difference or counting-on approach. The social and the linguistic contexts are very powerful determinants of action.

Rapid recall is important for freeing up mental energy. When children have rapid recall of the facts that link trios of numbers like 3, 8 and 11, it is possible for them to condense the stages of calculations without spending time on calculating basic facts. The child no longer needs to expend mental energy on $8 + 3$ in the addition $38 + 43$.

The main purpose of rapid and accurate recall of number facts is not to collect gold stars, or for 'beating' other children who cannot yet manage fast recall. Instead, the purpose is one of economy of effort, fluency, automaticity and linkage. It is to train the mind and thus, free it of the burden of lower order tasks so that attention can be given to higher order conceptualisation.

Resources and further reading

Andrews, P. (1997) A Hungarian perspective on mathematics education. *Mathematics Teaching*, MT 161, December, pp. 14–17.

Askew, M., Brown, M., Rhodes, V., Wiliam, D. and Johnson, D. (1997) *Effective Teachers of Numeracy: Report for the Teacher Training Agency*. London: King's College, University of London.

Assessment of Performance Unit (1991) *APU Mathematics Monitoring (Phase 2)*. London: School Examination and Assessment Council.

Beishuizen, M. (1993) Mental strategies and materials or models for addition and subtraction up to 100 in Dutch second grades. *Journal for Research in Mathematics Education*, 24(4), pp. 294–323.

Beishuizen, M. (1998) Which mental strategies in the early number curriculum? A comparison of British ideas and Dutch views. *British Educational Research Journal*, 24(5), pp. 519–539.

Brousseau, G. (1997) *Theory of Didactical Situations in Mathematics*. Dordrecht: Kluwer Publications.

Claxton, G. (1999) *Wise Up: The Challenge of Lifelong Learning*. London: Bloomsbury.

Cockcroft, W.H. (1982) Mathematics Counts: Report of the Committee of Enquiry into the Teaching of Mathematics in Schools. London: HMSO.

Donaldson, M. (1978) *Children's Minds*. London: Fontana.

Foxman, D. and Beishuizen, M. (1999) Untaught mental calculation methods used by 11-year-olds: some evidence from the assessment and performance unit survey in 1987. *Mathematics in School*, 28(5), pp. 5–7.

Gattegno, C. (1985) Knowledge v experience. *Mathematics Teaching*, MT 110, March.

Harries, T. (1997) Reflections of a mathematics lesson in Kaposvar. *Mathematics Teaching*. 161, December, pp. 11–13.

Merttens, R. (ed.) (1996) *Teaching Numeracy*. Maths in the Primary Classroom. Leamington Spa: Scholastic Limited.

Piaget, J. (1952) *The Child's Conception of Number*. London: Routledge & Kegan Paul.

Plunkett, S. (1979) Decomposition and all that rot. *Mathematics in School*, 8(3), pp. 2–5.

Shuard, H. *et al.* (1990) *PrIME: Children, Mathematics and Learning*. London: Simon & Schuster.

Skemp, R. (1986) *The Psychology of Learning Mathematics*. Harmondsworth: Penguin.

Walkerdine, V. (1988) *The Mastery of Reason: Cognitive Development and the Production of Rationality*. London: Routledge.

Watson, A. (1993) Russian Expectations. *Mathematics Teaching,*. 145, December, pp. 5–9.

13 Gaining access to children's learning

Learning is not directly accessible. In fact I make the argument elsewhere in the book (see page 87) that often learning takes place in the time and space *between* lessons rather than *within* a lesson. So finding ways to gain access to children's learning is a fascinating challenge for teachers. It is for me, why I enjoy working with children in the Early Years, where staying in touch with children's learning is most challenging. This chapter explores some strategies for gaining access to children's learning in the least invasive ways possible.

Monitoring children's understanding through questioning and discussion

There is a useful distinction to be made between children who think they understand but do not, and children who will not declare that they understand, but do (often a lack of confidence). It is the children who think they understand but do not, who are likely to be among the more difficult to detect (and many of this group are likely to be boys).

Naturally, most parents want children to produce correct answers, but for the teacher, incorrect answers are a much better source of information about the boundaries of understanding. It is a major part of the effective teacher's style, to explore children's errors and misconceptions orally, through questioning and discussion, during all phases of the lesson. Often, an initial question combined with a follow up, can quickly help the teacher differentiate between areas where children have secure knowledge, and areas where they have difficulty. A correct answer (orally or written) leaves one wondering whether the answer was:

- guessed more or less at random;
- given with the intention of pleasing you – the child knows the correct answer but gives a different one;
- understood several months previously, in which case the child may not be excited or challenged by what is being taught today;
- copied, the child was repeating what they have heard or seen, but there is no evidence of any deep understanding;
- offered after some hard thinking resulting from the child working at a challenge level.

Errors and misconceptions are best worked on through discussion and the use of individual wipe boards prior to formal writing. When children come to practise examples in their books they are in a much better position to produce accurate answers. Children are much more likely to be proud of their work if you have helped them eliminate errors prior to writing in their books.

Developing a repertoire of questions

Developing taxonomies of questions is useful for gaining insight into children's understanding. If I am in the middle of a lesson and want to assure myself that someone is listening, or has understood something that I have just taught, I may only need to ask a question that will produce an answer which is repetitive of what I have just said. For example, having looked at the set of numbers:

12, 24, 41, 41, 57, 57, 57, 57, 57, 68

and explained that we can find the *mode* by looking for the number that appears the most often in our list, I may ask a child to simply repeat as nearly as possible, what I have just said.

Question: 'Seema. *How* do we find the mode of a set of numbers?'
Seema: 'We look for the number that appears the most often in our list.'
'And the mode is?' … ('Fifty-seven').

I may respond by thanking the child, perhaps repeating her answer, and then moving on to another idea. Often, it is necessary to initiate a discussion that entices those who are not yet secure in their thinking, and who are cautious about answering.

A question for Sarah. Sarah, can you repeat Seema's answer? (Seema can say it again if you need her to.). … Sarah, Can you repeat it now? Does it feel comfortable? Does it make sense to you? If it doesn't feel right, can you say why not?
A question for Salomon. Can you repeat Seema's answer? Please ask Seema a question of your own, about what she said.
Julie. Did you hear Seema's answer? Do you think she's right? Can you say why you think she's right?

Quite often, especially where the children are not too challenged by the work – perhaps it is something we are revising, I am inclined to shift to a different type of question: one that demands reorganisation rather than repetition. I will also employ this slightly more challenging question for those children in the class who are robust enough in their thinking to manage something slightly harder.

A supplementary question for Assim. Assim, in your own words can you say how we find the mode? Try to tell us using your own words, instead of the words that Seema used. Imagine you're telling your mum over the phone. Can you tell me the mode from the data you've got?

It is very easy for children to perceive the teacher as the mathematician and themselves as weak learners with little insight or understanding. The most effective teachers try to avoid this classroom climate aiming instead for being mathematically self-effacing, whilst remaining pedagogically strong. We should try to create a climate in which the children build their self-image as confident explainers of mathematical ideas and problems.

Question, to a less confident child. 'Merryn, would you like to ask Assim or Seema a question about what's going on here?' The intention here is to allow Merryn to utter the question (directed at another child) that I anticipate she may not have the confidence to ask me. If Assim or Seema cannot manage an answer unaided, I can help them.

Encouraging another child to explain an idea is sometimes more effective than an answer which comes directly from the teacher. There is potential for dialogue and the sharing of explanations between children without the teacher being directly involved. Children themselves are more likely to be seen as sources of knowledge.

It is useful for us to have taxonomies of questions in our heads. They enable us to ask a range of questions in order to provoke different types of response. Some responses promote discussion, others provide us with a brief check that we are being understood, others challenge children's thinking in a most productive way. We can organise a range of question types to include questions that require:

- *literal* responses, brief and succinct, so we can quickly check understanding and move on;
- *re-organisation* of information allowing children to present answers in various ways;
- *interpretation*. 'Did you hear what Melinda said? Is she right to say that?';
- children to *infer* something from what has gone before. 'Here's a tricky problem! Here's another set of numbers: 2, 3, 4, 4, 4, 5, 6, 7, 7, 7, 8, 9, what might the mode be?';
- an *opinion* to be given. 'Seema. How do you like to work when you're trying to find the modal value of a set of numbers?'

Monitoring children's understanding through classroom observation

Mathematics lessons that involve practical activity are not just beneficial for supporting children's learning. Practical tasks and activities usually interpose an object between teacher and learner, for example, objects to be measured or counted. The gaze of both the teacher and the children is likely to be on the equipment and the resources being manipulated. If eye contact can be avoided this gives children a lot more thinking time.

Eye contact is associated with direct communication and in some cultures it is rude to speak to an adult and look directly at them. In the classroom, eye contact between child and teacher triggers an expectation of question and response or discussion. This means that where direct eye contact can be avoided, there is less expectation of immediate verbal interchange. Avoiding direct eye contact with children who are engaged in practical tasks is relatively easy, useful and may be less disruptive for them.

Try it out when you have set up a practical, table-top activity, as part of a lesson. Quietly go up to a pair of children who are absorbed in their task. Crouch down until you make direct eye contact with them. Chances are, they will stop what they are doing and wait for you to speak – or speak directly to you. Then go to another pair. Stand beside them but avoid looking directly at them. Chances are that they will look up to see what you are doing. If they see that you do not want to make eye contact with them, they will probably assume you do not want to talk. They are likely to return to their task, unless of course they want to tell you something!

Carrying a notepad and a pencil with you is another way of avoiding eye contact when you are close to children and can overhear and observe them. You can sit quite close and even be at eye level without interrupting them. Sitting sideways on to them is useful, so is looking as though you are writing. The curious ones may want to know *what* you are writing about them, but after a couple of lessons, they will ignore you when you are in note-taking mode.

What do you want to observe? There are some general benefits to be gained from good observation.

- Is my lesson going the way I want it to?
- Is the pace right for them: are they ready to move on to the next part of the lesson?
- Am I achieving what I think I am?
- Do the children understand the lesson objective and are they achieving it?
- What can I find out that will help me improve the next bit of this lesson, and the lesson that follows?
- What can I find out that other teachers and parents would find useful?

There is always a tension between the *quantity* and the *quality* of data that can be obtained in a busy classroom. It is possible to collect a lot of data quickly so long as it is not complex and detailed. It is possible to collect a small amount of rich, complex data, but we are unlikely to be able to collect lots of complex data in one single lesson. However, the quality of the data we do collect, improves considerably with practice.

Focus first, on getting a lot of useful but simple data. We need to know who is absent, because they are likely to need extra guidance when we next tackle the topic. Lessons should be pitched at a level where they challenge most of the children, that is, the work is challenging rather than trivial, and ideally, everyone can demonstrate success (which is not the same as saying that everyone is doing work of exactly the same level of difficulty).

Once we have observed the children during the lesson, we will be able to make much more secure judgements about how to support individuals and what we need to teach during our next lesson. A simple tick sheet is sufficient for this level of detail. It could contain, for example:

- the names of the children, probably grouping together the names of those who are working together;
- the lesson objective, written in words that children understand, 'I can find the mode of a set of numbers by finding the most frequent…'

A simple code can be used (Figure 13.1) to record whether children:

- I have sufficient understanding, to work independently and to extend the level of difficulty themselves;
- / can tackle the work independently, when given prior guidance and support;
- — lack understanding and can only work with support;
- o are absent from the lesson.

Lesson objectives / Names				
Assim	/	/	/	/
Merryn	O	O	—	—
Rasheed	I	I	I	I
Seema	/	/	/	I

Figure 13.1 Record showing how children responded to the lesson content and tasks.

Our long-term aim is to improve our teaching skills so as to provide lessons where all children, irrespective of ability, can achieve success in the actual tasks we set them. The record above would suggest that Merryn is a cause for concern, either because absence could be affecting performance, or maybe performance is affecting attendance. We realise as a result of these few observations that we need to support Merryn more effectively in future. We should be thinking about ways to provide more opportunities for her to be successful.

Rasheed is a cause for concern, because we may be wasting his time. It is not clear from this record whether he is consolidating and practising already acquired skills – perfectly legitimate classroom behaviour – or whether these lessons are just too easy. Maybe he is not being challenged or extended.

We can supplement this data with richer and more complex information. One way to collect richer data is to observe a target group in detail, in addition to the information gained from more general observations of the whole class. Group observations can be more detailed, especially where we keep a group under observation for a whole week, across different curriculum areas.

A more elaborate code is useful if it makes sense to you and you can use it. You could include a column for ability (high A to low E) and one for effort (high 5 to low 1). So someone you assess as A1 really needs you to provide something more stimulating and someone who is E5 means you and they are onto something pretty good, so congratulations are needed all round. This type of personal record keeping has one important use: to improve our teaching by maximising our understanding of children's performance. The best way to do this is to record regularly and then to look for trends over time. If we have a good system, we should be able to spot children making steady improvement, those who make a rapid improvement, those who are wobbly and those who are in decline.

We benefit from making systematic classroom observations and keeping records, because we are better informed about:

- judgements made within a lesson;
- deciding whether to change our questioning, or the pace, the focus, and the length of each part of the lesson;
- what needs to be planned for future lessons.

Using written work to support understanding

The theoretical underpinning of the National Numeracy Strategy (NNS) follows Vygotsky, and includes the assumption that learning is an interactive, social process. Language is not seen as solely communication. Language is taken to be the essential structuring medium for thinking and understanding: language and thought are regarded as indistinguishable. This theoretical perspective therefore does not value written work for its own sake. Written work has to contribute to the restructuring of language and thought, for it to be valuable.

From this perspective, learning is not seen as dependent upon an extensive writing process or the repetitive practice of routines. Rather, writing *extends* understanding only when the writing process helps:

- to develop the use of language and thought, and support the conceptualisation of mathematical ideas;
- as a means of challenging current thinking and reformulating existing mental structures and processes (similar to Piaget's conceptualisation of *assimilation* and *accommodation* but with language as the mechanism by which conceptual development is driven);
- aid reflection and review, since writing captures *current* thinking, whereas *reading what one has written* takes us back to our previous thoughts;
- move the children towards automaticity.

Writing is *unhelpful* when the writing task interferes with the thinking process – for example:

- when there is no clear connection in the child's mind between writing, practical mathematical tasks and current modes of thought;
- where writing is distracting and an additional physical or mental burden;
- where the writing demands are trivial;
- where writing involves the over-practising of written routines that are already automatic.

Children can learn to use written work to extend their thinking when they are taught to write discriminately. Most young children find writing a complex and demanding task. They need to devote considerable mental energy to the process, and it can easily become the dominant task, leaving the mathematical objectives sidelined.

We need to plan carefully so that written work is focused and appropriate. Mathematical development is hampered by engagement with trivial writing tasks that are uninspiring, distracting and seen as irrelevant by children. By contrast, Helen Williams experimented with getting her 4-year-old Reception children to write for a purpose. She asked them to put some interesting things in a yoghurt pot. She wanted them to count them carefully, and asked who would remember what they had done when they came to school the next day. She asked if they could draw something on a piece of paper and use the paper to cover their yoghurt pots. 'Draw something that will remind you of how many things are inside'. Like the children in Martin Hughes' work, they invented a range of solutions. They drew diagrams, pictures such as three little houses to represent three bricks, symbols such as spirals. One or two invented tally lines, and one or two wrote numerals. The discussion the following morning was very interesting as the children talked about what their writing meant to them and how it helped them remember what they had put in their pot.

Henry Liebling advocates scribing as a powerful modelling tool. If a record is useful, and particularly where the mathematical task is taking up much of the children's available attention, the adult can suggest to the child:

- 'You do the thinking and I'll do the writing';
- 'Think to me';
- 'Say what you see'.

Public scribing results in writing which belongs both to the original author and to the group or class as well. This means that, with the teacher's help where necessary, the child, the group or the class can read, review and validate or discuss using the notes and diagrams as prompts and reminders of what was suggested or claimed. They are working notes and can be reused or changed. They are not decried, but can be put to one side if another child has an idea that challenges the first bit of writing. If more needs to be said, then the cycle starts again. The two sets of notes can then be compared.

Rather than automatically expecting writing as an outcome, we need to consider writing for a range of purposes. Is it going to support the development of knowledge, understanding and skills? Effective writing includes:

- informal jottings to support memory and recall, during a series of complex steps;
- diagrams, patterns, pictures and sketches (e.g. when faced with the need to calculate $84 - 39$, a child senses the possibility of using a counting-on procedure and creates a number line from 39 to 40 and then from 40 to 84, and deduces an answer of $1 + 40 + 4$ or 45);
- prose, where children reflect on an activity and explain how a problem has been solved, or how a generalisation has been reached, for example, when a child writes, 'We built models with cubes using a cross pattern with one red one in the centre and four whites on the arms of the cross. We found out that we needed four more cubes to make each new model. We discovered a rule to work out how many cubes we needed for each model. Our rule is – think of which model you want to build, times this by four then add the one in the middle. (You can also write it 4 times x plus 1, or $4x + 1$).'

Monitoring children's written work

Monitoring written work is perhaps the second most important source of information after monitoring the interactions between children themselves and between them and the teacher. As far as possible, teachers should monitor written work in discussion with children during the lesson. The best quality written work gives the best information. Good quality written work arises in one of two ways:

- as part of the children's own decision-making (with prompts and encouragement from adults) when they realise that they need to make jottings to support their reasoning, to carry out calculations, and to communicate their ideas;
- as part of the teacher's planning of activities and tasks to support children's reasoning, accuracy and communication.

The evidence gained from monitoring children's written work is likely to be poor and misleading where writing tasks do not arise out of a genuine need. This occurs mainly when the teacher sets poor quality tasks, sets demands for written work arbitrarily and for no real purpose, and where children are not taught to initiate jottings and written routines for themselves to support their thinking.

Monitoring for evidence of understanding can be done in different ways depending on what the teacher needs to check up on. Where there is concern for an individual or a small group, then targeting the individual or group is the best strategy. Where there is a need to check that a new routine has been written correctly, a more superficial scan of the whole class will suffice.

During the introduction to a lesson teachers can:

- invite children to write answers and ideas on a class white board, or on individual boards;
- model some possible approaches to solving a problem and invite children to choose the type of recording that best helps them.

During the main activity, teachers can:

- work briefly with a previously targeted group, in order to examine what has been written;
- withdraw from a target group for a couple of minutes and visit all other groups;
- draw the class together for a brief review in mid-lesson, and ask one or two children to read out their written work (this is an effective way of sharing good strategies for recording);
- spend five minutes where children exchange books and mark each others work against clear criteria given by the teacher (the marking child can code the book to show that the work is either satisfactory or not, ✓ or ☹, then the teacher can sort the books knowing which ones to concentrate on after the lesson);
- when children look at each other's work, they give feedback to one another that focuses on constructive criticism.

During the plenary, teachers can:

- ask individual children to explain their reasoning and show their written work, or show their understanding by writing the answer to a further example on the class white board or an individual board.

Summarising what you learn from children's classroom activity

The indiscriminate collection of poor quality evidence is a major time waster. Teachers need to build up useful records over time, perhaps with one or two pieces of evidence per child per term. The key is to find and keep the smallest amount of good quality evidence that allows you to assess the child's knowledge and understanding in the topic being taught.

So long as there are no more than four or five groups per class, focusing on one target group per week becomes manageable. You can then target each group once every half term.

You and the child (scribing for younger children where necessary) can then photocopy and annotate one example of written work per child during the week when that child is part of the focus group.

As soon as possible after the lesson, brief notes can be made, for example, on the current five-day planning sheet, (using a different coloured pen) or on a group record sheet (see the example sheet on page 184).

Careful monitoring of written work contributes to teachers' judgements about whether children have:

- grasped mathematical ideas and can reason;
- learned routines and problem-solving strategies;
- communicated their ideas effectively.

It might be administratively useful and valuable for short-term behavioural management purposes, to give children written work in order to keep them quiet while you work with other groups. As a strategy it does not produce much cognitive learning. Alternative strategies can be much more effective in promoting learning. It is more productive, for example, to provide a worksheet that asks children to work in pairs to invent as many ways as possible of making 50p, rather than designing an individual worksheet containing twenty specific calculations. Most effective of all, is to ensure there is regular opportunity for children to engage with open-ended practical tasks.

Requiring children to carry out lots of written calculations does not, of itself, improve their understanding or mathematical competence. Boredom and over-practice is likely to lead to more errors rather than fewer.

As a general training point, it is worth saying that in the early stages of training, trainers need to show you how to develop effective ways of interacting with individual children, a group or the whole class. You should expect to become very effective, very quickly, given a well-run school and good training.

What is sometimes missing from training, and is more appropriate for inclusion towards the end of the training period and during the Newly Qualified Teacher (NQT) year, is for the trainee to learn how to raise the quality of the work in those groups where there is no direct interaction for several minutes during a lesson.

Initially, you may find that the groups who are given tasks to do whilst you are busy working with another group, will not perform as well as you want. For many trainees, the biggest gains in teaching effectiveness come from learning how to organise, monitor, support and guide those groups which you are expecting to work away from your direct control.

The quality of teaching only really begins to take off, when teachers can achieve high levels of effectiveness without direct and continual intervention with a group. 'Teaching from a distance' is a crucial (though later) skill to be developed: and depends for success on you acquiring a really deep understanding of *scaffolding* in all its forms.

Brainstorming and concept mapping

Brainstorming is now acknowledged as a highly effective method of getting access to the knowledge and skills held by individuals in a group. Its power lies both in its speed of effectiveness and also in the diversity of solutions produced when problems need to be solved. It has its limitations, one of which is that it requires a relatively sophisticated level of tolerance of the group as a social entity. Another limitation, which is sometimes overlooked, is that production of private knowledge into the public arena of the group does not mean that everyone in the group can use the knowledge and skills that emerge.

Group brainstorming is made more effective by following it with a second, individual task, where each person in the group is helped to map the connections between the pieces of new knowledge and skills produced by the first stage. Teachers find group brainstorming more effective when they follow it with an individual concept or mind mapping activity.

Suppose we tackle the problem of wanting to make a school flag with a group of Reception children – a real problem if there is already a school flag and it is in a poor state. It is at the top of a flagpole and is therefore inaccessible (which is a real *advantage* when trying to promote a discussion). Brainstorming is best done in short stages, using large photos of the individual children involved (easy these days with digital cameras). You could record the individual children's ideas and save them to a web page so that clicking on the child's image results in hearing them 'say their bit'.

It is quite easy to generate some ideas about:

- how to get the old flag down;
- how long the flagpole would be if it was taken down and laid in the playground;
- how much new rope will be needed to replace the old one;
- what sort of design could be created for the new flag.

If it is not convenient to use a digital camera and computer to store children's photos and speech, the teacher will probably want to scribe children's ideas as speech bubbles, mount them as part of a display, and then read them to the children at a later date.

The next stage with Foundation age children is to organise the replacement of the old flag over several days. Teachers frequently plan projects that develop over time where children are involved in different ways at each step. There is often a large interactive display associated with such work that helps teachers to get young children to recall the recent past and to separate out certain aspects of experience for reflection. Although this is not a formal mind map, the teacher often uses the display as part of a project with the display illustrating the connections between the different elements.

With older children, it is possible to review a topic and assess children's understanding by getting them to produce more formal concept maps. Concept maps promote a *connectionist* approach to teaching and learning. The King's Study (Askew *et al.*, 1997) showed that teachers who help children make connections between different areas of their experience produce some of the best gains in children's mathematical knowledge and understanding.

The advantages are that the brainstorm can be used effectively to trawl for a wide range of ideas and possible solutions; whilst the concept map allows individual children time for reflection, absorption of new ideas and an opportunity to represent their current knowledge.

A brainstorm activity about length will lead to the production of many related words and ideas, some of which may not be entirely accurate. Naturally, few if any children will have access to all the knowledge and understanding that the brainstorm generates. From the brainstorm, the teacher will have access to a list of words and ideas related to the measurement of length. One way of proceeding is to provide individual children with a copy of the ideas that have been generated, in the form of cards, for example. Individual children can then make a concept map by arranging their set of cards in a way that makes sense to them.

A typical brainstorm about *measurement* might produce the following words:

> stones, centimetres, weight, ruler, tape measure, scales, angles, protractor, degrees, daytime and night time, speed camera, amount, balance, quantity, bank machine, counter, heavy, light, nanosecond, light year, kilometre, ton, tonne, …

It is really helpful if any puzzling words are dealt with first. If I do not understand *scales* (because I'm thinking of fish and not sure how fish fit in to this activity). I need to ask the person who provided the word to explain (… 'We've got some in our kitchen and we use them to weigh sugar and stuff like that.'). When we are happy with the results of the brainstorm and the words that have been produced, we can begin to organise the information by grouping the words under headings. Which words seem to go together?

Associating and categorising is the next stage. Humans are good at making connections between apparently unrelated ideas. Having a label for a group of related items is powerful because recalling the label can trigger associations with the contents of the groups. This is an efficient learning process especially where *the learner* is the one who has decided the groupings. Let the children organise words and phrases which seem to them to go together. When the data has been grouped and some heading suggested, then you can encourage them to work for clarification of any ambiguities that remain.

After a period of collaborative organising of the data the next stage needs to be an individual activity where each person uses the brainstorm results to construct their own concept map of the information. For this, they need a large sheet of paper and time to transfer the brainstorm data into their own personal map, which will uniquely reflect the blobs of knowledge they securely hold, and the connections between the blobs. Combining a digital camera and an interactive white board can make brain storm results quickly available to everyone.

Concept maps are powerfully visual and also strongly connective. They help us reveal for ourselves and others the way we connect different pieces of knowledge that we have acquired. Children start with two or three words, concepts or ideas, that 'go together' and which they know are connected in some way. They write the words and draw a line to join them, then most important, write the connection along the joining line, trying wherever possible to make a sentence which joins the two concepts, but a single verb will often be sufficient.

Gradually they incorporate as many of the brainstorm words as they can, until they have a concept map that represents a structured account of their subject knowledge and understanding.

This dual stage activity can be motivating because it demonstrates to children:

- the wealth of knowledge that they already have;
- how valuable it is to work as a team to pool knowledge, strategies and ideas;
- how important it is to organise knowledge to maximise its usefulness and accessibility.

Concept maps encourage the negotiation of meanings and are useful both at the start and the end of a topic or series of lessons. Perhaps the two most important and exciting challenges for teachers in respect of children's cognitive knowledge are:

1   to make difficult ideas easily accessible to children, but without dumbing down;
2   to devise teaching strategies that help children build mental connections between what they already securely know, and what is recently familiar but not yet secure.

If we succeed in these two challenges, then we deserve to be regarded as pretty smart at our job. Concept maps support connectionist teaching very well (Figure 13.2).

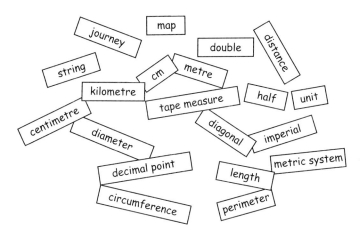

Figure 13.2 A set of cards generated by brainstorming and used for making a concept map.

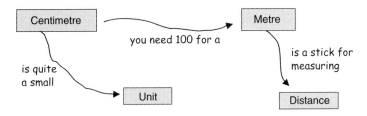

Figure 13.3 Building up a concept map.

Children are taught to think of ways in which words can be linked and to join related words with an annotated line. The lines and their annotations are just as important as the words. Individual children then draw lines to represent the connections between words producing a map of the concepts they have which relate to the topic. The concept map may begin to take the form shown in Figure 13.3.

The concept map is useful as a review activity because:

- both teachers and children can interpret the map to see the extent of the knowledge and understanding;
- strengths, weaknesses, errors and gaps can be diagnosed easily;
- reviewing concept maps helps teachers to be economical and focused in their review lessons.

Resources and further reading

Black, P. and Wiliam, D. (2002) *Inside the Black Box: Raising Standards Through Classroom Assessment.* London: King's College (Department of Education and Professional Studies).

Brown, T. (1998) *Coordinating Mathematics Across the Primary School.* London: Falmer Press.

Cockburn, A.D. (1999) *Teaching Mathematics with Insight: The Identification, Diagnosis and Remediation of Young Children's Mathematical Errors.* London: Falmer Press.

Connor, C. (ed.) (1999) *Assessment in Action in the Primary School.* London: Falmer Press.

Cooper, B. and Dunne, M. (2000) *Assessing Children's Mathematical Knowledge.* Buckingham: Open University Press.

Gipps, C. (1997) *Assessment in Primary Schools: Past, Present and Future.* London: British Curriculum Foundation.

Headington, R. (2000) *Monitoring, Assessment, Recording and Accountability: Meeting the Standards.* London: David Fulton.

Hughes, M. (1999) *Closing the Learning Gap.* Stafford: Network Educational Press.

Torrance, H. and Pryor, J. (1998) *Investigating Formative Assessment: Teaching, Learning and Assessment in the Classroom.* Buckingham: Open University Press.

Wright, R., Martland, J. and Stafford, A. (2000) *Early Numeracy: Assessment for Teaching and Intervention.* London: Paul Chapman.

14 Recent thinking about learning

Why is mathematics taught in schools at all? Most people in adult life do not use algebraic notation, nor do they need detailed knowledge of advanced geometry. There has to be a reason for teaching mathematics other than mere utilitarianism. Pleasure is a factor for many children who are involved in high quality lessons with teachers who have embraced the philosophy of the National Numeracy Strategy (NNS). Pleasure in one's own learning, is still undervalued in schools. I have never been comfortable with the badge-wearing 'maths is fun' viewpoint. For me maths is often hard work, frustrating and difficult. I see children experiencing pleasure in lessons where teachers make them aware that they are acquiring intellectually stimulating, new ideas. Gaining a sense of personal achievement should be a main ingredient of schooling. The purpose of education must be to demonstrate success.

Another case for teaching mathematics can be made if one reads recent studies of brain function and considers what we now understand about brain function and learning.

> The organism's engagement with an object intensifies its ability to process that object sensorily and also increases the opportunity to be engaged by other objects – the organism gets ready for more encounters and for more-detailed interactions. The overall result is greater alertness, sharper focus, higher quality of image processing.
>
> (Damasio, 1999: 182–183)

We can contrast Damasio's description with that of a learner who has developed a fear reaction to persistent failure. If this occurs, then we have to ask ourselves what contribution has schooling made to the learner's life. Teachers teach mathematics most effectively when they engage children's intellectual capabilities, not when they teach facts and just measure what has been memorised. The most effective way is to teach mathematics as a problem-posing–problem-solving cycle of activity, with the teacher introducing new knowledge and techniques to help children ask increasingly challenging questions, and use increasingly complex processes to solve problems. This is perfectly possible in pre-school settings with skilled practitioners and should be part of the skills of all teachers in primary schools.

The unique learning demands that are created when mathematics is taught as a problem-posing–problem-solving cycle come primarily through the need for intense engagement with the object under study. When working on maths problems it is important to see the big picture, and still remain immersed in the detail. For 3-year-olds this could be arranging a set of numerals in correct order, to illustrate the words of a song like Five Little Ducks.

To be effective, the practitioner finds an appropriate time to engage the children in discussion about how the numerals can represent the key mathematical elements in the song.

The argument made throughout this book is that mathematics *is* a language. It is a symbolic representation of a mode of thinking about the world, and a genuine discourse between teacher and children is an essential and continuing medium of exploration. Mathematics lessons should be some of the noisiest lessons that teachers teach. Damasio argues that engagement with the *object* increases our ability to process the object sensorally. I am arguing that engagement is particularly rewarding in mathematics because:

- maths is intellectually demanding – it invites commitment to engagement;
- engagement is easily provided in primary school if we use the full range of senses, because children naturally use all their senses to explore their engagement with objects of study;
- children are intrigued by their discovery of the paradoxical nature of mathematics, first meetings with the notion of infinity are experienced alongside an awareness of mathematics as offering closure and defining perfection.

Because maths is essentially a system of symbolic representation it is uniquely placed to provide a representation of objects of study. So for children who have explored the symbolism of numerals to represent what is happening in the song about the five little ducks, the teacher's pointing to the number three as the song is sung provides metonymic access to the whole story and to 'what comes next'.

As shown in the example immediately above, maths acts not only as a symbolic representation of the number system or of calculation, rather it can become a representation of the whole story – it provides access to 'the narrative of the event' not just to the mathematical features of the event.

To paraphrase Damasio, I argue that by engaging children with a complex object like a maths problem and working on a solution, the teacher is using mathematics to help children organise and represent an experience like a song. The neural consequence (as opposed to the fun aspect) is that the children, (Damasio's *organism*) develop their brain functioning. They are helped to get ready for more encounters and for increasingly complex interactions with their world. 'The overall result is greater alertness, sharper focus, higher quality of image processing' (*ibid.*).

Two qualifications need to be added to this discussion. One is that *language* is central to this increasing facility to use the brain and *discourse* is the vehicle that the best teachers use. By *discourse* I am distinguishing a process that is qualitatively different from, but obviously subsumes, good questioning, responding appropriately to children's questions and answers, introducing and using the necessary mathematics vocabulary, and introducing children to mathematical terms such as, addition, division, square, oblong... etc.

For me, discourse is qualitatively more than this because teachers' discourse is, *engagement with children* through the whole range of language processes, with the intent to promote enquiry, rather than simply to seek closure or check the accuracy of children's current thinking.

The second qualification involves the argument that emotional energy is of a higher order than the energy available for cognitive processing: emotions can swamp cognitive processes. Research into brain function suggests that our sense of self is a major determinant in how we function cognitively, even when learning a so-called 'rational' subject like mathematics.

How we feel about ourselves generally, and more especially, how we feel about our core selves during a mathematical activity, significantly affects our cognitive functioning, and potential for the memorisation of mathematical ideas and processes. Because mathematics is a generalisable, symbolic system that can be applied in a whole host of specific situations ($y = mx + c$ can have an infinite number of values), it may be that mathematical symbols can also be attached to affective and psychic elements within our thinking. (cf. the account by David Pimm (1994) of Laura, a very young child disturbed by the arrival of Pimm as a visitor, who increased the size of the family group to three again some months after her father's death).

Claxton outlines a process that involves a dual processing of experience, a study of the object and a parallel monitoring of the subject (our selves).

> We become conscious of stimuli … because they are being referred to a special part of the neural network which corresponds to our self-image, to see if they fit comfortably with the sense of who we are, and with the ongoing life story in which we see ourselves as taking part.
>
> (Claxton, 1997: 159)

An important idea developed through Claxton's book is that there is evidence for an *undermind*, an 'intelligent unconscious, that works quietly below, and in some cases ahead of, conscious apprehension' that is most effectively integrated into our thinking, when intuition and the slower more contemplative ways of knowing are allowed to operate alongside the rational. The importance of harmony in teaching is illustrated by the need to nurture the function of *undermind* so that emotional energy is harnessed to support and extend rational thinking.

> The more self-conscious we are – the more fragile our identity – the more we shut down the undermind. As people feel increasingly vulnerable, so their access to, and reliance on, information that is faint or fleeting declines. They become not just physically but also mentally clumsy, losing access to the subtler ways of knowing.
>
> (*Ibid.*: 128)

The jury is still out when it comes to the effectiveness of the various popular ideas about improving children's effectiveness as learners. There are many books and programmes that claim to *understand the mind, accelerate learning, transform learning* and *exercise the brain*, (Dennison and Dennison, 1986; Honey and Mumford, 1992; Buzan, 1993, 1995; Smith, 1996; Carter, 1998; De Bono, 1998; Caviglioli and Harris, 2000; Dryden and Vos, 2001)

The professional teacher needs to study these ideas and resources carefully by:

- remaining critical of new ideas (by that, I mean, checking them out thoroughly, trying them out in classrooms, discussing their effectiveness with colleagues and remaining sceptical until there is clear evidence of their effectiveness);
- being open to new ideas, not just sticking to tried and tested methods through habit;
- resisting advice to give up successful ways of working, just because they are 'unpopular' or out of style.

To conclude, there is evidence to suggest that studying maths is good for us *because* it requires considerable focus of attention when engaging with new problems and ideas, if we are to gain mastery. According to Damasio, the struggle for mastery is, in itself, a brain-enhancing activity. From Claxton, we recognise that there is good reason for engaging in mathematical problem solving within an environment where the self is seen and felt as a successful problem-poser and problem-solver. This is most likely to happen in classrooms where the teacher ensures that learners recognise that it is OK to make mistakes, and that mistakes are seen as real opportunities for moving on in our thinking.

Mathematical problem solving involves an inner dialogue between rational thought and the more intuitive 'undermind', but the evidence produced from very recent studies of brain function may just be leading us to similar conclusions that philosophers have drawn previously. Because mathematical problem solving involves an inner dialogue, it can support both 'calculative' and 'meditative' thinking.

> The approaching tide of technological revolution in the atomic age could so captivate, so bewitch, dazzle and beguile, ... that calculative thinking may someday come to be accepted and practised as the only way of thinking. What great danger then might move upon us? Then there might go hand in hand with the greatest ingenuity in calculative planning and inventing, indifference toward 'meditative' thinking, total thoughtlessness. And then? Then man would have denied and thrown away his own special nature – that he is a meditative being.
>
> (Heidegger, 1969)

What teachers need to do, if they accept the view that to be *ourselves*, in Heidegger's sense of the word, we need to retain our own special nature, we need to engage children in more than one kind of mathematical thinking. We can include opportunities for meditative thought within mathematics lessons by studying the use to which mathematics is put in architecture, music and by studying the way different cultures use and have used mathematics in the past. That this way of working not only satisfies a philosopher's concern for the future of humankind, but also accommodates research evidence of individual brain function – is more than just serendipitous.

What are the key skills?

From the discussion in the previous section, it is clear that the ability to exercise some conscious control over our choice of thinking mode is a key skill. A new and exciting development is the training material for teachers emerging from the NNS teams. These materials take both a *pedagogical* and a *knowledge-based* stance and tackle issues of teaching and learning head on.

In 1999, the Qualification and Curriculum Authority (QCA) identified key skills as:

- application of number (numeracy skills);
- effective communication;
- use of computers;
- improving one's own learning performance;
- effective interaction with others;
- meeting needs and solving problems.

(QCA, 1999: 8)

There is considerable resonance between these key skills and the requirements of the National Curriculum (NC) for mathematics with its emphasis on *problem solving, communicating* and *reasoning*. The key features of Ma1 *using and applying* are described in the opening sections of Ma2 *Number*, Ma3 *Shape, Space and Measures*, (and beyond Key Stage 1 (KS1)) in Ma4 *Handling Data*.

The same three themes appear each time: *problem solving, communicating and reasoning*. On pages 62 and 67 of the NC there is the claim that:

> The mathematics programmes of study and the National Numeracy Strategy *Framework* are fully aligned. The *Framework* provides a detailed basis for implementing the statutory requirements. . . .
>
> (DfEE and QCA, 1999)

I have always taken the view that *using and applying* is also a description of effective teaching. We need to review our teaching to see whether we provide the opportunities for children to meet the expectations listed, rather than just look for evidence that children can do the things listed. A useful way of using the NC Programmes of Study is to:

1   Read the Programmes of study (PoS) statements in terms of pupil entitlement.
2   Ask ourselves tough questions about our ability to make appropriate provision in our classrooms.

We can review the extent to which our classroom is an environment for effective learning by prefacing each of the statements in the *using and applying* PoS with the same question: 'How do I create opportunities in my classroom for my children to be successful?' For teachers at KS1 this means providing a classroom environment where children can:

> . . . develop flexible approaches to problem solving and look for ways to overcome difficulties . . .
> . . . use the correct language, . . .
> . . . communicate in spoken, pictorial and written form . . .
> . . . understand a general statement and investigate whether particular cases match it . . .
> . . . explain their methods and reasoning when solving problems . . . .
>
> (Taken from using and applying PoS: Mathematics Key Stage 1: 62)

If we take this proactive stance to what we are capable of providing, we can view *using and applying* as a mechanism for professional development of effective teaching of mathematics. What we force ourselves to consider are the ways in which we can make changes to our teacher behaviour, our classroom organisation and the classroom climate we create. If we get it right, children can practice on a daily basis what is listed in the PoS statements.

Communication and literacy

The NNS Framework, and to a lesser extent the NC, espouse a view of mathematical understanding based upon an extended view of *literacy*. What does this mean for teaching and learning?

Many teachers and children get no further than thinking that the relation between mathematics and literacy extends no further than ensuring that lessons contain access to referrents, such as; cube, cuboid, sphere, equation, numeral, graph, hundred square, etc. To see this is to recognise that there is a vocabulary of mathematical objects and labels, and that access to this vocabulary provides a useful way to refer to objects and ideas that are common in maths lessons. These words are useful labels and children gradually build up a vocabulary that allows for useful reference to the objects themselves, to discussion about calculation, to the development of mathematical thinking.

Access to a vocabulary is not sufficient in itself and children will not become mathematicians by practising their vocabulary, however diligently. What is needed in addition to this knowledge, is the understanding produced through *discourse*. Discourse in mathematics lessons includes an essential extra ingredient – it is self-referential. Discourse enables both parties to link their own ideas to the speech, action and thought (of at least), one other interested party, in a vital way that supports and promotes independent thinking and opportunity for debate and argument.

The responsibility for providing discursive contexts for learning lies with the adults in the teaching environment – the teacher and others. Engagement with mathematics occurs primarily at the instigation of the teacher who creates puzzlement, and who promotes problem-posing and problem-solving by mediating problematic situations, that is, by explaining where potential problems lie and how they might be tackled. For example, by telling the children that the Maths Monster has visited the classroom overnight and muddled up the number line, so that it is not in a fit state to be used. The teacher then extends the discussion by posing questions like, 'How do I know the number line has been mixed up? What do we need to look at to make sure it is in the right order? What can I do to fix it?'

The teacher also orchestrates the provision of necessary skills and techniques so that the children can realistically tackle the problems posed: but without committing intellectual piracy: stealing the children's ideas, or putting words into their mouths in order to get them to utter correct answers in an unthinking way.

Children need to be taught how to *read mathematics* as part of the process of developing their mathematical literacy. When I use the word *read*, I include knowing how *to look* at words or number sentences with comprehension when written, where to start and finish the decoding process, how *to say* number sentences with meaning, how *to hear* mathematical discussion with understanding.

In an early algebra activity, I emphasise that being able to act sensibly on what we hear, is important when tackling maths problems. I use the chip shop as a (fairly) familiar context. Children need to be able to *read*: 'Two cod and chips. One plaice and one chips. Wrapped.', in a way that allows them to interpret the accompanying actions of the fishmonger who translates the order into action to complete the purchase.

According to one interpretation, the result could be; two separately wrapped parcels each containing a piece of cod and some chips, with a separate parcel containing a piece of plaice, and another parcel containing chips. There may be variations in different parts of the country, based on different local readings and of course the whole statement might produce dramatically different results in other cultures where fish is not battered and chips are not made from deep fried, sliced potato.

The discourse will include; utterances, mathematical assumptions and tacitly agreed local meanings, together with their associated actions. Now try,

$$((5 - 6) + (-7 + 2)) \times (-5)^2$$

Quite a few answers are possible, depending on how one invents and applies rules governing the use and meaning of the symbols, including brackets.

Children need opportunities to:

- work with provocative teachers;
- have extended dialogue with teachers about the teacher's actions and utterances;
- practise explaining their own thinking to themselves and to others;
- link thought and action.

The philosophy behind the daily maths lesson as conceived in the NNS Framework includes a Vygotskian perspective on language and discourse as a structuring process. Language organises thinking and contributes to the construction of conceptual understanding. From a pedagogical perspective, this notion of dialogue emphasises the crucial role that language plays in effective teaching. It claims that involving children in discourse also gives teachers access to the child's:

- current thinking processes;
- errors and misconceptions;
- reasoning;
- communication skills;
- level of knowledge of relevant vocabulary;
- current connections between different pieces of mathematics being used to solve a particular problem.

It is also predicated on the assumption that children benefit because the process of discourse enables them to utilise language to:

- make sense of experiences;
- integrate new and previous knowledge by exploring possible connections between currently disconnected ideas and actions;
- produce mental structures and frameworks for thinking that limit the role of memory whilst emphasising connectivity;
- apply vocabulary to novel (and perhaps unanticipated) situations;
- provide structures for reflection and review of actions and ideas.

If we accept the above argument, then we should realise that one important consequence of using discourse as the primary means by which teachers bring children to an inner understanding of *self-as-mathematician* is that mathematics lessons have to be among the noisiest lessons that we teach. The main mode of teaching must be interaction and dialogue, open discussion, exploration and argument. It needs to be said, of course, that periods of calm and silence are also required for inner thought, concentration on detailed calculation, contemplation and reflection. The two key points are:

1   That discourse requires dialogue (conversation between two or more persons) and invites explanation by all those involved.
2   The above discussion should not be read as implying that teachers should talk the most, or that children should listen the most.

Recording and communicating in maths lessons

Successful maths lessons call upon a wide repertoire of teaching skills, including the ability to:

- model
- demonstrate
- show
- describe
- explain
- tell
- ask.

The child's repertoire of learning skills needs to include all the above. In addition, most children have the ability to:

- copy
- mimic
- adapt the given
- interpret meaning
- assume and extrapolate
- reproduce the original ideas in new contexts.

The result of discourse on a mathematical idea or problem is that the teacher and pupils can arrive at new insights. As the lesson proceeds, the teacher may realise that children need more opportunities to incorporate new ways of working, or need more time for practice. Children may realise that they have new skills and new knowledge.

Within a single lesson, some children are unlikely to construct a meta-awareness of what has been achieved. Discourse is a powerful vehicle for, and promotes, meta-awareness. One opportunity presented by the plenary period at the end of a lesson is to help children locate and attend to what it is, that has been produced in the lesson for and by the different actors involved, and how what has been produced fits with the teacher's intentions for the lesson.

If temporarily, we make a distinction between the recording of mathematics for the purposes of supporting learning, and the purpose of providing evidence by which teachers demonstrate their adherence to external requirements, then recording must originate with the teacher and flow towards the point where children can adopt and adapt what the teacher has demonstrated, modelled and produced.

A further distinction is also necessary. Teachers can model ways of recording the *result* of mathematical thinking and activity, or they can go further and try to include something more ephemeral but crucial for understanding, by attempting to record the process of *mathematical thinking*.

In Foundation classrooms, recording might involve carrying out an activity then revisiting it through discussion and role play, for example, by showing children that by organising people and objects, we can all have a chair to sit on and a piece of fruit to eat, or that if we pair up with a friend, we can play an enjoyable game. Recording often takes the form of paintings, drawings, 3-D models from modelling materials, or the use of plastic toys to represent events.

At Key Stage 1 (KS1), it could include straightforward 'watch me' demonstrations by the teacher, of how to make life easier by using number lines and jottings to support memory and to avoid *counting* in favour of *calculating*. This could be demonstrated by the teacher through discussion and action, using a flipchart and pens, where the teacher models by drawing and talking, how to combine the use of a number line with known facts such as 6 and 4 make 10, to find the answer to:

- 26 and 4 more makes;
- 36 and 4 more is;
- 46 and 4 equals;
- $56 + 4 =$

Utterances are accompanied by the drawing of a number line, the recording of a starting number, a representation of the addition of four more by drawing a curved line, the recording of a final number. Recording in maths lessons has several important features:

- each type of recording is likely to originate with the teacher scribing, whilst uttering a story that complements the scribing, before it is adopted by the majority of children;
- the teacher emphasises the connection between scribing and spoken utterances, and the mapping that is possible from spoken to scribed representation;
- the teacher requires children to imitate the uttering and the scribing, whilst encouraging them to add their own embellishments (you can say it slightly differently from me, if that helps your thinking);
- the teacher draws children's attention to what they have learned to do;
- the teacher draws children's attention to the potential for *applicability* by emphasising the *generality of the activity* (e.g. by emphasising that we can all draw a number line if we want to, to find out what 23 and 7 make because we already also know that 3 and 7 make 10);
- teachers can emphasise the inner structure inherent in a decimal counting system (we can use what we know about 3 and 7, to find the answer to 33 and 7, $43 + 7$, $53 + 7$, $123 + 7$).

Thus, recording in maths lessons:

- can accompany initial thinking about an aspect of maths that children may not have worked on before (i.e. recording does not have to *follow* an activity, and often precedes practical activity by children);

- is an aid to structuring our thinking;
- is an aid to monitoring some aspects of children's thinking, when teachers have such over-large classes as they currently do;
- relieves us from the burden of over-dependence on memory;
- helps us make sense of what we have been taught;
- can provide a shorthand record of thinking and activity;
- is a support to the *internalisation* of structures and patterns;
- reflects and duplicates the construction of mental frameworks (shapes, models and number line images are likely to stand in metaphoric or metonymic relation to the mathematical activity being represented and to the thinking process used to produce the mathematical result);
- is offered to children in a form that is easy for them to adopt (teachers are careful to offer economic models, that is, models where the number of steps and procedures employed avoid laborious over-detail, are minimalist, in the sense that children are offered the most (conceptually) for the least (in terms of finger-achingly tedious writing and drawing);
- can be adapted by children (you actually hear children saying in class, 'I think I'll use a hundred square to solve this') and reproduced by them in new contexts;
- requires repetition and regular practice if it is to be internalised in a form that makes it readily available and easily called to mind.

Because there are some novel ideas presented here, there is likely to be resistance to the adoption of some of the ideas and methods outlined. Resistance can come from:

- our initial caution;
- our own reluctance to adopt unfamiliar practices that contradict aspects of our learning experiences;
- children who are familiar with a different type of classroom experience and schooling;
- colleagues who have not adopted the philosophy inherent in the NNS;
- parents who lack direct experience of the changes that have taken place in classroom teaching since they were in primary classroom as learners.

One source of support for developing these ideas is an interesting section of the Department for Educations and Skills (DfES) website (supposedly for parents) which gives a clear view of the intentions behind the strategy to improve numeracy and the efforts to raise the quality of mathematics teaching.

Teachers are required to justify their professional work to external individuals and bodies. Parents, other teachers and external bodies such as Office for Standards in Education (OFSTED) are able to demand that teachers provide evidence of what children know, understand and can do, as a result of the schooling they have received. One source of evidence is children's own written work. We need to be very clear (and this is not always easy) whether the written work that we require of children, both during lessons and between lessons, is intended to promote children's knowledge, understanding and skills, and whether in addition, it is intended to justify to others what we believe is valid classroom activity.

Children's written work:

- provides a focus for feedback to individual children through marking;
- helps teachers monitor their teaching, by seeing what children can actually do as a consequence of the teaching they have received;
- provides a record of what has been achieved;
- shows children's errors and misconceptions, the analysis of which, can aid teachers' future lesson planning and planned intervention;
- provides a source of information for following teacher;
- provides evidence to parents of what has been taught and accomplished.

Resources and further reading

http://www.braindance.com/homepage.htm(Tony Buzan home page).

http://www.braingym.com

http://www.dfes.gov.uk/parents/curriculum/home.cfm (Department for Education and Skills).

http://www.ofsted.gov.uk/ (Office for Standards in Education).

http://www.thelearningweb.net (Learning revolution website).

Buzan, T. (1993) *Mind Map Book*. London: BBC Books.

Buzan, T. (1995) *Use Your Head*. London: BBC Books.

Carter, R. (1998) *Mapping the Mind*. Weidenfeld and Nicolson.

Caviglioli, O. and Harris, I. (2000) *Map Wise*. Stafford: Network Educational Press.

Claxton, G. (1997) *Hare Brain, Tortoise Mind: Why Intelligence Increases when you Think Less*. London: Fourth Estate.

Claxton, G. (1999) *Wise Up: The Challenge of Lifelong Learning*. London: Bloomsbury.

Damasio, A. (1999) *The Feeling of What Happens: Body and Emotion in the Making of Consciousness*. Sandiego, CA: Harcourt.

De Bono, E. (1976) *Teaching Thinking*. Harmondworth: Penguin.

De Bono, E. (1998) *Simplicity*. London: Viking (Penguin).

Dennison, P. and Dennison, G. (1986) *Brain Gym*. Ventura, CA: Edu-Kinaesthetics.

Dryden, G. and Vos, J. (2001) *The Learning Revolution*. Stafford: Network Educational Press. Sandiego, CA: Harcourt.

Heidegger, M. (1969) *Discourse on Thinking*. London: Harper Row.

Honey, P. and Mumford, A. (1992) *The Manual of Learning Styles*. Maidenhead: P. Honey.

Mitchell, C. and Williams, H. (1998) *Teaching Mathematics to Young Children: 4–7*. Cambridge: Chris Kington Publications.

Pimm, D. (1994) Another Psychology of Mathematics Education. In: Paul Ernest (ed.) *Constructing Mathematical Knowledge: Epistemology and Mathematical Education*. London: Falmer Press.

QCA (1999) 'New television series about key skills'. *ONQ Issue* 5 April 1999 (8).

Smith, A. (1996) *Accelerated Learning in the Classroom*. Stafford: Network Educational Press.

Williams, H. (2003) *Classworks: Reception*. Cheltenham: Nelson Thornes.

Williams, H., Skinner, C. and Barber, B. (2000) *Foundations Mathematics: Teaching the Early Years*. Numerary solutions. Oxford: Reed Educational and Professional Publishing Ltd.

PART IV

Meeting the Standards

How to monitor your progress towards the Standards

Because of the nature of mathematics and its position in the curriculum it is an ideal subject for exploring how to meet the Professional Standards. In the following pages all the Standards are reproduced in grids, with space for you to plan how to meet them and to record your achievements. This will help you when you discuss your training needs with class teachers, school-based mentors and training tutors. I recommend to the trainees with whom I work, that they regularly skim their copy of the Standards and use highlighter pens to record how they judge their progress. 'Use your intuitive mind. Decide quickly. Do not linger. Later you can review your decisions using a rational approach, perhaps in discussion with a friend who knows you and your situation.'

A traffic light system can be useful in breaking down the Standards into manageable chunks and taking control of them, rather than feeling that they rule your life. By highlighting words and phrases each week or two, you can colour code the Standards throughout your training. It can be useful to get out the green pen when your confidence is low and you think you have not made any progress recently.

Responding to a Standard

Green – I have met this Standard: Plan some easy ways of repeating what you have achieved in mathematics, with another ability group, in another subject, in another Key Stage, in another school. Review what you would have to do differently to achieve the Standard in different settings. Is it possible that there is another Standard that makes similar demands that will now be easier to meet? What else can you highlight as completed or close to completion?

Amber – I have not got this completely sorted: Is it lack of opportunity, a gap in maths subject knowledge, or perhaps a misunderstanding about what you have to do? Who might be able to help you? Do not be afraid to ask questions. Check to make sure when further opportunities will be available and put them into a diary. Need to build your subject knowledge?

Fix a time in your diary to work with someone else. Do not try to work all by yourself – the training process is too intense for a lot of independent learning. Share lifts for example and discuss issues in the car.

Red – I cannot do this yet: Reflect on why you have a problem, and whether the problem really is as big as it seems. Use a diary to plan some study time around your school-based work and other commitments. Identify specific and realistic periods of time in which to do things. Prioritise, because there is too little time to do everything. Arrange to meet with peers, tutors and mentors to discuss why you think you are not making progress. Identify specific action to take, rather than listing everything you think you can't do.

In the grids on the following pages there is space to write down the action that you need to take.

If you have highlighted a section of the Standards in

- green, you can ask yourself: how can I strengthen this further, achieve the Standard in another Key Stage or in other classrooms, or use it to help me meet another related Standard?
- amber, ask yourself what exactly you can do: how can I strengthen myself, what other Standards have I already achieved that help me here?
- red, you need to ask: what exactly is the nature of the block, am I being realistic and objective in my assessment of the situation, who do I need to talk to?

15 Meeting the Standards for Professional Values

The eight standards for Professional Values and Practice combine a broad range of attitudes and beliefs promoted by society in general and evidence from research, with children's legal entitlement. Your work in mathematics can make a big contribution to meeting these Standards.

> … these Standards outline the attitudes and commitment to be expected of anyone qualifying to be a teacher, and are derived from the Professional Code of the General Teaching Council for England.
>
> (DfES/TTA, 2002: 2)

The earlier Standards in government Circular 4/98 emphasised technical competence, and saw the delivery of curriculum knowledge and skills in a professional void, disconnected from the values, ethics and commitments. Pupils were represented as empty vessels to be topped up by teachers whilst teachers themselves were seen as technicians, either competent or not in applying a range of techniques.

In contrast, the current Professional Standards recognise teaching as a social act requiring more than skills and knowledge. The social themes which the current government considers to be paramount are expressed through the Standards. In general terms they emphasise

- the professional relationships that effective teachers establish with children (1.1, 1.2, 1.3);
- effective communication with parents, and carers (1.4);
- the need to take a full part in the corporate life of schools (1.5);
- seeking professional development through reflective practice and learning from colleagues (1.7).

The inclusion of Professional Values into the Standards, together with the removal of the requirement to train for a specialist subject, makes it more likely that trainees who are following school-based routes into teaching (e.g. School Centered Initial Teacher Training (SCITT) and Graduate Teacher routes) can fully meet the Standards.

The General Teaching Council (GTC) has suggested that it is the professional activity and conduct of trainees in school that need to be assessed against these Standards and the professional code of the GTC.

Table 15.1 Monitoring progress towards meeting the Standards for Professional Values

Précis of the Standards for Professional Values	*I need to take the following action:*
Expectations of pupils I have high expectations of all pupils; respect their social, cultural, linguistic, religious and ethnic backgrounds. I am committed to raising their educational achievement (1.1).	
Personal behaviour and relationships with others I treat pupils consistently, with respect and consideration. I am concerned for their development as learners (1.2).	
I demonstrate and promote the positive values, attitudes and behaviour that I expect from my pupils (1.3).	
I communicate sensitively and effectively with parents and carers. I recognise their roles in pupils' learning, and their rights, responsibilities and interests (1.4).	
I understand the contribution that support staff and other professionals make to teaching and learning (1.6).	
I am aware of, and work within, the statutory frameworks relating to teachers' responsibilities (1.8).	
Commitment to the school I contribute to, and share responsibility in, the corporate life of my school (1.5).	
Commitment to self improvement and professional development I work to improve my own teaching, by evaluating it, learning from the effective practice of others and from evidence. I am motivated and able to take increasing responsibility for my own professional development (1.7).	

You can meet the Standards for Professional Values in many different settings (Table 15.1). Do not just think of yourself as teaching mathematics in classrooms; include after-school maths clubs, Parents' Meetings, whole-class assemblies, school trips, visits and so on.

Exploring cultural roots

The teaching of mathematics in primary schools gives plenty of opportunities for meeting the Standards through the fostering of inclusiveness, high expectations and respect for cultural and ethnic diversity. Part of this process is to be open to the cultural diversity of the classrooms and schools in which you work.

At the heart of the Standards for Professional Values, is the belief that people are more likely to learn if they are respected, valued, believe in themselves, and are encouraged to celebrate their achievements. This is particularly important in mathematics. There is a powerful and problematic relationship between achievement in mathematics and self-esteem. Although written in 1981, Laurie Buxton's *Do You Panic at Maths?* is as informative today as it ever was. It tells the personal stories of several very able and successful professional people in different walks of life, all of whom hid the fact that they were maths phobic.

In mathematics lessons and after-school clubs there are a number of things you could do to acknowledge cultural diversity. Many parents, carers and older siblings teach counting rhymes to babies as part of play. You could set yourself the challenge of learning some simple counting rhymes in two or three new languages, from Europe, South-east Asia and Africa for example, and some unfamiliar counting rhymes in English from outside the UK. Do not forget about 'dipping rhymes' for choosing a leader for a game. Never mind that some of the numbers may be trivial for a class of 10-year-olds, what is important is the celebration of stories and rhymes from other cultures, preferably using the 10-year-old experts who have roots in those cultures, and who can teach you and their friends their games and stories. Write them on charts, tape record them, learn them yourself and teach them to your class.

Another way to start is by teaching lessons on counting and the way numbers are written and recorded in different cultures. Which systems use a 0 and which do not? What do Chinese numerals look like? How would you write the first 100 numbers in Bengali? Why do numbers in French, step in tens until 60 and then step in twenties from 60 to 80 to 100? In which dialects or languages can you find a pattern of scores (twenties) in England: what is counting in Cornish like, or in Northumbrian? Menninger's book contains a wealth of detail.

Pay particular attention to learning the counting systems used by children in your class who have connections with other cultures and who speak languages other than English. The PrIME File (Shuard *et al.*, 1990) is a valuable source of multicultural mathematics resources with photocopiable grids of counting systems. Journals such as *Mathematics in School* and *Mathematics Teaching* are a useful source of articles, resources and images. For example, *Mathematics Teaching* (MT 112: 53) shows geometric patterns from Madurai in southern India, which are drawn on the ground outside houses each day.

Mathematics is a wonderful vehicle for the celebration of different cultures. We use an Arabic numeral system, which Arab traders originally obtained from the Indian subcontinent. We still use a Roman numeral system, which has existed alongside calculation methods that were developed in Italy in the fourteenth century. We can use Chinese and Japanese abacus and sorobans for calculations. We can buy and play numerous games whose origins may be Chinese, African or early European. A useful reference is *Africa Counts* (Zaslavsky, 1990).

We use both solar calendars based on Roman methods, adapted by papal decree in the eighteenth century, and lunar calendars that record events in the Islamic year. Christians, Jews and Muslims count their years from different start dates. We know about, but have not entirely understood, the workings of the Mayan calendar from South America, despite the fact that it appears to have been more accurate than its counterpart in sixteenth century Europe.

We teach simple 2-D and 3-D shapes and can find examples of glorious geometrical designs in the Moorish architecture of Granada, in the pyramids of Egypt, the Byzantine domes of Russia and Asia, and in the traditional igloo buildings of the Inuit. Algebra has a long and well-documented history which is discussed elsewhere in this book.

There is no excuse for the teacher of mathematics to be monocultural. What is difficult, is managing the tensions that can exist between the different ethnic, religious and cultural groups that are present in the classroom, when our society promotes ambiguous images of sex, gender, race and culture, where some groups are 'invisible' – never represented in television advertisements for example, and where children remain one of the poorest and most socially disadvantaged groups in our society.

Meeting children's needs and rights

On first consideration, it appears reasonable that a professional teacher should promote the rights of the child, but even this is not so straightforward in practice. Many schools face considerable difficulty, managing children who present challenging behaviour. Many primary children have huge daily responsibility as carers, sometimes for adults in their family but more often for other children: we do not always know this, or know how to support them. Respecting their lived experience is part of the teacher's system of values but first we need to learn about their experience.

Stress is not an exclusively adult affliction. Children are as vulnerable to stress as adults and as easily damaged by it. Many children live in poverty, suffer under-privilege and are unable to access many of the benefits of our highly affluent society.

Even when we work with children who present us with few challenges, living up to the United Nations declaration of children's rights is very difficult in the current school structure because it requires us to respect the right of children to an opinion of their own, and accords them the right to be heard. With large classes, a highly prescriptive curriculum, and the conformist society that exists in Britain, this is difficult to manage, even when the child expresses a 'conforming' view. It is even more problematic where the child's expressed view is unorthodox, as well it might be, in a young child whose views are developing.

When we compare current state school curricula and opportunities for exploring children's rights, with the opportunities provided in private sector education, like Krishnamurti or Steiner schools, we are brought to a realisation of how prescriptive, bounded and highly regulated, teachers' behaviour has become in the state sector.

High expectations

Believing in the high ability of the children whom you teach, can actually change their ability, or at least can increase their willingness and confidence to work harder on difficult ideas. It is not surprising then, that the professional values listed in the first section of the Standards include references to motivational aspects of learning. The Hay McBer (2000) research showed how important teacher expectations are in raising standards.

Our professional values do not just affect our attitudes to children; they also influence our attitudes towards ourselves and our teaching. A professional teacher is self-driven to achieve, to improve on current levels of knowledge and skills and to develop classroom effectiveness, within realistic and achievable limits.

The professional teacher recognises the roles that are played beyond the classroom. They need to communicate sensitively with other adults, both inside and outside their school, and with parents. They should talk sensitively, and without favour or bias, about children's mathematical achievements and limitations. They should recognise the potential impact of their words on the aspirations of others and they need to tread a path that allows them to retain professional honesty without either being destructive or dismissive of children's achievements.

Resources and further reading

http://www.canteach.gov.uk/teaching/ (Teacher Training Agency for routes into teaching).

http://www.gttr.ac.uk/ (Graduate Teacher Training Registry GTTR – applications online for graduates).

http://www.dfes.gov.uk/index.htm (Department for Education and Skills).

www.gtce.org.uk (General Teaching Council).

Mathematics in School and *Mathematics Teaching* (Journal sources of images and articles on Multicultural education and inclusion).

Mathematics Teaching (MT 112: 53) (Geometric images drawn outside houses in Madurai, S. India).

Buxton, L. (1981) *Do You Panic at Maths?: Coping with Maths Anxiety*. London: Heinemann Educational.

Makarenko, A. S. (1936) *The Road To Life*. Vols 1–3. Moscow: Foreign Languages Publishing House.

DfES/TTA (2002) *Qualifying to Teach: Professional Standards for Qualified Teacher Status and Requirements for Initial Teacher Training*. London: DfES/TTA.

Shuard, H. *et al.* (1990) *PrIME: Children, Mathematics and Learning*. London: Simon & Schuster.

Zaslavsky, C. (1990) *Africa Counts: Number and Pattern in African Culture*. New York: Lawrence Hill, Hill Books, Chicago.

16 Meeting the Standards for knowledge and understanding

The information contained in this section of the Standards covers the following:

Different types of knowledge	Standards
Subject knowledge	in relation to teaching children (2.1) in relation to passing the QTS skills tests (2.8)
Curriculum knowledge	in relation to the Foundation Stage, Key Stages 1 and 2 and the Literacy and Numeracy Strategies (2.1a, 2.1b, 2.2, 2.3)
Pedagogical knowledge	'know-how' in for example 'know how to use ICT effectively' (2.5)

> … these Standards require newly qualified teachers to be confident and authoritative in the subjects they teach and to have a clear understanding of how all pupils should progress and what teachers should expect them to achieve.
>
> (DfES/TTA, 2002: 2)

The Standards tend to rely on a fairly narrow, traditional view of knowledge and understanding. Of course, we need to look carefully at what the Standards require, but we also need to look beyond them, especially to recent research in the study of brain function, learning strategies and the way we organise personal knowledge, which has led to new ideas about how classrooms and teaching can be made more effective.

Recent ideas about how we learn are not fully represented in the Standards even though trainees are expected to consider how pupils' learning can be affected by their physical, intellectual, linguistic, social, cultural and emotional development (2.4), a requirement which demands deep and thorough knowledge of recent research. In one sense, the current Standards could be seen as a minimum which many trainees will in fact exceed.

The main knowledge emphasis in the Professional Standards is on cognition, although there is recognition that affective knowledge is important; trainees should know a range of strategies to promote good behaviour and establish a purposeful learning environment (2.7).

We need to be aware of the work of people like Howard Gardner and Daniel Goleman and writers like Guy Claxton who has produced excellent summaries of what we currently know about learning. There are also a huge number of national and local initiatives and school-based projects, such as *A Place 2 Be*, which provides counselling for children in schools.

The range and quantity of knowledge required by teachers to function effectively is enormous. Classifying it into different categories can be very useful because it helps us to monitor our own professional development, not only through the initial training period but beyond, after gaining Qualified Teacher Status.

An important influence on the classification of knowledge for teachers and teaching has been the work of Shulman (1987) and this has been used very effectively more recently by Turner-Bisset (1999).

Although it is impossible to strictly categorise knowledge using completely impermeable boundaries, each of Shulman's categories does have a distinct 'flavour' that can help us think about our developing knowledge and understanding (Table 16.1).

Table 16.1 Classifying the wide range of knowledge that teachers need to develop

Knowledge categories based on Shulman (1987)	Examples of the knowledge and understanding that belongs in each category
Content knowledge	Being well informed and having knowledge of mathematical topics and general ideas. A personal enthusiasm and a feeling for mathematics that extend beyond the classroom and what you teach children. Interest could be expressed in personal enjoyment of things like statistics from sporting almanacs, astronomy, calendars from different cultures, designing your own knitting patterns, making your own clothes, writing codes and code-breaking, writing software.
Curriculum knowledge	Familiarity with the mathematics contained in the NC and the NNS. Knowledge of the mathematics content of a school's medium term planning. Knowledge of useful resources to support teaching and learning.
General pedagogical knowledge	Knowledge and a grasp of general teaching strategies for working with children. Know-how that helps you set up learning groups, organise children and resources for a clear purpose and in pursuit of effective learning. Skill with techniques such as; story-telling, using puppets, role-play, direct exposition, doing practical activities, making up songs, teaching introductions and plenary sessions. It implies knowledge of theories of learning and models of teaching.
Pedagogical-content knowledge	Managing the specific challenges we face when teaching and learning maths. Knowing how to adapt general pedagogical strategies for organising learning. Selecting appropriate strategies to meet the specific demands of learning mathematics. How to organise and employ teaching strategies around the most effective resources and discourse. Knowing several very different ways to teach conversion of decimals, fractions and percentages.
Knowledge of learners and their characteristics	Knowing about individuals as people and their learning styles. How to help a new arrival cope with their new class. An understanding of child development, children's personal interests, and their age-related games and activities, learning strengths and difficulties. Issues relating to SEN and the more able.

(Continued)

Table 16.1 Continued

Knowledge categories based on Shulman (1987)	Examples of the knowledge and understanding that belongs in each category
Knowledge of practical contexts for learning, schools as communities and schools in relation to the wider community	Knowing how to explore different aspects of a maths topic in PE, in the school hall, in the playground, using a table-top game. Knowing why children can be more disruptive in certain teaching contexts than others, how the same class needs to be managed differently in different places; indoors in a practical session, the playground, swimming pool, school visit, assembly. Knowing how the school promotes mathematics beyond the classroom.
Knowledge of educational ends, purposes, values.	Saying what you believe in terms of children's entitlement and why you want to teach. (It may be easier to explore educational aims following the introduction of the Standards relating to Professional Values.)

Content knowledge

Shulman (1987) describes content knowledge by referring to teaching as a learned profession with teachers' knowledge 'resting on two foundations: the accumulated literature and studies in the content areas, and the historical and philosophical scholarship on the nature of knowledge in those fields of study' (p. 9). It implies that we need a broad, informed world view of the current and historical impact of mathematics on our own culture and other cultures: a feeling for the subject throughout the subject domain.

Curriculum knowledge

Knowledge of the National Curriculum (NC) Orders and the National Numeracy Strategy (NNS) Framework, for example, allows us to judge what will be covered over the Key Stage, the year and each half-term. It indirectly guides us to other material. If, for example, we feel unprepared to teach some aspects of statistics in Y6, we know that we need to achieve a deeper knowledge of the curriculum if we are to teach the topic successfully. It includes knowledge of the way the curriculum is presented in work books and text books and other published materials and resources.

General pedagogical knowledge

We could say generalisable, rather than stick with Shulman's word – general. As we train, we rehearse and build a wide repertoire of teaching techniques. For example, we can quickly organise a whole class plenary using an interactive whiteboard, following a practical activity session where children worked in pairs and small groups. We can teach a formal and interesting lesson for 45 minutes on using an angle measurer and compasses and can transfer our skills to a very different teaching context. We learn how to explain, discuss and question children in classrooms, and help individuals to use these same strategies to talk about mathematics to their peers.

Having acquired these techniques and strategies, we need to take a further step. We need to learn how to call upon them in very different contexts: so that we do not think of using puppets only in art and drama but also in mathematics. We need to integrate our teaching strategies so that they become available as professional choices when we plan lessons across the curriculum. We can achieve this only when our full repertoire of techniques is available to us during planning for a particular class or group of children, and in relation to the particular aspect of mathematics we intend to teach. When we can do this, we have gone beyond the basic practising of techniques. We have subordinated the techniques to our own learning.

Pedagogical–content knowledge

This knowledge base develops out of, and depends on the others. Working creatively with this knowledge base is how we demonstrate professional expertise in action. It occurs when expert teachers intuitively explore the interactions between the other knowledge bases and draw these different forms of knowledge together to inform their know-how, their performance, their art.

Many beginning teachers work towards this very rapidly in some subjects and contexts during training, but evidence suggests (Turner-Bisset, 1999) that some beginning teachers tend not to be able to call up all the relevant knowledge bases and integrate them to solve a particular set of problems they may face with certain lessons and children. This may be because of an inability to synthesise fully or successfully; but is more likely to be caused by one or more of the knowledge bases being weak, so that there is not sufficient knowledge available to be drawn on.

Pedagogical-content knowledge is the blending of content and pedagogy into an understanding of how particular topics or problems can be organised into lessons and learning opportunities. Two very different examples of sources in mathematics to support this knowledge integration, are Deboys and Pitt (1992) who explore links between the internal hierarchy of mathematical ideas, and the way that children build conceptual knowledge and skills. A second example is the NNS support material *Teaching Mental Calculation Strategies* (1999), which shows how the use of the number line to teach mental calculation strategies requires us to combine our understanding of the metaphorical representation of mathematical relations through the use of number lines, with knowledge of the conceptual challenges facing children when they tackle number calculation in this way.

Knowledge of learners and their characteristics

To teach effectively, we need to know something of child development and the way these ideas can shape teachers' decisions about the organising of classroom experiences for effective learning and teaching. Notions of why and how to support (scaffold) learning, for example, can be drawn from the work of Vygotsky (1978) and from developments of Piaget's ideas, by Bruner (1986: 95–98); Donaldson (1978), and particularly in mathematics, by Hughes (1986) and Skemp (1989).

We also acquire other important and more general knowledge of learners. What are 8-year-olds generally like? What do many 10-year-olds love to read? What is the latest craze sweeping the playground? Why is it that if we are over-protective or dismissive of the concerns of distressed children ('Never mind dear, I'm sure it'll be alright soon.') some may react by confiding more with their peers and much less with us? Social knowledge allows us to tune in to particular age groups and become aware of how they typically respond in class and group situations. A teacher who has planned a competitive class game as part of a maths lesson may choose to modify this into quiet paired work, on a day when the children are excited by the arrival of the school photographer.

Knowledge of practical contexts for learning

We need to know how to use the resources and physical spaces to teach mathematics effectively and the time needed by different learners to engage in meaningful learning. We learn how differently children behave in different settings: how some settings calm them whilst others stimulate them. We learn to use breathing, stimulation, relaxation and yoga techniques to aid concentration and mindfulness, particularly when children are tired, excited or anxious.

We learn to organise the space in which we work to achieve our goals. Knowledge of educational contexts also implies knowledge of how we respond best during school-based training, how mentors may try to support us and why they might not give the support we expect. We learn about how to behave in school as a privileged adult with the right of access as a professional, how to respond to parents, to the head teacher's expectations of us in relation to the school. We learn that despite being geographically close, two schools can feel entirely different. We learn about catchment areas, class sizes, children's and teacher's attitudes to mathematics, the time given over to mathematics in the curriculum, the role and expectations of mathematics coordinators or subject leaders.

Knowledge of educational ends, purposes, values

It has been notoriously difficult to discuss national educational purposes in Britain without creating a duality where discussion gets stuck between opposing notions of development of the individual (where nurturing, flowering and blossoming metaphors are often used), and notions of utilitarianism which argue for developing skills in the workforce and ensuring appropriate training for the next generation of workers and wealth creators. The introduction of the Standards for Professional Values may make for more fruitful discussion in future and less polarised debates on the purposes of education.

The training process is very demanding in terms of new learning. Thinking about knowledge and understanding in the above categories can give structure to your own learning process and provide a useful focus. It is impossible to learn all that is made available during training: trainees need to be very selective in relation to need. Identifying personal needs is easier when we can think about categories of knowledge and skills. This approach helps us to

- organise what has to be learned to meet the Standards;
- develop our strengths;
- work on areas of need;
- organise our learning efficiently.

The Standards for knowledge and understanding

The eight standards for knowledge and understanding make demands which can be read in terms of Shulman's areas. Some of the Standards are very focused and demand knowledge in one particular area, others are more complex and meeting them requires knowledge across several of Shulman's categories.

When tackling the more complex Standards you will need to build up and draw together the different related knowledge that is required for meeting the Standard. Shulman's categories show us where to go to build up these different areas of knowledge.

It is not a good idea just to write down what you cannot do. The approach is too negative and the result can be a block to further action. Where you have not met a Standard in full, highlight the part that you have met, then try to describe what you actually need to do to fully meet it. If you have only met the Standard in a narrow sense and want to become more robust in that area of your training, write down the action that you need to take.

A positive way to start is by thinking about the areas where you tend to feel most comfortable. A personal commentary might read: I know a lot of history, geography and science. I am really interested in music. I have never really understood school timetables and how the whole school is organised – how all the bits fit together. I really love helping individuals to learn but I am nervous about trying to organise a whole class of 8–9 year-olds. Based on your personal statement, consider what your priorities should be (Table 16.2).

Table 16.2 Monitoring progress towards meeting the Standards for knowledge and understanding

Précis of the Standards for knowledge and understanding	*I need to take the following action:*
These Standards demand curriculum knowledge together with a deeper and wider knowledge of mathematics content that goes beyond the classroom.	
• I have a secure knowledge and understanding of the subjects for which I am training to teach (2.1).	
• In relation to specific phases which are relevant for me: … I know and understand … the Curriculum Guidance for the Foundation Stage and for Reception children, the frameworks, methods and expectations set out in the National Literacy and Numeracy Strategies … (2.1a).	
• I know and understand the curriculum for each of the National Curriculum core subjects, … the NLS and NNS. I have sufficient understanding of a range of work across [the non-core subjects] to be able to teach them in the age range for which I am trained, with advice from an experienced colleague where necessary (2.1b).	
• I know and understand the Values, Aims and Purposes and the General Requirements set out in the NC Handbook…. I am familiar with the National Curriculum Framework for Personal, Social, and Health Education [which for KS1 and KS2 includes Citizenship] (2.2)	
• I am aware of expectations, typical curricula and teaching arrangements in the Key Stages or	

(Continued)

Table 16.2 Continued

Précis of the Standards for knowledge and understanding	*I need to take the following action:*

phases before and after the ones for which
I am trained to teach (2.3).

This Standard requires knowledge of learners
  and their characteristics.
- I understand how pupils' learning can be affected
  by their physical, intellectual, linguistic, social,
  cultural and emotional development (2.4).

This Standard requires pedagogical-content
  knowledge of ways to teach ICT and
  knowledge of practical contexts for learning
  to use ICT in varied settings.
- I know how to use ICT effectively, both to
  teach and to support my wider professional
  role (2.5).

This Standard requires pedagogical-content
  Knowledge of how to support SEN children
  in maths lessons, knowledge of learners and
  their characteristics so as to meet individual
  needs, knowledge of practical contexts for
  learning, schools as communities and schools in
  relation to the wider community so as to be
  able to reduce individual difficulties and
  recognise social and cultural factors related to
  English as an additional language when
  teaching mathematics.
- I understand my responsibilities under the SEN
  Code of Practice, and know how to seek
  advice from specialists on less common types
  of special educational needs (2.6).

This Standard demands general pedagogical
  knowledge of general strategies for the
  management of individuals and groups within
  maths lessons, pedagogical-content knowledge
  in order to teach maths topics effectively and
  know why children can find the subject
  problematic, Knowledge of learners and their
  characteristics so that potential problems can
  be planned for, in advance. Knowledge of
  practical contexts for learning so that changes
  in routine, use of resources maximises interest
  and motivation.
- I know a range of strategies to promote good
  behaviour and establish a purposeful learning
  environment (2.7).

This Standard requires Content Knowledge of
  mathematics beyond what you may be teaching
  in school.
- I have passed the Qualified Teacher Status skills
  tests in numeracy, literacy and ICT (2.8).

Resources and further reading

http://www.canteach.gov.uk/teaching/ (Teacher Training Agency for routes into teaching).

http://www.dfes.gov.uk/index.htm (Department for Education and Skills).

www.gtce.org.uk (General Teaching Council).

http://el.webportalpro.com/comdir/cditem.cfm?NID=259 (*A Place 2 Be*).

Bruner, J. (1986) *Actual Minds, Possible Worlds*. Cambridge, MA: Harvard University Press.

Claxton, G. (1999) *Wise Up: The Challenge of Lifelong Learning*. London: Bloomsbury.

Deboys, M. and Pitt, E. (1992) *Lines of Development in Primary Mathematics*. Belfast: Blackstaff Press.

Donaldson, M. (1978) *Children's Minds*. London: Fontana Press.

Gardner, H. (1999) *Intelligence Reframed: Multiple Intelligences for the 21st Century*. New York: Basic Books.

Goleman, D. (1996) *Emotional Intelligence: Why it Can Matter more than IQ*. London: Bloomsbury.

Hughes, M. (1986) *Children and Number: Difficulties in Learning Mathematics*. London: Basil Blackwell.

Shulman, L. S. (1987) Knowledge and Teaching: foundations of the new reform. *Harvard Educational Review*, 57, 1–22.

Skemp, R. (1989) *Mathematics in the Primary School*. London: Routledge.

Turner-Bisset, R. (1999) Knowledge Bases for Teaching. *British Educational Research Journal*, 25(1), 39–55.

Vygotsky, L. (1978) *Mind and Society*. Cambridge, MA: Harvard University Press.

17 Meeting the Standards for teaching

The Standards for teaching are organised into the following three sections.

1   Planning, expectations and targets
2   Monitoring and assessment
3   Teaching and class management.

These are the most complex and demanding of the published Standards. Teaching draws together all the various skills learnt during training. To teach effectively teachers need to synthesise curriculum knowledge, pedagogical knowledge, knowledge of learners and contexts for learning. They need to integrate this knowledge with their understanding of the way in which the school functions as a community and how it relates to other communities.

Teaching

> … these Standards relate to skills of planning, monitoring and assessment, and teaching and class management. They are underpinned by the values and knowledge covered in the first two sections.
>
> (DfES/TTA, 2002: 3)

To teach effectively, teachers need to establish good professional relationships quickly, both with other professionals and with children. Trainees need to understand themselves well enough to know how they can prepare themselves to teach, learn how to produce detailed lesson planning, how to organise groups, deploy resources, assess children and evaluate their own performance.

They need to gain a working knowledge of each school's curriculum documents and materials and build up their own resources so that they can act as autonomous professionals who are not dependent on the immediate availability of key materials that may be in limited supply or being used by somebody else.

Trainees need to be able to differentiate support within the classroom and make difficult decisions in-the-moment about how to proceed with their lesson and with the management of their children. They need to become efficient at record keeping and managing all the paperwork related to school and to their own training.

Teacher attitude

By observing children and working with them, one can get a sense of their intellectual powers in the most unexpected situations. I arranged a visit to an infant school in Southampton
for a group of trainee teachers from Winchester and some American elementary school vis-
itors from Illinois. I was observing a 4-year-old with a metre stick working outdoors by the
school pond. He was dipping the stick into the pond then removing it, and looking at the
numbers where the stick changed from wet to dry. He could read the whole centimetres in
the range 20–80 and was obviously able to approximate, because he was looking at the nearest whole centimetre to the watermark. He then said the number out loud to himself before
repeating the activity. He could feel, as he prodded, that the bottom of the pond was uneven
and he dipped the stick at a different angle each time. Nevertheless he persisted for several
minutes and was very absorbed in the task. I asked him what he had found out. He said he
was thinking about how much water was in the pond. I asked if he thought he would be
able to find out by using the stick. After a few seconds thinking time, he said that he would
need to know how much water was under the stick each time he put the end of the stick
onto the surface of the pond. I was impressed by this, because he was able to see how to
modify his initial activity. He had created a mind picture of a small column of water beneath
the stick. Then what clinched it for me was his final statement. 'They'd all be different. You'd
need to touch the stick onto the water lots and lots of times until you'd touched it every-
where, then you'd know.' Anyone who has tried to think about calculus will recognise the
insight that this 4-year-old had expressed. He was on the edge of summing to infinity, as
well as somewhat precariously, on the edge of the pond.

   Research from Hay McBer (2000) suggests that classroom climate is a key factor in high performance. It is useful to compare these findings with those of Carol Dweck reported by Guy
Claxton (1990) . One of the key influences of climate is teacher attitude and the expectations
of teachers in relation to children's performance. Children who work in classrooms with teachers who believe in their intellectual skills, tend to produce those intellectual skills. Children, who
are thought to be meagre intellectually, tend to end up that way. We have to tell children, 'You
can do it!' We also need to believe that they can, and we need a very high level of professional
skill to provide the learning context that makes high achievement possible.

Effective planning

At the beginning of training, planning may mean being able to decide how to get yourself
and some resources ready, in order to work with a small group of children on part of a lesson topic organised by a practising teacher.

   By the end of training, planning will mean something very different and you will need
to demonstrate high levels of skill. Planning will then involve a long and complex set of
inter-related skills and decisions. In the check list below, there are some examples of the
complex skills and strategies that need to be acquired over time.

   It is useful to make a positive statement about your own development, against each
example. You could use the traffic light approach by colour coding in green what you can
do. Only use red and amber for fairly intractable difficulties that you do not seem to be able
to resolve and for which you need to take action. It is not necessary or helpful to colour

examples when you have not had the opportunity to practice. Remember, the whole point of training is to provide opportunities to steadily acquire the skills – and most of us do this, if we take responsibility for our own actions and look for ways to create opportunities for ourselves.

Effective management

As a trainee you need to manage a variety of groups of children in many different physical spaces and move them from one space into another quickly and quietly. You will need to establish your own style and way of doing things, within the general class rules and school policy, so the children get to enjoy learning with you. The more classroom routines you can establish and the earlier you establish them, for example, handing out resources, moving children from one part of the classroom to another, the more likely you and the children will become free to teach and learn.

When children know the routine for beginning and ends of lessons, when they know who does the tidying up, how the chairs are arranged and when equipment is handed out and put away, these aspects of teaching become automated and relegated to the level of important but routine.

When children know what to expect during the lesson, they are calmer and more focused. Putting up a notice at the beginning of each lesson in a conspicuous place and reading it to the children, 'In this lesson we will be …' is very useful in focusing their attention. When the routines are established, the focus of the lesson is learning.

Maintaining a balance between management and teaching

When management issues become the major points of discussion between teacher and children and lessons are dominated by telling children when they should and should not talk, who has to clear up, and so on, then the quality of lessons can deteriorate quickly.

- Teaching and learning may not get started, or may occupy only a tiny part of the lesson.
- Children who want to work cannot think about the mathematics because class discussion is mainly about who has got the pencil sharpener, how long before the bell goes, and who is talking, who should not be.
- The children get bored and annoyed and can become steadily more and more difficult to control.

The one thing that children are very clear about is that they hate teachers who constantly shout. They can be happy with very strict teachers, easy going teachers, consistent teachers, but shouting teachers are unpredictable, scary and upsetting.

The nosedive in lesson quality, when it happens, is rapid. It can only be avoided by balancing management and control issues against moving the lesson forward and maintaining pace. Getting on with teaching something interesting and achievable, with good pace, is the only solution to re-stimulating bored and fractious children.

Initially, we may be nervous about letting the children do things independently, and we continue to talk to them for far too long, because we are anxious about how to control less formal situations and practical activities. We may be unconsciously avoiding the start of the less formal, more fluid part of the lesson.

Most of us have experienced a difficult period at the beginning of training when it feels as though the only thing we are doing is nagging the children. Control, discipline and constant reminders of the rules occupy large chunks of lessons. We need to persist in demanding high standards, but crucially, there is also an urgent need to produce really simple but absorbing lessons so that children are distracted from misbehaving by the excitement of learning. We need to make learning the easy option.

The lessons must contain activities which allow children to practise the class and school rules, which must not be in contravention of wider rules of society that children are expected to keep as part of their cultural and ethnic origins. The lesson content has to have a good pace and be

- sufficiently interesting to absorb the children's attention;
- sufficiently difficult to be intellectually challenging;
- easy enough for everyone to achieve some success;
- accessible for those of different language and social backgrounds;
- respectful of individual children's values and beliefs, their cultural identities and their religious affiliations.

Classroom organisation differs across Europe. In many countries, furniture is organised to allow whole-class teaching where every child can see everyone else's face. This is usually achieved by organising in a U shape. The purpose is to help sustain discussion. We find it easier to support extended discussion when we are facing the person we are talking to. Ask the class teacher's advice about moving the furniture and be prepared for resistance on occasions. There is something symbolic about classroom layout as well as practical. It is a personalised space, even when this is not recognised by the teacher who occupies it. You may find you meet a curious resistance when you suggest alterations to the layout of the classroom. Nevertheless, it is worth persisting because we react so personally to the space around us. One teacher will find a particular configuration supportive whilst another will find the same arrangement disruptive to their teaching. Do not constantly change the layout, but at different times and over a period of time, try U-shaped arrangements, groupings of 4–6, pairs, circles, and so on. Monitor the children's reactions to the space as well as your own preferences.

The need to meet the Standards progressively

Where there are distinct phases to training, it is more productive to phase the acquisition of knowledge and professional ability. Like other institutions that care for their trainees, The College of St Mark and St John in Plymouth have successfully[1] tried to stage the introduction and meeting of the Standards over the training period in relation to different school-based training opportunities. Each phase of the training is organised to maximise the opportunities for steady professional development.

The first school-based training opportunities tend to be shorter, orientating experiences, where trainees gain familiarity about how classrooms and schools function in general terms.

Table 17.1 Part of the School Experience Profile showing progressive working towards the Standards over three phases of training (St Mark and St John, Plymouth)

Planning	Phase 1	Phase 2	Phase 3
Matching of work to children	With guidance matches work to class or age group. Has respect for, and expectations of children's work. Aware of pupils' special educational needs.	Sets some challenging tasks. Demonstrates appropriate expectations. Considers IEPs in planning. Plans for positive behaviour.	Sets tasks for whole class, individual and group work, including homework, which challenge pupils and ensure high levels of pupil interest. Sets appropriate and demanding expectations for pupils' learning, motivation and presentation of work. Identifies pupils who have special educational needs, including specific learning difficulties, are very able, are not yet fluent in English. Knows where to obtain help in order to give positive and targeted support in En, Ma, Sc, ICT and relevant foundation subjects.
Classroom organisation and resources: physical and human	Adequate preparation of resources and classroom organisation. Thinks ahead and plans ahead. Plans to avoid potential hazards.	Plans the work of other contributing adults. Plans to vary organisation of classroom to match activities and lesson objectives. Adequate organisation of a widening range of resources including ICT.	Organises pupils, resources and space to provide for class, group and individual learning. Familiar with subject-specific health and safety requirements where relevant, and plans lessons to avoid potential hazards.

They are often focused on particular themes. One of the themes in the first phase of training could be about working with groups of children of very different ability within a single class. In contrast, whole-class teaching may not be such a key issue as it will be in later phases. Standards can be worked on systematically and this approach helps to reduce the feeling of being overwhelmed.

By setting out the Standards and their component knowledge and skills in a developmental way, trainees can experience progress during each phase of training and between successive phases. They can see the progress they make by using their personal copy of the institution's training profile and by recording their achievement. They are expected to take responsibility for self-assessment and to record their own development against phase-related statements like the ones shown in Table 17.1.

Table 17.2 Monitoring progress towards meeting the Standards for teaching

Précis of the Standards for teaching	I need to take the following action:
This is a very hard standard to achieve because of its complexity. It demands curriculum knowledge together with general pedagogical knowledge and pedagogical-content knowledge, combined with knowledge of learners and their characteristics, and knowledge of practical contexts for learning.	
• I set challenging teaching and learning objectives based on knowledge of pupils, knowledge of expected performance for the age group, and the appropriate type of work that should be provided for the age range (3.1.1).	
These Standards demand curriculum knowledge relating to assessment, pedagogical-content knowledge in relation to SEN, knowledge of learners and their characteristics, and knowledge of practical contexts for learning, schools as communities and schools in relation to the wider community.	
• I plan for individual lessons and sequences of lessons, showing how pupils will be assessed. My teaching is supportive, sensitive to needs, and ensures the progress of boys and girls from all ethnic groups (3.1.2). • I plan and use resources effectively, and with sensitivity to children's interests, language and cultural backgrounds (3.1.3).	
This Standard demands curriculum knowledge, pedagogical-content knowledge, knowledge of learners and their characteristics, knowledge of practical contexts for learning, schools as communities and schools in relation to the wider community.	

(Continued)

Table 17.2 Continued

Précis of the Standards for teaching	*I need to take the following action:*

- I collaborate with teachers in school, contribute to the school community, guide and direct other adults within lessons (3.1.4).

This Standard demands, content knowledge, knowledge of practical contexts for learning, schools as communities and schools in relation to the wider community.

- I plan to use a wide range of contexts for learning, in school and beyond (3.1.5).

These Standards demand curriculum knowledge, pedagogical-content knowledge, and knowledge of learners and their characteristics.

- I reflect on monitoring and assessment to improve practice. I use a range of strategies to evaluate children's progress (3.2.1).
- I monitor and assess during teaching. I provide immediate constructive feedback to promote success, and I can show children how to reflect, assess and evaluate their own learning (3.2.2).
- I assess progress against early learning goals and foundation stage frameworks, NC level descriptions, NC assessment frameworks and national objectives, for my phase of training, with guidance from experienced colleagues where necessary (3.2.3).
- I give appropriate differentiated support to children of high, average and below average achievement, and those experiencing problems through behavioural, emotional and social difficulties, with guidance from experienced colleagues where necessary (3.2.4).
- I identify levels of attainment in English when it is being used as an additional language, and analyse language demands [in relation to mathematics teaching and learning]. I ensure appropriate intellectual challenge, give language support [and ensure full access to the mathematics curriculum] (3.2.5).
- I systematically record children's progress and achievements, and provide evidence of attainment and progress over time using a range of work. I discuss children's progress with them, review their assessed work and help children plan and set targets (3.2.6).
- I use records as a basis for accurately reporting children's attainment and progress, orally and in writing to parents, carers, other professionals and to the children themselves (3.2.7).

(*Continued*)

Table 17.2 Continued

Précis of the Standards for teaching	*I need to take the following action:*
These Standards demand curriculum knowledge, general pedagogical knowledge, pedagogical-content knowledge, knowledge of learners and their characteristics, knowledge of contexts for learning.	

- I have high expectations of children. I build successful relationships centred on teaching and learning, and a purposeful learning environment where diversity is valued and where children feel secure and confident (3.3.1).
- In relation to my phase of training, I can *competently and independently*, teach the required knowledge, develop children's understanding and skills, covering all six areas of learning in the Foundation Stage Guidance, NLS and NNS for Reception children, and for children at KS1 and KS2, the relevant core subjects (of English and the NLS, mathematics and the NNS, and science).
  For all other curriculum subjects included in my training, I can teach a range of work independently, with advice from experienced colleagues where necessary (3.3.2).

These Standards demand, curriculum knowledge, general pedagogical knowledge, pedagogical-content knowledge, knowledge of learners and their characteristics, knowledge of contexts for learning.

- I motivate children through the teaching of clearly structured lessons. I make learning objectives clear to children, encourage collaborative work, use interactive teaching methods, promote active and independent thinking, and encourage children to take responsibility for their own learning (3.3.3).
- I differentiate my teaching to meet the needs of all pupils including the most able and those with SEN, with advice from experienced colleagues where necessary (3.3.4).
- I support children with English as an additional language [to ensure full access to the mathematics curriculum] with advice from experienced colleagues where necessary (3.3.5).
- I organise and manage teaching and learning time effectively (3.3.7).
- I organise and manage resources, equipment and the physical space safely and effectively, with the help of experienced colleagues where necessary (3.3.8).

(Continued)

Table 17.2 Continued

Précis of the Standards for teaching	*I need to take the following action:*
• I have taken responsibility for a class or classes over a sustained and substantial period, and I can teach across the age and ability range for which I have been trained (3.3.11).	
• I encourage children to work independently by providing homework and other work beyond the classroom which consolidates and extends work carried out in class (3.3.12).	
• I work collaboratively with colleagues including specialist teachers. With the help of colleagues where necessary, I manage the work of teaching assistants and other adults (3.3.13).	
These Standards demand curriculum knowledge, general pedagogical knowledge, knowledge of learners and their characteristics, knowledge of practical contexts for learning, schools as communities and schools in relation to the wider community.	
• I help girls and boys make good progress by taking account of their varying interests, experiences and achievements, and their cultural and ethnic backgrounds (3.3.6).	
• I set high expectations for children's behaviour, establish clear framework for classroom management and discipline, manage children's behaviour constructively, anticipate potential problems, and promote children's self-control and independence (3.3.9).	
• I recognise and respond effectively to equal opportunities issues as they arise in the classroom. I challenge stereotyped views, bullying and harassment. I follow relevant policies and procedures (3.3.14).	

Note

1 Extract from OFSTED report on assessment. Arrangements for the assessment of trainees are coherent and well-managed, particularly at the pass/fail borderline. Assessment is well integrated with the training, for example, the evaluation by schools of each block of school experience is used to adjust training to remedy any common weaknesses identified by the schools.

18 Moving from initial training into the NQT year

In several ways, the NQT year begins before the training programme is finished. Applications and interviews for jobs can coincide with a long final school placement during the summer term. Most trainees are exhausted at this time. Long teaching days, full class responsibility, sore throats, lack of sleep, final assessment and, as the student group disperses at the end of the training period, the anticipated loss of recently found friends all contribute to an emotionally demanding time.

Not surprising then that an increasing number of trainees choose to travel abroad for a year rather than seek a post immediately. However, for the majority who intend to start work in school immediately, this is the point when your career begins to take off. Energy levels soar again once you receive the invitation to attend the interview.

There are several books and resources that you can draw on for detailed guidance and support through the transition to qualified teacher and into the first year of teaching as a NQT. A useful book will help you

- make a successful application to a job of your choice;
- revisit your values and confirm why you chose teaching as a career;
- consolidate what you have learnt during training;
- develop your *praxis* – your own personal way of putting theory into practice;
- extend your knowledge into new areas;
- help you integrate fully into the new workplace, whether it be a traditional setting in school or elsewhere;
- interpret the paperwork and expectations that come with the new job.

In *Getting Started*, Henry Liebling (1999) provides detailed information about the induction process: what your responsibilities and your entitlements are. He looks at the first year in terms of

- establishing yourself as a class teacher with full responsibility for a group of children for the year;
- organising yourself;
- managing behaviour;
- assessing and evaluating your performance as a NQT;
- different models of teaching;

- learning styles;
- what has been learned about learning from neuroscience;
- using knowledge about learning to become a more effective teacher;
- interpersonal and intrapersonal dynamics.

Applications and interviews

Finding advertisements for posts in school is relatively easy these days. There are many online web addresses to look at and the Times Educational Supplement has maintained its major role in advertising posts. Local authorities will send publicity and recruitment material to your training provider, either directly to the Primary Course Office or to the Careers Section.

The interviews for most posts which are advertised by schools, take place in front of school governors and usually in the school itself. In some of the larger cities there are interview 'pools' where the Local Education Authority (LEA) organises the initial selection. Education officers usually conduct these interviews in collaboration with experienced teachers and head teachers who are looking for new recruits to their school, so how you come across at these interviews can be more important than it might appear. This selection process often ends with a period of negotiation between successful applicants and the head teachers of local schools. You do not have to accept the first school that is offered but you do have to be diplomatic if you are going to keep your options open within the LEA.

Career Entry Profiles

Hopefully, mathematics will feature as one of your strengths. This does not mean that you are expected to have a formal qualification in mathematics, although for some people it will include an 'A'-level qualification or something equivalent. It does mean that you have shown that you can make a significant contribution to children's learning in mathematics within your chosen age range.

The Career Entry Profile (CEP) is an important document and you should be completing it as you move into the final phase of training. You will need to discuss it with your school-based mentor, the class teacher and possibly the head teacher. It is useful to include discussions about the CEP when you have meetings to evaluate the final phase of your school-based training. What you write in negotiation with your mentor should reflect and illustrate your professional strengths and achievements. It is vital that it also contains the areas that you intend to develop during your NQT year. These are not weaknesses and you should not identify them as such. The idea behind the CEP is that it supports a smooth transition from initial to continuing training. All teachers are required to engage in professional career development and for you, during the NQT year, the areas for development will be those which you consider will make the greatest impact to your professional effectiveness in the coming year.

Head teachers are expected to identify the development needs of all their staff in their School Development Plans, so they will want to hear from you as part of the interview what your continuing training needs will be. They should not encourage you to talk about weaknesses and you should avoid presenting them as such.

Preparing an application

Completing the application form properly and producing a good letter of application is crucial. You have to find a style which is positive but not too showy or pushy. Many people seriously undersell themselves at this point. If you have good ICT skills then download advice from the Internet and make a professional-looking CV.

Most advertisements ask for a letter of application to be included. I suggest avoiding writing lengthy paragraphs about 'my philosophy of teaching' even if you are asked to provide one. They can become very 'tacky' – it has been my life's ambition to work with children – and it is easy to be woolly and vague about what you can actually do. An alternative is to prepare the letter in a different way. Write down in note form just for yourself, what you believe in and what is important to you in teaching. Think about what you

- need for your own professional satisfaction;
- want to achieve for the children you teach;
- need a school to provide in order to work in the way that suits you best.

When you have done this, think about important incidents from your teaching experience during training. Choose incidents that show you putting your beliefs into practice and working in harmony with the school and its staff. Write these into your letter as very short (one line) examples of your effectiveness. Then match each one with a brief statement from your philosophy notes, about your beliefs and values. Treat these as 'philosophy in action' and present them as your personal achievements.

What this style of writing shows is that you are not an air-head, you can actually put your values into your teaching. The resulting letter becomes more personally confirming: what you are saying is, I have achieved these things during my training and they mean something important to me as a person and as a teacher. If necessary you can start this section of your letter with a sentence like: 'I will discuss my philosophy by referring to recent achievements in my teaching'. Share your letter and your completed application with a friend or a mentor so that you can check the style, accuracy, spelling and so on.

Interviews

When it comes to interview day, make sure that you see children at work, teachers in the staff room, parents in the playground and children at play. If you go for a pool interview this opportunity will come later when you are offered a school.

Try to get a sense of the whole school picture. You may well be asked to prepare and teach a lesson as part of the interview day. This is more difficult if you are invited to choose a lesson of your own, but discuss things with the school beforehand so you know exactly what is expected. The purpose of watching you teach is not to catch you out – it is to give every interviewee a similar experience to talk about during the formal interview.

People will want to see how you relate to children, rather than whether you know everything there is to know about division of fractions and the use of a calculator. So it is important to plan a lesson where there will be a lot of opportunity for informal activity and talk as well as formal interaction. Just keep things as simple as possible, let your personality be the thing that comes through.

When you are offered a job, do not automatically accept it, even though you may be under enormous financial and family pressure to get a job. A year in the wrong school can be miserable and the NQT year needs to be a success. Make sure you talk to the mathematics coordinator or subject leader about their current role and what they see are the big challenges ahead for the school. Check to see what might be expected of you and whether it fits what you want to be doing. Often NQTs are expected to shadow the subject leader during the year, to learn some part of the subject leader's job and to take some of the burden.

If possible, get into your new school during the term before you are due to start work and work with the children whom you will be teaching. This will calm their nerves as well as yours. Meet your induction tutor or mentor and discuss how you will work together. Take your CEP with you so that you can begin to discuss your strengths and needs in detail.

You will need to gather a large amount of information during early visits. The head teacher and your induction tutor will help you sort out the important, the urgent and the things that can be left until later. There are various sources of information that you will need. A typical list includes

- the general brochures, booklets and policy statements;
- the school handbook and prospectus;
- the current version of the development plan, into which your staff development needs will need to be fitted;
- curriculum documents, and schemes of work;
- data about the children you will be teaching;
- staff lists and contact numbers,
- a calendar for the coming period, with timetables if appropriate.

Organising yourself

Getting classroom routines established is a priority if you have a permanent appointment and your early efforts should pay dividends throughout the year. You may find you are not getting the teaching established as soon as you like. You need to remind yourself that even during the final training placement there is usually a class teacher who is continually supporting the teaching and the classroom management. Now it is just you. So get the management and organisation right. This will free you in a little while, to teach effectively.

You are the sole spokesperson for your class, so there will be a lot more items on your agenda when you are working full time than there were when you were training. You must manage your time creatively, if you are to survive and then add value to the class and the school. Along with time management skills, a further crucial skill is to make good decisions about important issues.

Organising your computer and your data files is crucial. Computers are central to teaching, learning, assessment and record keeping. It is vital that you become really efficient at managing the data that you need to access.

Resources and further reading

Bubb, S. (2000) *The Effective Induction of Newly Qualified Primary Teachers: An Induction Tutor's Handbook.* London: David Fulton.

Claxton, G. (1999) *Wise Up: The Challenge of Lifelong Learning.* London: Bloomsbury.

DfEE (1998) *Induction for New Teachers: A Consultation Document*. London: Department for Education and Employment.

DfES/TTA (2002) *Qualifying to Teach: Professional Standards for Qualified Teacher Status and Requirements for Initial Teacher Training*. London: DfES/TTA.

Hay McBer (2000) *A Model of Teacher Effectiveness*. Report by Hay McBer to the Department for Education and Employment – June 2000.

Liebling, H. (1999) *Getting Started: An Induction Guide for Newly Qualified Teachers*. School Effectiveness Series. Stafford: Network Educational Press.

O'Hara, M. (2000) *Teaching 3–8: Meeting the Standards for Initial Teacher Training and Induction*. London: Continuum Press.

Tickle, L. (2000) *Teacher Induction: The Way Ahead*. Buckingham: Open University Press.

References

Abbott, L. and Nutbrown, C. (eds) (2001) *Experiencing Reggio Emilia: Implications for Pre-school Provision.* Buckingham: Open University Press.

Abelson, H. (1986) *Turtle Geometry: The Computer as a Medium for Exploring Mathematics.* MIT Press.

Ainley, J. (1996) *Enriching Primary Mathematics with IT.* London: Hodder & Stoughton.

Ainley, J. (1999) *Doing Algebra type Stuff: Emergent Algebra in the Primary School.* Paper given at Psychology of Mathematics Education 1999, published in Proceedings of the 23rd Conference of PME, Vol. 2 1999 (2-9–2-16).

Alexander, R. (2000) *Culture and Pedagogy: International Comparisons in Primary Education.* Oxford: Blackwell.

Andrews, P. (1997) A Hungarian perspective on mathematics education. *Mathematics Teaching*, MT 161, December, pp. 14–17.

Anghileri, J. (ed.) (1995) *Children's Mathematical Thinking in the Primary Years.* London: Cassell.

Ashdan, C. and Overall, L. (eds) (1998) *Teaching in Primary Schools.* London: Cassell.

Askew, M. (1998) *Teaching Primary Mathematics.* London: Hodder and Stoughton.

Askew, M., Brown, M., Rhodes, V., Wiliam, D. and Johnson, D. (1997) *Effective Teachers of Numeracy: Report for the Teacher Training Agency.* London: King's College, University of London.

Assessment of Performance Unit (1991) *APU Mathematics Monitoring (Phase 2).* London: School Examination and Assessment Council.

Ball, S. J. (1990) *Politics and Policy-making in Education.* London: Routledge.

BEAM (Be a Mathematician: Exploring Series). www.beam.co.uk

Beishuizen, M. (1993) Mental strategies and materials or models for addition and subtraction up to 100 in Dutch second grades. *Journal for Research in Mathematics Education*, 24(4), pp. 294–323.

Beishuizen, M. (1997) Mental arithmetic: mental recall or mental strategies? *Mathematics Teaching*, 160, September, pp. 16–19.

Beishuizen, M. (1998) Which mental strategies in the early number curriculum? A comparison of British ideas and Dutch views. *British Educational Research Journal*, 24(5), December, pp. 519–539.

Bettelheim, B. (1976) *The Uses of Enchantment: The Meaning and Importance of Fairy Tales.* Thames and Hudson.

Black, P. and Wiliam, D. (2002) *Inside the Black Box: Raising Standards Through Classroom Assessment.* London: King's College (Department of Education and Professional Studies).

Blinko, J. and Graham, N. (1994) *Mathematical Beginnings: Problem Solving for Young Children.* Claire Publications.

Briggs, M. and Pritchard, A. (2002) *Using ICT in Primary Mathematics Teaching.* Exeter: Learning Matters.

Britzman, D.P. and Pitt, A. J. (1996) Pedagogy and transference: casting the past of learning into the presence of teaching. *Theory into Practice, Situated Pedagogies*, 35(2) Spring. College of Education, Ohio State University.

Brousseau, G. (1997) *Theory of Didactical Situations in Mathematics*. Dordrecht: Kluwer Publications.

Brown, M. (1996) The context of the research – the evolution of the national curriculum for mathematics. In: D.C. Johnson and A. Millett (eds) *Implementing the Mathematics National Curriculum: Policy, Politics and Practice*. London: Paul Chapman.

Brown, M. (1999) Swings of the roundabout. In: I. Thompson (ed.) *Issues in Teaching Numeracy in Primary Schools*. Buckinghamshire: Open University Press.

Brown, M. (2001) Numeracy policy. In: M. Askew and M. Brown (eds) Teaching and learning primary numeracy: policy, practice and effectiveness. *BERA Review*. British Educational Research Association. Southwell: Nottinghamshire.

Brown, T. (1998) *Coordinating Mathematics across the Primary School*. London: Falmer Press.

Bruner, J. (1986) *Actual Minds, Possible Worlds*. Cambridge, MA: Harvard University Press.

Bruner, J. (1996) *Culture and Education*. Cambridge, MA: Harvard University Press.

Bubb, S. (2000) *The Effective Induction of Newly Qualified Primary Teachers: An Induction Tutor's Handbook*. London: David Fulton.

Burton, L. (2002) Reconsidering curriculum – a reflection on values and vision. *British Educational Research Journal (Thematic Review)*, 28(5), October 2002, pp. 723–729.

Buxton, L. (1981) *Do You Panic at Maths? Coping with Maths Anxiety*. London: Heinemann Educational.

Buzan, T. (1993) *Mind Map Book*. London: BBC Books.

Buzan, T. (1995) *Use Your Head*. London: BBC Books.

Carter, R. (1998) *Mapping the Mind*. Weidenfeld and Nicolson.

Caviglioli, O. and Harris, I. (2000) *Map Wise*. Stafford: Network Educational Press.

Central Advisory Council for England (1967) *Children and Their Primary Schools* (Plowden Report). London: HMSO.

Clarke, S. (1998) *Targeting Assessment in the Primary Classroom: Strategies for Planning, Assessment, Pupil Feedback and Target Setting*. London: Hodder & Stoughton.

Clarke, S. and Atkinson, S. (1996) *Tracking Significant Achievement in Primary Mathematics*. London: Hodder & Stoughton.

Claxton, G. (1990) *Teaching to Learn: A Direction for Education*. London: Cassell.

Claxton, G. (1997) *Hare Brain, Tortoise Mind: Why Intelligence Increases When you Think Less*. London: Fourth Estate.

Claxton, G. (1999) *Wise Up: the Challenge of Lifelong Learning*. London: Bloomsbury.

Cockburn, A.D. (1999) *Teaching Mathematics with Insight*. London: Falmer Press.

Cockcroft, W.H. (1982) *Mathematics Counts*. Report of the Committee of Enquiry into the Teaching of Mathematics in Schools. London: HMSO.

Connor, C. (1999a) Two Steps Forward, One Step Back: progression in children's learning. *Primary File* 36, pp. 141–144.

Connor, C. (ed.) (1999b) *Assessment in Action in the Primary School*. London: Falmer Press.

Cooper, B. and Dunne, M. (2000) *Assessing Children's Mathematical Knowledge*. Buckingham: Open University Press.

Croll, P. and Hastings, N. (eds) (1996) *Effective Primary Teaching: Research Based Classroom Strategies*. London : David Fulton.

Damasio, A. (1999) *The Feeling of What Happens: Body and Emotion in the Making of Consciousness*. Sandiego, CA: Harcourt.

Day, C. (ed.) (2000) *The Life and Work of Teachers: International Perspectives in Changing Times*. London: Falmer Press.

Dearing, R. (1993) *Interim Report on the National Curriculum and its Assessments*. London: DfEE.

De Bono, E. (1976) *Teaching Thinking*. Harmondworth: Penguin.

De Bono, E. (1998) *Simplicity*. London: Viking (Penguin).

Deboys, M. and Pitt, E. (1992) *Lines of Development in Primary Mathematics*. Belfast: Blackstaff Press.

Dennison, P. and Dennison, G. (1986) *Brain Gym*. Edu-Kinaesthetics.

DES (1985) *Better Schools*. Presented to Parliament by the Secretary of State for Education and Science. London: HMSO.

DfEE (1998a) *Induction for New Teachers: A Consultation Document*. London: Department for Education and Employment.

DfEE (1998b) *Teaching: High Status, High Standards*. Circular 4/98. London: DfEE.

DfEE (1999a) *National Numeracy Strategy: Framework for Teaching Mathematics from Reception to Year 6*. London: DfEE.

DfEE (1999b) *National Numeracy Strategy: Mathematical Vocabulary*. London: DfEE.

DfES (2001) *Guidance to Support Pupils with Specific Needs in the Daily Mathematics Lesson*. London: DfES.

DfES/TTA (2002) *Qualifying to Teach: Professional Standards for Qualified Teacher Status and Requirements for Initial Teacher Training*. London: DfES/TTA.

Dickson, L., Brown, M. and Gibson, O. (1984) *Children Learning Mathematics: Teacher's Guide to Recent Research*. London: Holt Education.

Donaldson, M. (1978) *Children's Minds*. London: Fontana.

Dryden, G. and Vos, J. (2001) *The Learning Revolution*. Stafford: Network Educational Press.

Edwards, C.P., Gandini, L. and Forman, G. E. (eds) (1998) *The Hundred Languages of Children: The Reggio Emilia Approach − Advanced Reflections* (second edn). Greenwich, Conn.: Ablex Publishing Corporation.

Ernest, P. (1991) *The Philosophy of Mathematics Education*. Basingstoke: Falmer Press.

Faux, G. (1998a) What are the big ideas in Mathematics? *Mathematics Teaching*. MT 163, June, pp. 12–18.

Faux, G. (1998b) Using Gattegno Charts. *Mathematics Teaching*. MT 163, June.

Fisher, R. (1990) *Teaching Children to Think*. Oxford: Basil Blackwell.

Foxman, D. and Beishuizen, M. (1999) Untaught mental calculation methods used by 11-year-olds: some evidence from the assessment and performance unit survey in 1987. *Mathematics in School*, 28(5), November 1999, pp. 5–7.

Frazer, J.G. (1907) *The Golden Bough: A Study in Magic and Religion*. London: Macmillan.

Gardner, H. (1999) *Intelligence Reframed: Multiple Intelligences for the 21st Century*. New York: Basic Books.

Gattegno, C. (1974) *The Common Sense of Teaching Mathematics*. New York: Educational Solutions.

Gattegno, C. (1985) Knowledge v Experience. *Mathematics Teaching*, MT 110, March 1985.

Gipps, C. (1997) *Assessment in Primary Schools: Past, Present and Future*. London: British Curriculum Foundation.

Goleman, D. (1996) *Emotional Intelligence: Why it Can Matter More Than IQ*. London: Bloomsbury.

Graves, R. (1997) *The White Goddess: A Historical Grammar of Poetic Myth*. Manchester: Carcanet.

Griffin, P. (1989) Teaching takes place in time, learning takes place over time. *Mathematics Teaching*, MT 126, March 1989, pp. 12–13.

Goulding, M., Rowland, T. and Barber, P. (2002) Does it matter? Primary teacher trainees' subject knowledge in mathematics. *British Educational Research Journal*, 28(5), October 2002.

Harries, T. (1997) Reflections of a mathematics lesson in Kaposvar. *Mathematics Teaching*, MT 161, December 1997, pp. 11–13.

Hay McBer (2000) *A Model of Teacher Effectiveness*. Report by Hay McBer to the Department for Education and Employment − June 2000.

Hayes, D. (2000) *Handbook for Newly Qualified Teachers: Meeting the Standards in Primary and Middle Schools*. London: Fulton.

Haylock, D. (2001) *Mathematics Explained for Primary Teachers* (second edn). London: Paul Chapman Publishing.

Headington, R. (2000) *Monitoring, Assessment, Recording and Accountability: Meeting the Standards*. London: David Fulton.

Heidegger, M. (1969) *Discourse on Thinking*. London: Harper Row.

Hemmings, R. and Tahta, D. (1984) *Images of Infinity*. Leapfrogs.

Hewitt, D. (1994) *The Principle of Economy in the Learning and Teaching of Mathematics*. Open University: PhD Thesis.

Hewitt, D. (1998) Approaching arithmetic algebraically. *Mathematics Teaching*, MT 163, June 1998, pp. 19–29.

Honey, P. and Mumford, A. (1992) *The Manual of Learning Styles* (third edn). New York: Plenum Press.

Hopkins, C., Gifford, S. and Pepperell, S. (1999) *Mathematics in the Primary School: A Sense of Progression* (second edn). London: David Fulton.

Hughes, M. (1986) *Children and Number: Difficulties in Learning Mathematics*. London: Basil Blackwell.

Hughes, M. (1999) *Closing the Learning Gap*. Stafford: Network Educational Press.

Hughes, M., Desforges, C., Mitchell, C. and Carré, C. (2000) *Numeracy and Beyond: Applying Mathematics in the Primary School*. Buckingham: Open University Press.

Huyton, M., Carruthers, E. and Wilkinson, M (1998) Emergent mathematics. *Mathematics Teaching*, MT 162, March 1998, pp. 11–23.

Joyce, B., Calhoun, E. and Hopkins, D. (1997) *Models of Learning – Tools for Teaching*. Buckingham: Open University Press.

Jung, C.G. (1964) *Man and his Symbols*. London: Pan Books.

Koshy, V. (1999) *Effective Teaching of Numeracy*. London: Hodder & Stoughton.

Koshy, V., Ernest, P. and Casey, R. (2000) *Mathematics for Primary Teachers*. London: Routledge.

Liebling, H. (1999) *Getting Started: An Induction Guide for Newly Qualified Teachers*. School Effectiveness Series. Stafford: Network Educational Press.

Makarenko, A.S. (1936) *The Road To Life*. Vols 1–3, Moscow: Foreign Languages Publishing House.

Mason, J., Burton, L. and Stacey, K. (1982) *Thinking Mathematically*. London: Addison-Wesley.

Mathematics with cubes. Claire Publications www.clairepublications.com

Menninger, K. (1969) *Number Words and Number Symbols*. Cambridge, MA: MIT Press.

Merttens, R. (ed.) (1996) *Teaching Numeracy*. Leamington Spa: Scholastic Limited.

Mitchell, C. and Williams, H. (1998) *Teaching Mathematics to Young Children: 4–7*. Cambridge: Chris Kington Publications.

Mooney, C., Briggs, M., Fletcher, M. and McCulloch, J. (2002a) *Primary Mathematics: Teaching Theory and Practice*. Exeter: Learning Matters.

Mooney, C., Ferrie, L., Fox, S., Hansen, A. and Wrathmell, R. (2002b) *Primary Mathematics: Knowledge and Understanding*. Exeter: Learning Matters.

Montague-Smith, A. (1997) *Mathematics in Nursery Education*. London: David Fulton.

Mosley, F. and O'Brien, T. (1998a) *Eyes Closed*. London: BEAM.

Mosley, F. and O'Brien, T. (1998b) *In The Hall*. London: BEAM.

Mosley, F. and O'Brien, T. (1998c) *On The Mat*. London: BEAM.

Mosley, F. and O'Brien, T. (1998d) *Numbers In Your Head*. London: BEAM.

MultiLink *Action Mats* (E. J. Arnold) www.nesarnold.co.uk

NNS/QCA (1999) *Teaching Mental Calculation Strategies*. London: Qualifications and Curriculum Authority.

NNS (2001) *Assessment and Review Support Materials*. London: DfES.

Nickson, M. (2000) *Teaching and Learning Mathematics: A Teacher's Guide to Recent Research and its Application*. London: Cassell Education.

Nunes, T. (2001) British research on the development of numeracy concepts. In: M. Askew and M. Brown (eds) *Teaching and Learning Primary Numeracy: Policy, Practice and Effectiveness*. A review of British research for the British Educational Research Association in conjunction with the British Society for Research in the Learning of Mathematics. Southwell, Nottinghamshire: BERA. pp. 10–14.

Nunes, T. and Bryant, P. (1997) *Learning and Teaching Mathematics*. Hove: Psychology Press.

Nunes, T., Schliemann, A. and Carraher, D.W. (1993) *Street Mathematics and School Mathematics*. Cambridge: Cambridge University Press.

O'Brien, T.C. (2002) *Problem Solving (1–6)* (Ginn Numeracy Extras). Oxford: Ginn & Co.

Office for Standards in Education (OFSTED) (2000) *The National Numeracy Strategy: The First Year.* London: OFSTED.

O'Hara, M. (2000) *Teaching 3–8: Meeting the Standards for Initial Teacher Training and Induction.* London: Continuum Press.

Orton, A. and Frobisher, L. (1996) *Insights into Teaching Mathematics.* London: Cassell.

Parsons, E. (ed.) (1999) *GCSE Mathematics Revision Guide* (Higher Level). Coordination Group Publications.

Piaget, J. (1952) *The Child's Conception of Number.* London: Routledge & Kegan Paul.

Pimm, D. (ed.) (1992) *Mathematics: Symbols and Meanings.* Open University Monograph (Course EM236). Milton Keynes: Open University.

Pimm, D. (1994) Another psychology of mathematics education. In: Paul Ernest (ed.) *Constructing Mathematical Knowledge: Epistemology and Mathematical Education.* London: Falmer Press.

Pimm, D. (1995) *Symbols and Meanings in School Mathematics.* London: Routledge.

Pirsig, R. (1974) *Zen and the Art of Motor Cycle Maintenance: An Enquiry into Values.* London: Bodley Head.

Plunkett, S. (1979) Decomposition and all that rot. *Mathematics in School,* 8(3) pp. 2–5.

Pound, L. (1999) *Supporting Mathematical Development.* Buckingham: Open University Press.

QCA (1999a) *Early Learning Goals.* London: Qualifications and Curriculum Authority.

QCA (1999b) New television series about key skills. *ONQ* Issue 5 April 1999, p. 8.

QCA (1999c) *National Curriculum: Handbook for Primary Teachers in England, Key Stages 1 and 2.* London: HMSO and QCA.

QCA (2000) *Curriculum Guidance for the Foundation Stage.* London: HMSO.

Rhydderch-Evans, Z. (1993) *Maths in the School Grounds: Learning Through Landscapes.* Southgate.

Richards, C., Simco, N. and Twiselton, S. (eds) (1998) *Primary Teacher Education: High Status? High Standards?* London: Falmer Press.

Rotman, B. (1987) *Signifying Nothing: The Semiotics of Zero.* New York: St Martins Press.

Rowland, T. (1997) Dividing by three quarters: what Susie saw. *Mathematics Teaching,* MT 160, September 1997, pp. 30–33.

Rucker, R. (1988) *Mind Tools: The Five Levels of Mathematical Reality.* Harmondsworth: Penguin.

Saenz-Ludlow, A. and Waldgrave, C. (1998) Third graders' interpretations of equality and the equal symbol. *Educational Studies in Mathematics,* 35, pp. 153–187.

Sayer, J. (2000) *The General Teaching Council.* London: Cassell.

Selley, N. (1999) *The Art of Constructivist Teaching in the Primary School: A Guide for Students and Teachers.* London: David Fulton.

SCAA (1997) *The Teaching and Assessment of Number at Key Stages 1–3.* London: SCAA.

Shuard, H., Walsh, A., Goodwin, J. and Worcester, V. (1990) *PrIME: Children, Mathematics and Learning.* London: Simon & Schuster.

Shulman, L.S. (1987) Knowledge and teaching: foundations of the new reform. *Harvard Educational Review,* 57, pp. 1–22.

Simco, N. and Wilson, T. (eds) (2002) *Primary Initial Teacher Training and Education: Revised Standards, Bright Future?* Exeter: Learning Matters.

Skemp, R. (1986) *The Psychology of Learning Mathematics.* Harmondsworth: Penguin.

Skemp, R. (1989) *Mathematics in the Primary School.* London: Routledge.

Smith, A. (1996) *Accelerated Learning in the Classroom.* Stafford: Network Educational Press.

Steiner, R. (1973) *Theosophy: An Introduction to the Supersensible Knowledge of the World and the Destination of Man* (fourth edn). London: Rudolf Steiner Press.

Stern, C. and Stern, M.B. (1949) *Children Discover Arithmetic.* New York: Harper & Row.

Stokoe, R. and Illushin, L. (1998) Identifying strengths within alternative systems. *Mathematics in School.* 27(3), May 1998 pp. 31–33.

Straker, A. (1999) The National Numeracy Project 1996–99. In: Ian Thompson (ed.) *Issues in Teaching Numeracy in Primary Schools.* Buckingham: Open University Press.

Swee Fong, N. (1998) Can you please help us see what is a fraction divided by another fraction? *Mathematics Teaching*, MT 165, December 1998, pp. 28–29.

Tahta, D. (1998) Counting counts. *Mathematics Teaching*, MT 163, June 1998, pp. 4–11.

Tickle, L. (2000) *Teacher Induction: The Way Ahead*. Buckingham: Open University Press.

Thompson, I. (1997a) *Teaching and Learning Early Number*. Buckingham: Open University Books.

Thompson, I. (1997b) Mental and written algorithms: can the gap be bridged? In: Ian Thompson (ed.) *Teaching and Learning Early Number*. Buckingham: Open University Books.

Thompson, I. (1999) Mental calculation strategies for addition and subtraction (Part 1). *Mathematics in School*, 28(5), November 1999, pp. 2–4.

Thompson, I. (2001) British research on mental and written calculation methods for addition and subtraction. In: M. Askew and M. Brown (eds) *Teaching and Learning Primary Numeracy: Policy, Practice and Effectiveness. A review of British research for the British Educational Research Association in conjunction with the British Society for Research in the Learning of Mathematics*. Southwell, Nottinghamshire: BERA. pp. 15–21.

Torrance, H. and Pryor, J. (1998) *Investigating Formative Assessment: Teaching, Learning and Assessment in the Classroom*. Buckingham: Open University Press.

TTA (2000) *Using Information and Communication Technology to meet Teaching Objectives in Mathematics: Initial Teacher Training Primary*. London: TTA.

Turner-Bisset, R. (1999) Knowledge bases for teaching. *British Educational Research Journal*, 25(1), pp. 39–55.

Turner-Bisset, R. (2001) *Expert Teaching: Knowledge and Pedagogy to Lead the Profession*. London: David Fulton.

Vygotsky, L. (1962) *Thought and Language*. MIT Press.

Vygotsky, L. (1978) *Mind and Society*. Cambridge, MA: Harvard University Press.

Walkerdine, V. (1988) *The Mastery of Reason: Cognitive Development and the Production of Rationality*. London: Routledge.

Watkins, C. and Wagner, P. (2000) *Improving School Behaviour*. Paul Chapman Publishing.

Watson, A. (1993) Russian expectations. *Mathematics Teaching*, MT 145, December 1993 pp. 5–9.

Whitehead, A.N. and Russell, B.A.W. (1910) *Principia Mathematica*. Cambridge: Cambridge University Press.

Williams, E. and Shuard, H. (1997) *Primary Mathematics Today*. Harlow: Longman.

Williams, H. (1989) *Tuning in to Young Children: An Exploration of Contexts for Learning Mathematics*. Unpublished MPhil Thesis. Walton Hall: Open University.

Williams, H. (2003) *Classworks: Reception*. Cheltenham: Nelson Thornes.

Williams, H., Skinner, C. and Barber, B. (2000) *Foundations Mathematics: Teaching the Early Years*. Numeracy solutions. Oxford: Reed Educational and Professional Publishing Ltd.

Wragg, E.C. (1993) *Class Management*. London: Routledge.

Wright, R., Martland, J. and Stafford, A. (2000) *Early Numeracy: Assessment for Teaching and Intervention*. London: Paul Chapman.

Zaslavsky, C. (1990) *Africa Counts: Number and Pattern in African Culture*. New York: Lawrence Hill, Hill Books, Chicago.

Websites

www.atm.org.uk

www.m-a.org.uk

http://www.canteach.gov.uk/teaching/ (Teacher Training Agency for routes into teaching).

http://www.braindance.com/homepage.htm (Tony Buzan home page).

http://www.dfes.gov.uk/parents/curriculum/home.cfm (Department for Education and Skills).

www.gtce.org.uk (General Teaching Council).

http://www.gttr.ac.uk/ (Graduate Teacher Training Registry GTTR – applications online for graduates).

http://www.ofsted.gov.uk/ (Office for Standards in Education).

http://www.thelearningweb.net (Learning revolution website).

Index